The Visionary Tarot:
A Universal Guide

The Visionary Tarot:
A Universal Guide

Rosemary Ellen Guiley

Visionary Living, Inc.
New Milford, Connecticut

The Visionary Tarot: A Universal Guide

By Rosemary Ellen Guiley

© Copyright Visionary Living, Inc., 2016
New Milford, Connecticut
www.visionaryliving.com

All rights reserved.
No part of this book may be reproduced in any form or used without permission.

Cover design: Robert Michael Place
Back jacket and interior design by Leslie McAllister

ISBN: 978-1-942157-12-0 (pbk)
ISBN: 978-1-942157-01-4 (e-pub)

Published by Visionary Living, Inc.
New Milford, Connecticut
www.visionaryliving.com

Other books by Rosemary Ellen Guiley available from Visionary Living

Guide to Psychic Power
Calling Upon Angels: How Angels Help Us in Daily Life
Dreamwork for Visionary Living
Dream Messages from the Afterlife
Pocket Dream Guide and Dictionary
Develop Your Miracle Mind Consciousness
Angel Magic for Love and Relationships
Christmas Angels: True Stories of Hope and Healing
Soul Journeys: Past and Future Lives
Haunted by the Things You Love
The Djinn Connection
The Art of Black Mirror Scrying
Guide to the Dark Side of the Paranormal
Ouija Gone Wild

Table of Contents

Introduction — ix

1. Mysterious Origins — 1
2. The Kabbalah Connection — 21
3. The Golden Dawn Influence — 43
4. The Return of Alchemy — 57
5. Symbols in the Tarot — 67
6. The Major Arcana — 93
7. The Minor Arcana — 119
8. Tarot Rituals — 139
9. Reading the Cards — 151
10. Spreads — 161
11. Developing Your Psychic Ability — 183
12. Meditation, Visualization, and Affirmations — 191
13. Dreams and the Tarot — 213

Appendix: Glossary of Symbols — 221

About the Author — 233

Bibliography — 235

Introduction

Working with the Tarot is a magnificent spiritual journey. The cards continually reveal new information, insights, and discoveries. My own involvement with the Tarot began many years ago when I had a reading with a Tarot psychic. I was immediately entranced by the card images, which conveyed much more than was apparent on the surface. Intrigued, I wanted to learn the language of the symbols so that I, too, could read the cards. I studied the Tarot, learned how to read the cards, and began giving readings. Like many Tarot enthusiasts, I started with the Waite-Smith deck (also known as the Rider-Waite deck). Over time, my work with the Tarot expanded to include other decks, and I experimented with new ways to use the cards.

Around 1989-90, I met Robert Michael Place, a wonderful artist, jewelry designer, and expert on alchemy, a subject I was studying myself. Bob was at work on a Tarot deck that incorporated alchemical symbolism. We struck up a friendship and collaboration that produced two book and deck sets, The Alchemical Tarot and The Angels Tarot. I tell the full story later on in this book—it was an amazing experience of profound dreams, visions, and creative inspiration.

Of all the decks I have used, I still prefer The Alchemical Tarot, a versatile and powerful deck. I also still use the Waite-Smith deck. I have written this book as a universal guide to be used with any deck. Every themed deck has its individual details, but the fundamental meanings of the cards remain the same.

Using the Tarot is a rich and rewarding experience, constantly unfolding and never ending. We can approach the Tarot in two fundamental ways: to preview the future and discover meaning behind the events and forces in our lives, and as a tool for spiritual growth. The first approach, to divine the future, can be fruitful, but is only one dimension of the Tarot. The Tarot is well suited to discovery, and through it we can gain knowledge of the Self, which helps us realize our fullest potential.

Mysticism is the belief in, or pursuit of, unification with the One. It is also the immediate consciousness of the Divine. And, it is the direct experience of spiritual Truth. Through the Tarot, we can contemplate and experience all of those things.

As profound, mystical, and mysterious as the Tarot is, however, there is no reason why a guide to its mysteries cannot be simple and straightforward. That is the reason for writing this book: to provide a clear and uncluttered path of study for the Tarot. My intent is to help the beginner get a solid grasp of the cards and make rapid progress in using them, and to help the experienced student advance to new and higher levels.

Both beginner and experienced Tarot student can benefit from this book. It will teach you how to maximize your work with the cards, regardless of which deck you use. The means for this are universal techniques for developing psychic and meditative skills, understanding symbols, and making use of the psychology of ritual and patterns. The book also features clear interpretations of the cards, a guide for meditating with the Tarot, effective card spreads, and tips for designing your own spreads.

The Tarot lends itself to innovation and creativity, and your work with the cards will undoubtedly inspire you in many ways. May your journey be one of wonder.

How to use this book

The Visionary Tarot is a universal guide, and so I have not used the images of any particular deck throughout the book. Select your deck, and use the book to expand upon the images in each card.

I highly recommend *The Alchemical Tarot Renewed 4*, which is the fourth edition of *The Alchemical Tarot* created by artist Robert Michael Place. Bob and I worked on the original book and deck set, published in 1995, the story of which I tell in this book. If you are familiar with the Waite-Smith deck, one of the most popular and widely used decks of all, you will appreciate *The Alchemical Tarot*, which incorporates Arthur Edward Waite's vision with the profound symbolism of alchemy.

The Temperance card from *The Alchemical Tarot Renewed 3* is featured on the cover of this book, and more about it and Bob can be found at the end.

1

Mysterious Origins

Anyone who has examined a Tarot deck for the first time feels an indescribable attraction to the card images. The symbols seem at once foreign and arcane and also strangely familiar. The cards speak directly to the soul, awakening a timeless wisdom hidden somewhere within the deep recesses of consciousness, perhaps even deeper still within the collective unconscious of all humanity. No matter what the theme of the deck—and there are many, each based on a particular theme or motif—the Tarot evokes a sense of awe.

Who created these cards, and for what original purpose? No one knows the exact answer. Today's Tarot, in all its incarnations, has been handed down through a mysterious history. The true origin and purpose are obscure and will remain so, perhaps forever. Numerous theories have been put forth since the eighteenth century, some of them plausible and some highly speculative. As the late occultist and Tarot authority Arthur Edward Waite once observed, much of the Tarot's alleged history is negative and clouded by "reveries and gratuitous speculations." In all likelihood, we will never know the truth about the origins of the cards, and will be left with only our most educated guesses. It is difficult not to imagine that the cards were given some deliberate, occult significance, for whatever their origin, the Tarot cards contain ageless, esoteric truths couched in symbols.

The Tarot is complex, and has been related to alchemy, the Kabbalah, archetypes, the elements, mnemonics, astrology, and Jungian psychology. It has been reinterpreted in hundreds of decks with different themes.

Composition of the Tarot

The modern Tarot is a deck of seventy-eight cards bearing images and symbols. It has been one of the most popular systems of divination since the eighteenth century. The Tarot is divided into two parts, a Major Arcana, or Trumps, consisting of twenty-two cards, and a Minor Arcana consisting of fifty-six cards, almost as though two separate types of decks were blended together, as some speculate was the case.

The Major Arcana present images which express qualities, truths, and stages of enlightenment. These allegorical images varied in earlier times, but have been fairly uniform since the mid-eighteenth century. Today the Major Arcana cards have a specific order with numbers and names:

   0 The Fool
   1 The Magician
   2 The High Priestess
   3 The Empress
   4 The Emperor
   5 The Hierophant
   6 The Lovers
   7 The Charioteer
   8 Justice
   9 The Hermit
   10 The Wheel of Fortune
   11 Strength
   12 The Hanged Man
   13 Death
   14 Temperance

15 The Devil
16 The Tower
17 The Star
18 The Moon
19 The Sun
20 Judgement
21 The World

Sometimes the Justice and Strength cards, numbers 8 and 11 respectively, are reversed, with Justice being 11 instead of 8 and Strength being 8 instead of 11. The cards are numbered from 0 to 21. The first card, The Fool, originally had no cipher—the 0 was added later in Tarot development. Also, The Fool has not always been the beginning of the Arcana.

The Minor Arcana of fifty-six cards is divided into four suits of ten cards each, pips and court cards, and resembles today's playing cards. The traditional names of the suits are wands, cups, pentacles, and swords, though artists often give them variant names. Regardless of the suit names, the suits are consistent in their relation to the four elements of air, earth, water, and fire. They each have ten cards numbered one through ten (called the pips) and four court cards, traditionally named the page, knight, queen, and king.

In order to fully appreciate how the occultists of the eighteenth and nineteenth centuries perceived and developed the Tarot, we must first take a look at alchemy.

Alchemy and the Tarot

Alchemy is an ancient path of spiritual purification and transmutation. The Tarot, while much younger, also deals with transformation: the expansion of consciousness and the development of insight and psychic perception through images.

Alchemy has both spiritual and physical dimensions. From its spiritual perspective, alchemy is the art of transformation of the alchemist himself. From a physical perspective, alchemy concerns processes for transmuting base metals into silver and gold. Traditionally the spiritual side has been the true goal of alchemy; those who were interested only in amassing fortunes were considered pretenders to the true art.

Both alchemy and the Tarot are steeped in mysticism and mystery. Both present to the initiate systems of eternal, dreamlike, esoteric symbols that have the power to alter consciousness and connect the human soul to the Divine. Through alchemy, the Tarot comes into full power.

History and concepts of alchemy

Alchemy is the precursor of modern chemistry and metallurgy, and is more than 2000 years old. Both Western and Eastern systems of alchemy developed; here we will consider the Western path, which has had the greatest influence upon the Tarot.

The word "alchemy" is derived from the Arabic word *alkimia*. *Al* is the definite article (the), which in Arabic is normally attached to the noun. *Kimia* has two possible derivations. First, *kmt* or *chem* was the ancient Egyptians' name for their land; it meant "the black land" (meaning black or fertile earth in contrast to desert). In this case, the Arabic name would mean "the Egyptian Art." The second possibility is the Greek word *chyma*, which means to fuse or cast metal.

Western alchemy is based on the Hermetic tradition, a syncretism of Egyptian metallurgy and Neoplatonism, Gnosticism and Christianity. The core text is the Emerald Tablet, a mystical tract attributed to the legendary Hermes Trismegistus ("Thrice greatest Hermes"), the original alchemist. The central tenet of the Emerald Tablet is "as above, so below": humanity is a microcosm of the macrocosm of heaven, and correspondences exist between the two. One reflects the other.

The Emerald Tablet may be the oldest surviving alchemical text, though its origins are unknown. It is said to be inscribed with the whole of the Egyptian' philosophy, including the magical secrets of the universe. It is cited as the credo of adepts, particularly the alchemists, who interpreted it as a description of the transmutation process. According to one legend, the Emerald Tablet was found clutched in the hand of the body of Hermes Trismegistus in his cave tomb.

Other Hermetic works of importance, which were published much later, are known as the Corpus Hermeticum and the Hermetica.

The Egyptians developed one of the basic fundamentals of alchemy, that of "first matter," that is, that the world was created by divine force out of a chaotic mass called Prima Materia, or First Matter. All things can be reduced to first matter through a process called *solve et coagula,* "dissolve and combine," and then transmuted to something more desirable. This transmutation was accomplished through the joining of opposites. The entire chemical process was based on the assumption that all things in nature evolve into their purest and highest form. Thus imperfect base metals eventually become gold on their own. Alchemy speeds up the process.

According to early alchemy, all things have a hermaphroditic composition of two substances: sulphur, which represents the soul and the fiery male principle, and mercury, which represents spirit and the watery female principle. Later European alchemy added a third ingredient, salt, which corresponds to body. The transmutation process involves separating these three essentials and recombining them into a different form. The process must be done according to astrological auspices.

By the third century, alchemy was widely practiced, and had replaced many of the disintegrating mystery traditions. Zosimos (c. 250-300), a Greek author of numerous alchemical texts, traced alchemy to Biblical origins, an idea that gained popularity as alchemy reached its peak in medieval times. Zosimos also emphasized the transmutation of metals in his treatise *The Divine Art of Making Gold and Silver.*

Western alchemy suffered a setback in 296, when the Roman Emperor Diocletian ordered the burning of Egyptian and Hermetic alchemical texts, thus destroying a great deal of knowledge. However, the Emerald Tablet had by then passed into Arabic culture, where it continued to evolve. Alchemy was a highly respected science, practiced by adepts who wrote their treatises and manuals in deliberately obscure language. The term "gibberish" is derived from the name of a medieval alchemist, Jabir ibn Hayyan, known as Geber (c. 721-815), whose writings were difficult to comprehend. Alchemy thrived in Moorish Spain, where from the twelfth century on it spread throughout Europe, along with teaching of the Kabbalah.

By the fifteenth century, the practice of alchemy in Europe emphasized the quest for gold and amassing fortunes. It was a thriving, but not always reputable, practice, pursued by secretive men called "puffers," after their chemical procedures in their laboratories. Prague became one of the capitals of alchemy. Alchemy also took hold in England. Some European rulers and nobles became obsessed with transmuting metals into gold in order to finance their personal wealth and their war chests, especially for the expensive Crusades, and hired alchemists to produce gold. Fraudulent alchemists skipped about Europe, promising results long enough to make personal gains and then fleeing when patience with them ran out. Some made no escape, and were imprisoned or executed by irate patrons.

The agent of transmutation for both spiritual and physical alchemy is the Philosopher's Stone, a mysterious and elusive substance that was never described in direct terms. The Philosopher's Stone also is the Elixir of Life that would bestow immortality. The process of creating the Philosopher's Stone is the Great Work or Magnum Opus. The Philosopher's Stone is both the beginning of the Great Work, the Prima Materia, and the end result.

In physical alchemy, base metals were first reduced to a formless mass by melting or by placing them in a bath of mercury, the universal solvent. The mass then went through four stages of change: *nigredo*, characterized by blackness; *albedo*, a whiteness; *citrinitas*, a yellowing; and *rubedo*, a redness. The final stage yielded gold as well as the Philosopher's Stone. The Stone was highly concentrated, and when added into the alchemist's furnace of molten metals, it encouraged the rapid transmutation to gold—or so it was claimed.

Alchemists jealously guarded their secrets, and alchemical texts were written in obscure terms, as well as in images and symbols that had to be interpreted intuitively by the individual alchemist. The *Mutus Liber*, or *Silent Book*, is perhaps the best example of alchemy explained only through images. The hermaphroditic nature of alchemy was often expressed in erotic art, though there is no evidence that actual sexual rites were practiced in Western alchemy. Thus, we can see how alchemy and the Tarot complement each other in their primary language of symbols.

The ability to make gold out of lead was more legendary than fact, but numerous stories circulated about the alleged successes of some alchemists. In the course of their pursuits, alchemists were responsible for many discoveries important in metallurgy, chemistry, and medicines. However, in the early nineteenth century, alchemy fell out of favor after the discoveries of oxygen and the composition of water. Alchemy was reduced to the level of pseudo-science and superstition and was replaced by physics.

The spiritual side of alchemy is similar in approach. The "base metal" or imperfect person, is spiritualized through a transformation process of study and practice, and learning the great esoteric secrets. Thus, a person attains the gold of enlightenment.

In the Western tradition, the Hermetic philosophy became the basis for magical practices. Grimoires, or magical handbooks, contained many principles of correspondences for the casting of spells. The traditions of ceremonial magic, or high magic, are paths of enlightenment based on the balancing of the masculine and feminine principles, and the perfection of the whole being.

Jung's influence

Modern Western interest in alchemy was revived by Carl G. Jung (1875-1951), who understood both the spiritual and physical dimensions of alchemy, and especially saw the language of alchemy in the dreams of his patients. He noted that many dream symbols were alchemical in nature, even if the dreamer had no knowledge of alchemy. Thus, alchemy was deeply embedded in the collective base of human knowledge and experience, which he called the collective unconscious.

Jung studied the new field of psychology with Sigmund Freud, working closely with him from 1907-13. He then broke away to develop his own ideas, delving deeply into dreams, mythology, and then alchemy. He pioneered many concepts, among them, for our purposes here, ideas on the archetypes, or universal images that reside in the collective unconscious, the repository of all human experiences. Alchemy led to one of his most important concepts, individuation, which is the process of becoming whole.

Jung's interest in alchemy grew out of his intense interest in Gnosticism, and his desire, as early as 1912, to find a link between it and the processes of the collective unconscious that would pave the way for the re-entry of the Gnostic Sophia into modern culture. He found such a link in alchemy. Jung also was prompted to research alchemy by his own dreams. He collected a vast body of works on alchemy and immersed himself in study of the subject.

Jung saw alchemy as a spiritual process of redemption involving the union and transformation of Lumen Dei, the light of the Godhead, and Lumen Naturae, the light of nature. The alchemists' experimental procedure of *solve et coagula* symbolized the death and rebirth of the substances they used. The alchemist was part of the process himself, and transmuted his own consciousness into a higher state through symbolic death and rebirth. The alchemists' transmutation of base metals into gold and silver takes place within the psyche as the process of individuation, or becoming whole.

Jung had alchemical dreams and visions long before he knew what alchemy was about. Once he became immersed in it, he was able to understand dreams and visions from a new perspective, and he also was able to develop his theories on the personality. Through our experiences in life, we are challenged to integrate pieces of ourselves. Each one of us has a feminine side, the anima, and a masculine side, the animus, which must be brought into harmony with each other. In addition, we have the shadow, which consists of parts of us that are repressed. Individuation enables us to become conscious of both our smallness and our great uniqueness in the grand scheme of things.

Despite Jung's pioneering work uniting depth psychology and alchemy, interest in alchemy remained low until about the second half of the twentieth century, when study of it as a spiritual path revived.

Alchemical symbols are found in traditional Tarot designs because they are influenced by the engravings that accompany alchemical texts and other allegorical Renaissance literature. Today's Tarot drew on those roots and took defined shape in the eighteenth and nineteenth centuries, thanks to work by occultists who were steeped in esoteric knowledge, including alchemy, the Kabbalah, astrology, and the magical arts. Not all theories advanced about the Tarot were valid, but the alchemical nature of the Tarot was expressed in new card designs and ways of working with the cards to transform consciousness. We will see more about alchemy, symbols, and dreams later on.

The emergence of the Tarot

Tarot cards became popular for divination in the eighteenth century. Occultists created exotic theories that the cards were of great antiquity, perhaps descending from ancient Egypt, or the remnants of the fabled esoteric teachings of Hermes Trismegistus, the legendary Greco-Egyptian figure who gave humankind all its learning, and had been disseminated throughout Europe by Gypsies. More likely, the cards evolved out of the numerous decks of playing and teaching cards that spread throughout Europe as early as the fourteenth century, and were used primarily by nobility. Surviving decks from those times are incomplete, so we do not know exactly how the cards evolved into the present day Tarot.

The earliest surviving record of cards in the West dates to 1332, when Alfonse XI, the king of Leon and Castile, placed a ban on them. At that time, cards were making their appearance throughout Europe as gambling devices and were gaining great popularity. Since gambling was considered immoral, cards were banned by various rulers and condemned by the Church as instruments of the Devil. Playing cards were called—and still are by some—the Devil's Bible and the Devil's Picture Book.

There was no standard for the composition of these early decks of cards, and a great variety of designs and suits were employed. Even the number of cards differed greatly from one deck to another.

In 1377, a German monk identified only as "Johannes," a resident of a monastery in Breveld, Switzerland, left behind a Latin manuscript describing the arrival of a card game used at the monastery. He said he did not know who invented the game or where it came from, and he compared it to chess, "since in both there are kings, queens and chief nobles and common people." There were, however, more court cards than in the present playing card deck: six kings, four queens, and eight *marschalli* (knaves, which are now jacks). Johannes also speculated on the potential of the cards as a means of instruction in morality.

The appearance of other playing cards was recorded at about the same time elsewhere in Europe. Another early deck with suits, called the Hunting pack of Stuttgart, Germany, dates to around 1420, and has four suit signs: the hunting symbols of dogs, falcons, stags, and ducks.

Despite the opposition of the Church and the official bans on playing cards, Europe's royalty commissioned decks to be created for them, most likely for entertainment and amusement, and as forms of art. Most of the surviving early cards come from such specially commissioned, hand-painted decks.

Early Tarot cards appear to have been used primarily in games of chance and fortune telling. The earliest cards that may have been Tarot cards, and that still exist, may have been created and hand painted by Jacquemin Gringonneur in 1392 for the entertainment of King Charles VI of France. The Bibliotheque Nationale in Paris has on display seventeen cards said to be from the three decks created by Gringonneur, an allegation that has been disputed since 1848. The cards resemble the later Marseilles deck, published in 1748, which became the model for all subsequent Tarot decks, but have no inscriptions or numbers to indicate their order. Whether they are true Tarot cards remains a matter of disagreement. Waite believed them to be Tarot, and linked them to some of the Major Arcana, including The Fool, Emperor, Pope, Lovers, Wheel of Fortune, Temperance, Strength, Justice, Moon, Sun, Chariot, Hermit, Hanged Man, Death, Tower, and Last Judgement.

The oldest known Tarot decks are the Visconti-Sforza cards from early fifteenth-century Milan, Italy, designed for the Visconti and Visconti-Sforza families. Eleven versions are in existence, none of which are complete. One version, called the Pierpont Morgan-Bergamo deck, has seventy-four cards. The trumps bear no titles or numbers, and the Minor Arcana are divided into four suits of *spade* (swords), *bastoni* (wands), *coppe* (cups), and *denari* (coins or pentacles). One Visconti-Sforza deck, called the Cary-Yale deck, has sixty-seven cards, but in its entirety probably had eighty-six cards. Different artists created the various decks. The Pierpont Morgan-Bergamo pack, which is on display at the J. Pierpont Morgan Library in New York City, is believed to have been created by a Cremonese painter named Bonfacio Bembo. This deck has inspired some modem Tarot artists.

The name *Tarot* may have originated from fifteenth-century Italian decks. At that time, the trump cards were called *trionfi*, and by the early sixteenth century became known as *tarocchi* ("triumphs" or "trumps"), a name that eventually was extended to the entire deck of seventy-eight cards. *Tarot* is the French derivative of *tarocchi*. The carders, the guild of card makers in sixteenth-century Paris, referred to themselves as *tarotiers*. According to another theory, the word *Tarot* may have been derived from *tarock*, a German game with cards. Still another theory holds that the name derived from the term *tares*, small dots or points that bordered early playing cards, which were called *tarots*.

It is possible that Tarot cards, with their allegorical symbols of virtues, once were used as mnemonic devices for teaching. This purpose is suggested by the Tarocchi of Mantegna, fifty Italian cards that are believed to date to the late fifteenth century. The Tarocchi of Mantegna are divided into five series of ten cards each and are oriented to a theme: Twenty-two of the Mantegna cards bear a resemblance to sixteen modern Tarot cards, including thirteen of the Major Arcana and three court cards in the suits of swords, wands, and cups. Waite, however, found Tarot symbolism wanting in them.

By the end of the fifteenth century, Tarot decks in Italy, France, and elsewhere in Europe had evolved with different designs. From the fifteenth through the mid-eighteenth centuries, both Tarot and playing cards underwent additional changes in content, style, design, and size. The invention of the printing press in the mid-fifteenth century helped the proliferation of cards, which now could be printed from wooden blocks rather than painted individually by hand. Playing cards continued to evolve on their own to the present-day deck of fifty-two cards (the Page was dropped as a court card), and the Tarot incorporated playing cards.

By 1748, the French Marseilles Tarot deck had become standardized; it is now considered to be the grandfather of all modern Tarot decks and is still in use today. The Major Arcana were titled and numbered, with the exception of The Fool. A game of Tarot was played in southern France, Spain, Italy, and Germany, but at that time had not reached Paris.

By the end of the eighteenth century, Tarot cards were popular for fortune-telling, and occultists were incorporating them into magical studies and rituals.

The Egyptian connection

During that time, a theory crediting Gypsies with either originating the cards or introducing them to Europe was endorsed by some occultists. Though Gypsies were credited with the spread of the cards—and, as fortune tellers, they did make use of them—there is no evidence that they brought the cards out of ancient Egypt. Nonetheless, the Gypsy-Egypt theory was widely believed.

The earliest known record of the Gypsies in Europe dates to 1417, although it is likely that they arrived much earlier, perhaps as early as the tenth or eleventh centuries, probably emigrating out of northern India. They claimed to be Christian penitents who came from a land called Little Egypt. The Europeans dubbed them "Gypsies," a corruption of "Egyptians."

The chief promoter of the Egyptian connection was Antoine Court de Gebelin (1725-1784), a French archaeologist and Egyptologist, who claimed the Tarot symbols were fragments of an ancient Egyptian book, the Book of Thoth. As a high-grade Freemason, Court de Gebelin was well-versed in occultism, and was knowledgeable about ancient Egypt as well. But his theory was baseless because the Rosetta Stone, which provided the key to deciphering the first Egyptian hieroglyphics, had yet to be discovered.

Court de Gebelin said he stumbled upon the Tarot and uncovered its Egyptian origins by accident while calling upon "Madame the Countess of H_____," who was from Germany or Switzerland and was visiting in Paris. Upon the arrival of Court de Gebelin and his friends at the home where the Madame was staying, they found the countess playing a card game with several others. She informed her visitors that it was the game of Tarot. The countess pulled out a card that she said was "the world," though Court de Gebelin could not see any resemblance of the card's image to the name. He wrote later, however, that he immediately recognized the allegory:

> Everyone put down his hand and came to look at this marvelous card [the world] in which I saw what they had never before seen. Each person showed me another card, and in a quarter of an hour the deck had been gone through, explained and proclaimed Egyptian. And since this was not a figment of our imagination, but rather the result of selected and sensible knowledge of this game in connection with everything that was known about Egyptian ideas, we promised ourselves to surely make it known to the public one day; we were convinced that it would be pleased to have a discovery and a gift of this kind—an Egyptian book which escaped barbarism, the ravages of time, accidental and spontaneous fires and ignorance which is still more disastrous.

Court de Gebelin said that the word *tarot* was derived from two Egyptian words, *tar*, meaning "road," and *ro*, meaning "royal." (Remember, this "translation" of two alleged Egyptian words preceded the Rosetta Stone.) The Tarot, he said, represented the "royal road" to wisdom. Furthermore, the twenty-two trumps were representations of twenty-two stone tablets hidden in a temple that at one time had sat between the paws of the Great Sphinx, but had long ago disappeared into the sands. The cards were either allegories of Egyptian philosophy and religion expressed in hieroglyphics or told the history of the world, beginning with Mercury (Hermes). The four suits of the Minor Arcana represented four classes of Egyptian society. Swords were rulers and military nobility; wands were agriculture; cups were clergy and priests; and coins were commerce.

Court de Gebelin found additional Egyptian connections with the number seven, which was sacred to Egyptians: each suit of the Minor Arcana contained fourteen cards, or two times seven; the Major Arcana consisted of twenty-one numbered cards, or three times seven, plus the unnumbered Fool. He said the presence of The High Priestess confirmed their antiquity, as no modern deck would have such a pagan figure, and furthermore, she appeared with the horns of Isis. (It should be noted that horns are a common religious or esoteric symbol.)

According to Court de Gebelin, the Egyptians devised a card game with the Tarot, which they passed on to the Romans during the early Christian centuries. The game remained within Italy until the time of the Holy Roman Empire. The cards were dispersed throughout Europe by the Gypsies, who had saved all that was left of the ancient Egyptian writings.

If Tarot cards had existed in ancient Egypt, they would have been associated with Thoth, the god of magic, wisdom, learning, writing, healing, arithmetic, and astrology, who created the universe and transmitted his wisdom to mankind. An ibis-headed or baboon-headed deity shown in art with a pen-and-ink holder, Thoth was called the "Lord of the Divine Books" and "Scribe of the Company of Gods." According to myth, he restored the eye of Horus after it was torn to pieces by the evil Seth. Egyptian priests directed spells for the dead to him, because he recorded the weighing of the hearts of the souls in the underworld Judgement Hall of Osiris, and had the power to reanimate corpses.

The Greeks identified Thoth with their counterpart, Hermes, the patron god of magic, the messenger to other gods, and the courier of souls of the dead to the underworld. Thoth-Hermes in turn became identified with Hermes Trismegistus, the "Thrice-Greatest Hermes," a mythical figure credited with the authorship of from 20,000 to more than 36,000 sacred books of wisdom housed in the royal library of Alexandria, and as mentioned, earlier, the original alchemist. All but forty-two of the Hermetic books supposedly were lost in fires when Alexandria was sacked in the fourth century, and they survived through the ages as the Hermetica, the foundation of Western occultism, the secrets of which for centuries were said to be passed down orally from master to student. According to legend, Thoth presented the Book of Thoth, or the "Key to Immortality," to his successors. It is said to contain the secrets for immortality—the quest of alchemy— and the means by which mankind can come into the presence of the gods. The book supposedly served as a text to the ancient mystery cults that flourished during the Hellenistic era, and after the demise of the mysteries was removed to some unknown and distant land, where it is still held in safekeeping by certain adepts.

Such beliefs were held among many occultists of Court de Gebelin's day, but in fact, the Hermetica was not of ancient Egyptian origin, but a much later Christian authorship. This had been demonstrated at least a century earlier than the time of Court de Gebelin, but the ancient Egyptian theories were exotic and continued to have adherents, who preferred mystery to fact.

Court de Gebelin's Tarot theory, published as part of his nine-volume book, *Le Monde Primitif* (1773- 1784), had an enormous romantic appeal and became quite popular. But the "Egyptian Connection" was never substantiated. Court de Gebelin's twenty-two stone tablets and secret temple between the paws of the Sphinx have never been found.

The lack of Egyptian evidence did not prevent *Le Monde Primitif* from becoming a definitive source on the Tarot for the better part of a century, although the images Court de Gebelin reproduced were primitive and differed somewhat from the Marseilles deck. As for the Major Arcana, Court de Gebelin placed the unnumbered Fool card at the beginning and gave it a 0. He by no means had the last word on this.

The Egyptian theory was heavily promoted by an opportunistic follower of Court de Gebelin, a Parisian wigmaker named Alliette (1738-91), who began spelling his name backwards—Etteilla—and rose to great fame telling fortunes as *Le Celebre Etteilla*. Arthur Edward Waite labeled him an "illiterate and zealous adventurer." Etteilla caught the public's fancy with his story of how the Book of Thoth was produced in the 1828th year of Creation by seventeen Magi, one of whom was Tri-Mercury, a descendant of Mercury and a great-grandson of Noah.

Beginning in 1783, Etteilla inundated the public with his writings, claiming to have devoted some forty years to the study of Egyptian magic, the key of which had been discovered in the Tarot. Etteilla enthusiastically applied the Tarot to astrology, alchemy, and fortune-telling, and was a major influence in the raising of cartomancy to an exalted art.

Etteilla devised his own Tarot deck, distinct from other Tarot cards and apparently with little regard for any particular symbolism, and used them in his fortune-telling. He was later accused by the influential occultist, Eliphas Levi, of using his cards to hypnotize his clients.

Many occultists who followed Court de Gebelin and Etteilla blindly accepted and reiterated the alleged Egyptian origin of the Tarot. Finally, in 1910, Waite, who was an important figure in the Hermetic Order of the Golden Dawn in London—put it to rest once and for all. Writing in his own commentary, *The Pictorial Key to the Tarot* (1910), Waite stated:

> ...there is in fact no history [of the Tarot] prior to the fourteenth century. The deception and self- deception regarding their origin in Egypt, India or China put a lying spirit into the mouths of the first expositors, and the later occult writers have done little more than reproduce the first false testimony in the good faith of an intelligence unawakened to the issues of research.

As for Court de Gebelin, Waite said in another text:

> I respect M. de Gebelin for having conceived Egyptology by an act of the mind so long before it could have been conceived in any body of research; I respect him for having had, out of previous expectation, a vision concerning the Tarot, but as he did not marry his vision to any facts on this earth, I think he has only begotten a phantom son of the fancy.

The outlandish pronouncements of Court de Gebelin and Etteilla marked the beginning of a new stage in the evolution of the Tarot: the search for the truth about the purpose of the cards and their hidden meanings.

The astrology connection

The occultists who delved into the mysteries of the Tarot found a natural connection to astrology, an ancient system in which the positions of the planets and stars are used for prophecy and divination. Astrology has been practiced the world over, and in the West was considered a science through the Renaissance. It was readily accessible to the masses as well as adepts.

Astrology is based on the Hermetic principle "as above, so below." The ancients viewed earth and man as microcosms of the universe, a belief that endured through the Renaissance. Astrology holds that the celestial bodies exert forces and exhibit personalities that influence people and events below in the microcosm. These influences may be determined by mapping positions in the sky at various times. The influences also are used to determine the most auspicious times to undertake magical work and alchemical processes.

In Western astrology, the Chaldeans, as early as the fifth century BC, may have been the first to associate the positions of heavenly bodies with human birth times and personal destinies. The ancient Babylonians also practiced astrology, and either they or the Chaldeans codified the twelve constellations of the Zodiac around 3000 BC. From these studies emerged the horoscope, though it was the Greeks who perfected it and made it available to the general public. The stars were believed to govern not only personal destiny, but all manner of decisions and the courses of events.

Astrology was denounced by early Christians—in 333 the Emperor Constantine called it "demonic," and later St. Augustine opposed it as well—but it remained within popular belief. In the twelfth century, it enjoyed a comeback as a science, due in part, interestingly, to the work of Spanish Kabbalists (true Kabbalists), and did not fall out of favor as a science until after the mid-seventeenth century.

Popular cards in medieval and Renaissance Europe portrayed astrological associations. The cards alleged to have been painted by Jacquemin Gringonneur include one showing a crescent moon and two astrologers, clothed in long robes with hoods, holding a compass and a book bearing astrological symbols. The Tarocchi of Mantegna, from around the late fifteenth century, include a card called "Astrology" in one of its five series, and ten cards in another series devoted to the order of the heavens.

Symbols in the Major Arcana of the Marseilles deck of 1790 show correspondence to celestial bodies. There are, of course, the cards titled for celestial bodies—The Moon, The Sun, and The Star. Aquarius is evoked in Temperance, in which a winged figure pours water between two vessels, as well as in The Star, in which a naked woman pours water from two vessels into a body of water. The Moon includes a scorpion (perhaps evocative of Scorpio or Cancer), Strength a lion (Leo), Justice scales (Libra), The Sun twin children (Gemini), and so on.

Occultists of the eighteenth and nineteenth centuries matched the Tarot to the heavens. No two agreed. Etteilla corresponded the trumps to the Zodiac and seven planets (which in astrology include the moon and sun), which totaled only nineteen—he solved the problem by leaving three arcana unmatched. The occultist Oswald Wirth (1860-1943) drew up a table corresponding the Major Arcana to both the letters of the Hebrew alphabet and the constellations (including the twelve signs of the Zodiac) and a few stars; he placed The Fool last. He gave some of the cards multiple celestial associations:

MAJOR ARCANA	CONSTELLATIONS AND STARS
The Juggler (The Magician)	Orion—the Bull (Taurus)
The High Priestess	Cassiopeia
The Empress	The Virgin (Virgo)
The Emperor	Hercules, Lyra, Boreal Crown (Corona Borealis)
The Pope	The Ram (Aries)
The Lovers	Eagle (Aquila), Antinous, Sagittarius
The Chariot	Great Bear (Ursa Major)
Justice	The Balance (Libra)
The Hermit	The Ox-Driver (Bootes)
The Wheel of Fortune	Capricorn (opposed to Sirius)
Strength	Lion (Leo), Virgin (Virgo)
The Hanged Man	Perseus
Death	Dragon of the Pole (Draco)

MAJOR ARCANA	CONSTELLATIONS AND STARS
Temperance	Aquarius
The Devil	Goat (Capricorn), Coachman
Lightning-struck Tower	Scorpion (Scorpio), Ophiuchus
The Star	Andromeda, the Fishes (Pisces)
The Moon	Cancer, Sirius, Procion
The Sun	The Twins (Gemini)
Judgement	The Swan (Cygnus)
The Universe (The World)	Lesser Bear and Pole Star (Ursa Minor and Polaris)
The Foolish Man	Cepheus

The occultist Gerard Encausse, whose esoteric name was Papus (1865-1916), also applied his Tarot theories to astrology, stating in *The Tarot of the Bohemians: The Absolute Key to Occult Science* (1889) that such correspondences were necessary in order to prove the accuracy "of the principles upon which the construction of the Tarot is based." He based his analysis on the Egyptian year of four seasons, each with three months, and each month with three ten-day periods called *decani* (a five-day period was added to make a 365-day year). All of these things must be found in the Tarot, Papus said. He went on to correspond the suits of the Minor Arcana to the four seasons; the top three court cards of each suit to a figure of the Zodiac (the knaves were transition cards) and to a season; and each card in the Minor Arcana to a *decan*. The Zodiac signs and *decani* were in turn governed by planets. Papus also accepted Oswald Wirth's astrological correspondences to the Major Arcana. Upon this basis, Papus said, Tarot cards could be used to cast a horoscope.

Astrological correspondences became more overt after the turn of the twentieth century, when Waite reinterpreted the Tarot with his own deck and incorporated astrological symbols into his images. More recent decks also have incorporated astrological symbolisms, and spreads have been designed around the horoscope. However, there remains no definitive match between the Major Arcana and the signs of the Zodiac and planets, and correspondences vary considerably depending on the artist.

The Hermetic Order of the Golden Dawn, which formed in the late nineteenth century, placed great importance on the connections between astrology and the Tarot, although its approach differed from traditional astrology, and from associations made by earlier occultists. Only the seven planets of the ancients were used in the original correspondences: Mercury, Venus, Mars, Jupiter, Saturn, Moon, and Sun. Later decks related to the Golden Dawn added in the outer planets. Correspondences were made between the Major Arcana and the four elements, seven planets, and twelve Zodiac signs. The Minor Arcana were corresponded to planets in constellations.

Astrological correspondences have continued to play a role in many decks. Meanwhile, much more was yet to unfold in the development of the Tarot.

2

The Kabbalah Connection

In 1799, the Rosetta Stone was discovered by troops of Napoleon Bonaparte, and was named after Rosetta, Egypt, near where the slab was found. Its hieroglyphics were deciphered by Jean Francois Champollion in 1821 and were found to have nothing to say about anything connected to Tarot cards. That should have dashed Court de Gebelin's exotic theory to pieces, but romantic ideas die hard, and the Egyptian origin hypothesis resolutely survived. Some occultists, however, started looking elsewhere for explanations of the Tarot—and found them in the Kabbalah.

One of these individuals was Eliphas Levi (1810-1875), the pseudonym of Alphonse Louis Constant, a French philosopher, occultist, and an Abbe of the Roman Catholic Church, who helped revive interest in ritual magic. "Eliphas Levi" is a shortened version of Eliphas Levi Zahed, Constant's name in Hebrew, which he adopted for occult purposes. Arthur Edward Waite dismissed him as an intellectual lightweight—"only Etteilla a second time around in the flesh"—but Levi's peers regarded him as a man of great learning, and his theories were given much credence.

Levi's study of occultism included the Kabbalah and the doctrine of universal correspondences, by which he connected the Tarot to the Kabbalah.

To understand the development of the Tarot-Kabbalah connection, we must take a look at the history and fundamental concepts of the Kabbalah.

A mystical tradition

The term "Kabbalah" is derived from the Hebrew word QBL (*Qibel*), meaning "to receive" or "that which is received." It refers especially to a secret oral tradition handed down from teacher to pupil. "Kabbalah" was first used in the eleventh century by Ibn Gabirol, a Spanish philosopher, and has since become applied to all Jewish mystical practice. The Kabbalah is founded on the Torah, but is not an intellectual or ascetic discipline. It is a means for achieving union with God while maintaining an active life in the mundane world.

There are four main, overlapping branches of the Kabbalah:

1. The Classical, or Dogmatic, Kabbalah concerns the study of the Torah and the central texts of the Kabbalah, such as the Sefer Yetzirah and the Sefer Zohar.

2. The Practical Kabbalah concerns magic, such as the proper ways to make talismans and amulets.

3. The Literal Kabbalah concerns the relationship between the letters of the Hebrew alphabet and numbers. It features the deciphering of relationships and correspondences through *gematria*, a system for determining the numerical values of words and names; the finding of acronyms through *notarikon*, in which the first letters of words are used to make new words; and an encryption system called *temurah*, in which letters are transposed into code. Temurah plays a role in interpreting the Torah and in the making of talismans.

4. The Unwritten Kabbalah concerns the study of the Tree of Life, a system for the ascension of human consciousness.

Of the four branches, the Practical Kabbalah, Literal Kabbalah, and Unwritten Kabbalah are the most important to the Western magical tradition. Joined with Hermetic principles and philosophy, these parts of the Kabbalah create a philosophical, mystical, and magical system for the practice of ceremonial magic. This system, sometimes called the "Western Kabbalah" or "Western Qabalah," also plays a role in practical magic for the casting of spells.

History of the Kabbalah

According to lore, the Kabbalah originated from God's teachings to angels. After the fall of Adam and Eve, sympathetic angels taught the knowledge to Adam in order to provide man with a way back to God. The knowledge was passed to Noah, then to Abraham and Moses, who in turn initiated seventy Elders. Kings David and Solomon were initiates. Influenced by Gnosticism and Neoplatonism, the oral tradition was passed on into the tradition and literature of the Merkabah, early Jewish mysticism circa 100 BC-1000.

"Merkabah" means "God's Throne-Chariot" and refers to the chariot of Ezekiel's vision. The goal of the Merkabah mystic was to enter the throne world and perceive God sitting upon his throne. The throne world was reached after passing through seven heavens while in an ecstatic trance state. The passage of the mystic was dangerous, impeded by hostile angels. Talismans, seals, the sacred names of angels, and incantations were required to navigate through the obstacles.

The historical origin of the true Kabbalah centers on the Sefer Yetzirah ("Book of Creation"), attributed to Rabbi Akiba, whom the Romans martyred. The book's exact date of origin is unknown. It was in use in the tenth century, but it may have been authored as early as the third century. The Sefer Yetzirah presents a discussion on cosmology and cosmogony, and sets forth the central structure of the Kabbalah.

In 917, a form of Practical Kabbalism was introduced by Aaron ben Samuel in Italy, and spread through Germany and became known as German Kabbalism or Early Hasidim. It drew upon the Merkabah practices, in that it was ecstatic, had magic rituals, and had as primary techniques prayer, contemplation, and meditation. The magical power of words and names assumed great importance, and gave rise to the techniques of *gematria, notarikon* and *temurah*.

The Classical Kabbalah was born in the thirteenth century in Provence, France, and moved into Spain, where it was developed most extensively by medieval Spanish Jews. The primary work from which classical Kabbalah developed is the Sefer Zohar ("Book of Splendor"), attributed to a second-century sage, Rabbi Simeon bar Yohai, but actually written between 1280-86 by the Spanish Kabbalist, Moses de Leon. According to lore, the book comprises the teachings given to Rabbi Simeon by divine revelation.

The teachings of the Zohar became known as the Spanish Kabbalah and spread into Europe in the fourteenth and fifteenth centuries. After the expulsion of Jews from Spain in 1492, Kabbalah study became more public. Isaac Luria Ashkenazi (1534-72), called the Ari Luria, a student of the great Kabbalist, Moses Cordovero (1522-70), conceived of bold new theories that gave the Kabbalah a new terminology and complex new symbolism. Luria emphasized letter combinations as a medium for meditation and mystical prayer.

In the fourteenth century, a Practical Kabbalah developed involving magical techniques for making amulets and talismans, and for invoking spirits. The Practical Kabbalah is complex, and features the use of magical alphabets as secret codes for communication with angels.

Interest in the Kabbalah among Jews declined after the eighteenth century and then entered a cross-cultural renewal in the late twentieth century as part of a broad interest in esoteric subjects.

Western occult interest in the Kabbalah grew first out of German Kabbalism and then Lurianic Kabbalism. Christian occultists were attracted to the magical amulets, incantations, demonology, angelology, seals, and letter permutations, and used these as the basis for ritual magical texts called grimoires.

In the late fifteenth century, the Kabbalah was harmonized with Christian doctrines, which supposedly proved the divinity of Christ. The great occultist Cornelius Agrippa Von Nettesheim (1486-1535) included the Kabbalah in his monumental work, *Occult Philosophy* (1531). Also in the sixteenth century, alchemical symbols were integrated into the Christian Kabbalah. The Westernized Kabbalah is often spelled with a Q: Qabalah, to distinguish it from the original Jewish tradition.

The Tree of Life

Chief of importance to Kabbalah, as well as the Tarot-Kabbalah connection, is the Tree of Life, created by God, called Ain Soph ("without end" or "unending"), who cannot be known or named and is beyond representation. God created the world out of himself, but is not diminished in any way through the act of creation; everything remains within him.

The aim of man is to realize union with the divine. All things are reflected in a higher world, and nothing can exist independently of all else. Thus, man, by elevating his soul to unite with God, also elevates all other entities in the cosmos.

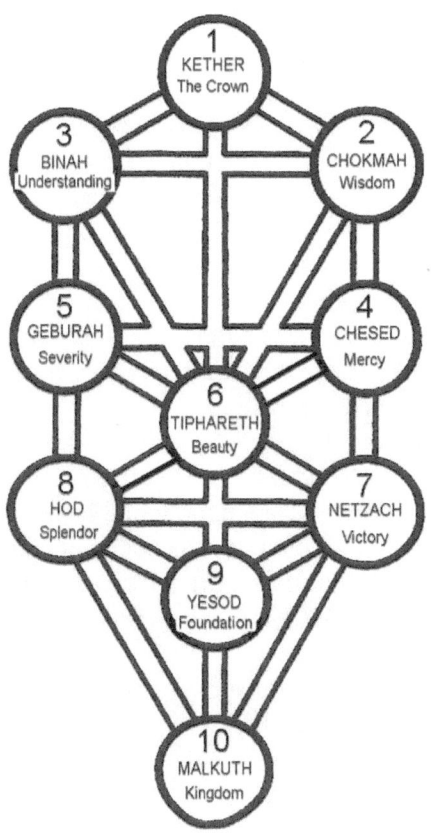

TREE OF LIFE

One of the mysteries of the Kabbalah is why God chose to create imperfect, lower worlds, though it is held that he did so because he wished to show the measure of his goodness. He created the world by means of thirty-two secret paths of wisdom, which are formed of letters and numbers: the twenty-two letters of the Hebrew alphabet and ten stations, or *sephirot* (from the Hebrew word for "sapphire"), which are vessels bearing the emanations of God, or are expressions of God. They form a language that substitutes for God. The *sephirot* are the source from which all numbers emanate and by which all reality is structured, represented by the Tree of Life.

The *sephirot* comprise the sacred, unknowable, and unspeakable personal name of God: YHVH (Yahweh), also called the Tetragrammaton. So sacred is the Tetragrammaton that other names, such as Elohim, Adonai and Jehovah, are substituted in its place in scripture. The letters YHVH correspond to the Four Worlds which constitute the cosmos:

- Atziluth is the world of archetypes and emanation, from which are derived all forms of manifestation. The *sephirot* themselves exist here. Atziluth is the realm of contemplation.
- Briah (also Beriyah) is the world of creation, in which archetypal ideas become patterns. The Throne of God is here, and God sits upon it and lowers his essence to the rest of his creation. It is the realm of meditation.
- Yetzirah is the world of formation, in which the patterns are expressed. It is the world of speech, and also the realm of ritual magic.
- Assiah is the world of the material. It is the realm of action in daily life.

In the Tree of Life, the *sephirot* form the central image of Kabbalistic meditation. The tree is a ladder map depicting the descent of the divine into the material world, and the path by which man can ascend to the divine while still in the flesh. The *sephirot* channel streams of divine light that become denser and coarser as they near the material plane. The divine light flows both down to the material world and up to God along these paths.

Each *sephirah* is a state of consciousness and a level of attainment in knowledge: mystical steps to unity with God. The ten *sephirot* are arranged in different groups, which facilitate the understanding of their meanings. The first *sephirah*, Kether (Crown), is the closest to Ain Soph, the Godhead, and is the source of all life and the highest object of prayer. Malkuth (Kingdom) penetrates the physical realm and is the only *sephirah* in direct contact with it. The lower seven *sephirot* are associated with the seven days of creation. Another division splits them into two groups of five, the upper ones representing hidden powers and the lower five representing manifest powers.

In another division, the top three—Kether, Chockmah (Wisdom) and Binah (Intelligence)—are associated with the intellect; the middle three—Chesed (Love), Geburah (Strength) and Tipareth (Beauty)—are associated with the soul; and the lower three--Netzach (Victory), Hod (Splendor) and Yesod (Foundation)—are associated with nature.

The *sephirot* are ineffable and descriptions of them cannot begin to approach their true essence. They can be reached only through the second *sephirah*, Chockmah (Wisdom), which is nonverbal consciousness. Binah (Intelligence) is verbal consciousness. One must learn to oscillate between Chockmah and Binah states of consciousness in order to grasp the *sephirot*.

The Tree is split into three pillars. The Right Pillar, masculine, represents Mercy and includes the Chockmah, Chesed, and Netzach. The Left Pillar, feminine, represents Severity and includes Binah, Geburah, and Hod. The Middle represents Mildness or Moderation and includes Kether, Tipareth, Yesod and Malkuth. The Middle Pillar alone also is called the Tree of Knowledge.

Sometimes an eleventh *sephirah* is included, Daath (Knowledge), located on the Middle Pillar below Chockmah and Binah, and mediates the influences of the two; it is also considered to be an external aspect of Kether. Daath made its appearance in the thirteenth century. When represented on the Tree, it is depicted as a sort of shadow sphere. Daath cannot be a true *sephirah*, for the Sefer Yetzirah, the key text of Kabbalistic philosophy, states that there can be only ten *sephirot*, no more, no less.

The pathways linking the *sephirot* have become more complex over time. Illustrations in the early sixteenth century, for example, depict only sixteen pathways. By the seventeenth century, there were twenty-two pathways, each of which was assigned a letter of the Hebrew alphabet. Thus, God's creation is made through the essences of numbers and letters.

Together the *sephirot* of the Tree of Life comprise a unity and create a five-dimensional continuum: the three dimensions of the physical world, plus time, plus the spiritual realm. Like the Akashic Records, they serve as a permanent record of everything that has ever taken place and ever will take place—the memory of God. The *sephirot* also serve as a means of communication with the unknowable God. The totality of the *sephirot* is expressed in the Tetragrammaton, the sacred and unspeakable name of God, given as YHVH (Yahweh), or "the Lord."

Here are the names and associations of the *sephirot*, as given in Agrippa's *Occult Philosophy*:

Kether
Number: One
Titles: The Crown; The Ancient One; The Aged; The Most Holy Ancient One; The Ancient of the Ancient Ones; The Ancient of Days; The Concealed of the Concealed; The Primordial Point; The Smooth Point; The White Head; The Inscrutable Height; The Vast Countenance (Macroprosopus); The Heavenly Man
Divine Name: Eheieh (I Am)
Archangel: Metatron
Angelic Order: Hayyoth (The Holy Living Creatures)
Archdemons: Satan, Moloch
Demonic Order: Thamiel (The Two Contenders)
Heavenly Sphere: Primum Mobile
Part of Man: Head

Chockmah
Number: Two
Titles: Wisdom; Divine Father; The Supernal Father
Divine Names: Jah; Jehovah (The Lord); Yod Jehovah (given by Agrippa)
Archangel: Raziel
Angelic Order: Ophanim (The Wheels)
Archdemon: Beelzebub
Demonic Order: Ghogiel (The Hinderers)
Heavenly Sphere: Zodiac
Part of Man: Brain

Binah
Number: Three
Titles: Intelligence; The Mother; The Great Productive Mother

Divine Names: Elohim (Lord); Jehovah Elohim (The Lord God)
Archangel: Tzaphkiel
Angelic Order: Aralim (The Thrones)
Archdemon: Lucifuge
Demonic Order: Ghogiel (The Concealers)
Heavenly Sphere: Saturn
Part of Man: Heart

Chesed
Number: Four
Titles: Love; Greatness
Divine Name: El (The Mighty One)
Archangel: Tzadkiel
Angelic Order: Hasmallim (The Shining Ones)
Archdemon: Ashtaroth
Demonic Order: Agshekeloh (The Smiters or Breakers)
Heavenly Sphere: Jupiter
Part of Man: Right arm

Geburah
Number: Five
Titles: Strength; Judgment or Severity; Fear
Divine Names: Eloh (The Almighty); Elohim Gabor (God of Battles)
Archangel: Camael
Angelic Order: Seraphim (The Fiery Serpents)
Archdemon: Asmodeus
Demonic Order: Golohab (The Burners or Flaming Ones)
Heavenly Sphere: Mars
Part of Man: Left arm

Tiphareth
Number: Six
Titles: Beauty; Compassion; The King; The Lesser Countenance (Microprosopus)
Divine Names: Eloah Va-Daath (God Manifest); Elohim (God)
Archangel: Raphael
Angelic Order: Malachim (Kings or Multitudes)
Archdemon: Belphegor

Demonic Order: Tagiriron (The Disputers)
Heavenly Sphere: Sun
Part of Man: Chest

Netzach
Number: Seven
Titles: Firmness; Victory
Divine Name: Jehovah Sabaoth (Lord of Hosts)
Archangel: Haniel
Angelic Order: Elohim (Gods)
Archdemon: Baal
Demonic Order: Nogah (The Raveners)
Heavenly Sphere: Venus
Part of Man: Right leg

Hod
Number: Eight
Titles: Splendor
Divine Name: Elohim Sabaoth (God of Hosts)
Archangel: Michael
Angelic Order: Bene Elohim (Sons of Gods)
Archdemon: Adrammelech
Demonic Order: Samael (The False Accusers)
Heavenly Sphere: Mercury
Part of Man: Left leg

Yesod
Number: Nine
Titles: The Foundation; Eternal Foundation of the World
Divine Names: Shaddai (The Almighty); El Chai (Mighty Living One)
Archangel: Gabriel
Angelic Order: Cherubim (The Strong)
Archdemon: Lilith (The Seducer)
Demonic Order: Gamaliel (The Obscene Ones)
Heavenly Sphere: Moon
Part of Man: Genitals

Malkuth
Number: Ten
Titles: The Kingdom; The Diadem; The Manifest Glory of God; The Bride (of Microposopus); The Queen
Divine Names: Adonai (Lord); Adonai Malekh (Lord and King); Adonai he-Aretz (Lord of Earth)
Archangel: Metatron in manifest aspect; also Sandalphon
Angelic Order: Issim (Souls of Flame)
Archdemon: Nahema (The Strangler of Children)
Demonic Order: Nahemoth (The Dolorous Ones)
Heavenly Sphere: Elements
Part of Man: Whole body

The Kabbalah/Qabalah and the occult revival

The revival of occultism that increased into the nineteenth century was fueled by a resurgence of interest in the Kabbalah and Westernized Qabalah, magical handbooks called grimoires, and a growing interest in the Tarot. Eliphas Levi was one of the figures at the forefront of the revival, and established correspondences between the Tarot cards and the Hebrew alphabet and the Tree of Life. As did some of his contemporaries, Levi related the Qabalah to the Tarot and numerology, and drew connections to Freemasonry, in which he saw a fusion of Judaic Kabbalism and neo-Platonic Christianity. The Qabalah, Levi said in his *The Book of Splendours: The Inner Mysteries of Qabalism* (1894), is one of three occult sciences of certitude; the other two are Magic and Hermeticism. Of the Qabalah, Levi said:

> The Qabalah, or traditional science of the Hebrews, might be called the mathematics of human thought. It is the algebra of faith. It solves all problems of the soul as equations, by isolating the unknowns. It gives to ideas the clarity and rigorous exactitude of numbers; its results, for the mind, are infallibility (always relative to the sphere of human knowledge) and for the heart, profound peace.

Correspondences

In his approach to the Tarot, Levi was particularly influenced by the writings of Cornelius Agrippa and the mystic Emanuel Swedenborg (1688-1772), on the doctrine of universal correspondences, a fundamental of early alchemy.

The doctrine of universal correspondences exists in some form in most esoteric texts and teachings. Most significantly, it is included in the central Hermetic text, the Emerald Tablet, which contains the whole of Western esoteric philosophy. (According to one version of the legend, the Emerald Tablet was discovered in a cave tomb clutched in the hand of the corpse of Hermes Trismegistus.)

The text has never been proved to be of ancient origin, but, like the rest of the Hermetic writings, was of later Christian authorship. The text is by and large inscrutable (and no two translations agree), but its opening is held to be the axiom of Western occultism: "That which is above is like that which is below and that which is below is like that which is above, to achieve the wonders of the one thing." It also states that "all things were produced by the one word of being, so all things were produced from this one thing by adaptation… Ascend with the greatest sagacity from the earth to heaven, and then again descend to earth, and unite together the powers of things superior and inferior."

From this axiom evolved occult systems of correspondences and sympathetic magic.

Agrippa expounded upon correspondences in On Occult Philosophy, in which he said that "every inferior thing should, in its kind, answer its superior thing…. Hence, every thing may be aptly reduced from these Inferiors to the Stars, from the Stars to their Intelligences, and from thence to the First Cause itself from the series and order whereof all Magic and all Occult Philosophy flows…."

Writing about two centuries later, Swedenborg placed great emphasis upon the importance of correspondences. In *Heaven and Hell*, he stated that to the ancients, "knowledge of correspondences was the chief of knowledges":

> By means of it they acquired intelligence and wisdom; and by means of it those who were of the church had communication with heaven; for the knowledge of correspondences is angelic knowledge. The most

ancient people, who were celestial men, thought from correspondence itself, as the angels do. And therefore they talked with angels, and the Lord frequently appeared to them, and they were taught by Him. But at this day that knowledge has been so completely lost that no one knows what correspondence is.

Since, then, without a perception of what correspondence is there can be no clear knowledge of the spiritual world or of its inflow into the natural world, nor any clear knowledge of the spirit of man, which is called the soul, and its operation into the body, neither of man's state after death, it is necessary to explain what correspondence is and the nature of it...

...The whole natural world corresponds to the spiritual world and not merely the natural world in general, but also every particular of it; and as a consequence everything in the natural world that springs from the spiritual world is called a correspondent....

Thus, correspondences were seen as the way back to the Source, the means by which all great religions and esoteric systems could be unified. For Levi, the origin of all esoteric teachings could be found in the Tarot and the correspondences between it and the letters of the Hebrew alphabet, the sacred name of God and numbers.

Levi accepted Court de Gebelin's Egyptian origin theory, and considered the Tarot to be a collection of symbolic hieroglyphs masking the inner truths of occultism. He was intrigued with the fact that there are twenty-two trumps and twenty-two letters in the Hebrew alphabet, which in turn have numerical values and correspond to the twenty-two paths of the Tree of Life. In 1856, Levi became the first occultist to correspond each Tarot trump to a Hebrew letter, and the four suits of the Minor Arcana to the Tetragrammaton—the four-letter name of God represented by YHVH. He devoted twenty-two chapters to these correspondences in his book, *Ritual of High Magic* (1856). In his book he stated:

> This Clavical [the Arcana] regarded as lost for centuries, has been recovered by us, and we have been able to open the sepulchres of the ancient world, to make the dead

speak, to behold the monuments of the past in all their splendor, to understand the enigmas of every sphinx and to penetrate all sanctuaries... Now, this was the key in question; a hieroglyphic and numeral alphabet, expressing by characters and numbers, a series of universal and absolute ideas...

The symbolical tetrad, represented in the Mysteries of Memphis and Thebes by the four aspects of the sphinx—a man, eagle, lion and bull—corresponded with the four elements of the old world [earth, air, fire and water]... Now these four symbols, with all their analogies, explain the one word hidden in all sanctuaries... Moreover, the sacred word was not pronounced: it was spelt, and expressed in four words, which are the four sacred letters, Yod... He[h]... Vau... He[h]...

The Tarot is a truly philosophical machine, which keeps the mind from wandering, while leaving its initiative and liberty; it is mathematics applied to the Absolute, the alliance of the positive and the ideal, a lottery of thoughts as exact as numbers, perhaps the simplest and grandest conception of human genius...

An imprisoned person, with no other book than the Tarot, if he knew how to use it, could in a few years acquire a universal knowledge and would be able to speak on all subjects with unequalled learning and inexhaustible eloquence.

Levi opined that the Tarot was handed down by "certain wise kabbalists" who preserved their sacred knowledge "first on ivory, parchment, on gilt and silvered leather, and afterwards on simple cards, which were always the objects of suspicion to the Official Church as containing a dangerous key to its mysteries." He described the Tarot as a miraculous book, the source of inspiration of all the sacred ancient books, and a perfect tool for divination "on account of the analogical precision of its figures and its numbers. In fact, the oracles of this book are always rigorously true, and even when it does not predict anything, it always reveals something that was hidden, and gives the wisest counsel to those who consult it."

He heaped praise upon Court de Gebelin for ferreting out the "truth" and criticized Etteilla.

Before he could draw his correspondences between trumps and letters, Levi had to decide where to place the unnumbered Fool card in the sequence of trumps. In order to get the synchronization he desired, he moved The Fool from the beginning to between the last two cards, XX Judgement, and XXI The Universe or World. This enabled him to correspond The Fool with the letter Shin, the symbol of Life-Breath of the Holy Ones, or the Holy Spirit. The insertion did not change the number of the final card, which remained XXI. The sequence of the cards changed one to twenty to zero to twenty-one. In *Ritual of High Magic*, Levi provided his keys to the Major Arcana and their corresponding Hebrew letters as follows:

I The Magician: Aleph
Being, mind, man or God; the incomprehensible object; unity mother of numbers, the first matter

II The Female Pope: Beth
The house of God and man, the sanctuary, the law, gnosis. Cabala, the hidden church, the binary, woman, mother

III The Empress: Gimel
The Word, the ternary, plenitude, fruitfulness, nature, generation of the three worlds

IV The Emperor: Daleth
The door of government among the Orientals, initiation, power, the tetragram, the quaternary, the cubic stone or its base [a symbol of the manifested universe; also, an alchemical symbol for salt, itself a symbol of the earth; also, a symbol of the fraternal Lodge]

V The Pope (The Hierophant): Heh
Indication, demonstration, teaching, law, symbolism, philosophy, religion

VI Vice and Virtue (The Lovers): Vau
Linking together, hooking, lingam, intermingling, union, embrace, struggle, antagonism, combination, equilibrium

VII The Chariot: Zain
Weapon, swords, flaming sword of the church, holy septenary, triumph, royalty, priesthood

VIII Justice: Heth
Balance, attraction and repulsion, life, fear, promise and menace

IX The Hermit: Teth
Good, fear of evil, morality, wisdom

X The Wheel of Fortune: Yod
Principle, manifestation, praise, manly honor, phallus, virile fecundity, the scepter of the father

XI Strength: Kaph
A hand in the act of taking and holding

XII The Hanged Man: Lamed
Example, teaching, public instruction

XIII Death: Mem
The heaven of Jupiter and Mars, domination and force, rebirth, creation and destruction

XIV Temperance: Nun
The heaven of the Sun, temperatures, seasons, movement, changes of life, always new and yet always the same

XV The Devil: Samech
The heaven of Mercury, occult science, magic, commerce, eloquence, mystery, moral strength

XVI The Tower: Ayin
The heaven of the moon, alterations, subversions, changes, weakness

XVII The Star: Phe
The heaven of the soul, thought emissions, moral influence of the idea on forms, immortality

XVIII The Moon: Tzaddi
The elements, the visible world, reflected light, material forms, symbolism

XIX The Sun: Quoph
Mixtures, the head, the summit, the prince of heaven

XX Judgement: Resh
The vegetative, earth's generative power, eternal life

0 The Fool: Shin
Sensibility, flesh, eternal life.

XXI The Universe (The World): Tau
The microcosm, the resume of all in all

Levi found Kabbalistic associations for the Minor Arcana by corresponding the four suits and the four court cards in each suit to the four letters of the Tetragrammaton:

> **Yod**: Sceptres (Wands); King; enterprise and glory
> **Heh**: Cups; Queen; love and happiness
> **Vau**: Swords; Knight; hatred and misfortune
> **Heh**: Pentacles; Page; money and interest

Levi also used the letter-manipulation technique of *temurah* to find meaning in the word *Tarot*. *Temurah*, as noted earlier, is the transposition of letters in a word to create new words. Thus, Levi found that "Tarot" could be transposed to *rota*, the Latin term for "wheel," and "Tora," an incomplete spelling of "Torah," the scripture and law of Judaism. The *temurah* codes were corroborating evidence to him that the Tarot was indeed a wheel of life or spiritual evolution, and was founded on Kabbalistic wisdom.

Levi represented this graphically. R stands for the Christ symbol, which lies between O and A, representing the Omega and Alpha, respectively, the end and the beginning. T stands for Tau, the cross of incarnation. Levi corresponded T to Yod; O to the first Heh; R to Vau; and A to the second Heh in the Tetragrammaton.

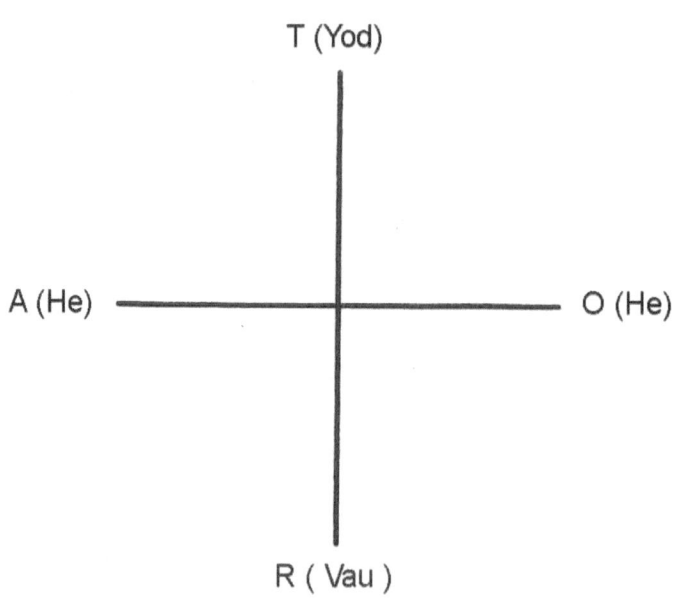

LEVI'S WHEEL OF LIFE

Levi's opinions on the Tarot were both hailed and dismissed, and supported and refuted, not only by the occultists of his day but those who came immediately after him. Some of those who refuted Levi did give him the benefit of the doubt, suggesting that he may have deliberately obscured occult information to fool the uninitiated. In esoteric teachings, blinds are not uncommon as a means of preventing information from falling into the wrong hands, either those who would seek to destroy the information, or those who are not yet prepared to receive it. Despite the debate over Levi's views, and regardless of the validity, Levi's interpretation of the Tarot became firmly ensconced in the development of the Tarot.

Later in his life, Levi concluded that the Tarot had originated in the Middle East and been brought to Europe by the Gypsies.

Levi's influence

Despite his critics, Levi had a profound influence on some of his students, as well as other occultists. His interpretations were expanded by Gerard Encausse, a physician who, as previously noted, went by the occult pseudonym, Papus, and who studied with Levi. As a leading Martinist and member of the Kabbalistic Order of the Rose-Cross, Papus, too, was steeped in occultism. He saw the Tarot as presenting the spiritual history of man: the emergence of the soul from the Source, descending to the material, then returning to the Source. In his most important work on the Tarot, *The Tarot of the Bohemians: The Absolute Key to Occult Science* (1889), he optimistically predicted that society was on the verge of incredible transformation, and that materialism was on the way out. What was needed was synthesis, in the fashion of the wisdom taught by the ancients.

In ancient times, Papus said, knowledge was transmitted only to those who had proved themselves worthy by passing tests of initiation. The knowledge was transmitted in the secret rites of the Mysteries, upon which the adept became known as a Priest or Initiate. There came a time when the Initiates realized that their knowledge might be lost forever, and they established three ways for preserving it: through secret societies, the "cultus," and the people. The secret societies originated primarily from Alexandria, the great ancient seat of learning, and included such groups as the Gnostics, alchemists, Knights Templar, Rosicrucians, and Freemasons. The cultus was the means by which the one true religion was translated to religions that would suit the temperaments of all peoples, each with its own tradition and scriptures. The people who were entrusted with preserving and transmitting occult doctrines were the Bohemians, or Gypsies, whose card game of Tarot was the "Bible of Bibles ... the book of Thoth Hermes Trismegistus, the book of Adam, the book of the primitive Revelation of ancient civilization," said Papus.

The key to the Tarot, he said (echoing Levi), was the Tetragrammaton, YHVH, each letter of which not only had Tarot correspondences, but also correspondences with Christian symbols: Yod = the episcopal crosier; Heh = the chalice; Vau = the Cross; and Heh = the Host. The Tarot itself was based on the word ROTA, arranged as a wheel, each letter corresponding to a letter in the Tetragrammaton: R = Vau; O = Heh; T = Yod; and A = Heh.

Papus adopted Levi's placement of The Fool between XX and XXI of the Major Arcana. And, like Levi, he denounced Etteilla's deck, describing it as "of no symbolic value" and "a bad mutilation of the real Tarot." Papus also laid great stress upon the Pythagorean system of numbers in deciphering the meaning of the cards.

According to Papus, his Kabbalistic explanation of the Tarot was "for the exclusive use of Initiates." This was in keeping with the teachings of the day, that certain levels of knowledge were only for those whose studies and participation in secret orders and societies entitled them to access. How this declaration prevented the uninitiated masses from reading Papus's book remains a mystery.

In 1889, the same year that Papus published *The Tarot of the Bohemians*, Oswald Wirth published a deck of Major Arcana whose twenty-two designs incorporated the twenty-two Hebrew letters. Papus and Wirth both influenced the teachings of the Kabbalistic Order of the Rose Cross, which evolved into Rosicrucianism.

Paul Christian, another Levi student, created a system combining Tarot with Kabbalistic astrology.

Thus, Levi, Papus, and their followers laid the foundation for a Kabbalistic Tarot, which was absorbed into the teachings of the Hermetic Order of the Golden Dawn, the greatest magical order of modern times, and the source of several of the most influential and favored Tarot decks still in use today.

Critical views

The Tarot-Hebrew alphabet association came under fire in ensuing years. The correlation works at times, but in some cases is forced. Manly P. Hall (1901-1990), the founder of the Philosophical Research Society and author of *The Secret Teachings of All Ages* (1928), termed such associations "far from convincing." Some Jewish Kabbalists and scholars understandably frown on what they consider to be misrepresentations of the true Kabbalah. One outspoken scholar was Gershom Scholem (1897-1982), who stated in his book, *Kabbalah* (1974):

The many books written on the subject in the nineteenth and twentieth centuries by various theosophists and mystics lacked any basic knowledge of the sources and very rarely contributed to the field, while at times they even hindered the development of a historical approach. Similarly, the activities of French and English occultists contributed nothing and only served to create considerable confusion between the teachings of the Kabbalah and their own totally unrelated inventions, such as the alleged kabbalistic origin of the Tarot cards. To this category of supreme charlatanism belong the many and widely read books of Eliphas Levi (actually Alphonse Louis Constant; 1810-1875), Papus (Gerard Encausse; 1868-1916), and Frater Perdurabo (Aleister Crowley; 1875-1947), all of whom had infinitesimal knowledge of Kabbalah that did not prevent them from drawing freely on their imaginations instead.

Such criticisms, however, have not dampened study of the Kabbalistic Tarot, for the correspondences between the letters and the trumps do seem to have an interesting significance. As Waite once observed, "The attempt to connect the symbols of the Tarot with the system of Kabalistic [sic] theosophy will seem in itself arbitrary, but it can, under certain circumstances, produce very curious results."

Are these results are mere coincidence, or do they hold hidden truths? At the very least, the Kabbalah-Tarot correspondences form a road map for expressing and exploring universal cosmic truths.

For detailed approaches to the Kabbalistic Tarot, see *The Tarot: A Key to the Wisdom of the Ages* and *The Book of Tokens* by Paul Foster Case (1934); *The Qabalistic Tarot* by Robert Wang (1987); and *A Practical Guide to Qabalistic Symbolism* (1978) by Gareth Knight.

3

The Golden Dawn Influence

The Hermetic Order of the Golden Dawn, established in 1888 in London, possessed the greatest store of Western occult and magical teachings of all time. It attracted the leading occultists, among them Arthur Edward Waite (1857-1942), Samuel Liddell MacGregor Mathers (1854-1918), William Butler Yeats (1865-1939), and Aleister Crowley (1875-1947).

The Golden Dawn placed the Hermetic Kabbalah and the Tarot at the center of its teachings.

The Golden Dawn was not originally intended to be a magical order, but a secret society for adepts who wished to complete their training in spiritual growth, drawn from studies in alchemy, Rosicrucianism, Freemasonry, the Kabbalah, and other esoteric arts. The primary purpose of the order was "to prosecute the Great Work: which is to obtain control of the nature and power of my own being." Some of the texts included Christian elements, such as the establishing of a closer relationship with Jesus, the "Master of Masters." Members circulated various Catholic and Anglican writings and sermons.

Ritual magical practices quickly became a focus of the Order. A great deal of magical knowledge flowed out from the Golden Dawn, as well as ground-breaking advances in the Tarot.

History

The history of the Hermetic Order of the Golden Dawn—usually known simply as the Golden Dawn—is colorful and explosive. It flamed into prominence like a bolide meteor, and by 1896 was in decline. Still, it lasted into the twentieth century, splitting into offshoots and continuing to inspire students of the occult to the present day.

The three principal founders were all both Rosicrucians and Freemasons: William Wynn Westcott, a London coroner; Samuel Liddell Macgregor Mathers, an occultist and author; and William Robert Woodman, a retired physician and horticulturist who was Supreme Magus of the Rosicrucian Society of Anglia. Woodman had a strong interest in and knowledge of the Kabbalah, which he had introduced to Rosicrucian studies. Westcott conceived the idea for the Golden Dawn and invited Woodman and Mathers to cofound it with him. Woodman was old enough to be the "gentleman" of the society and lend it an air of Victorian respectability.

Traditionally, secret societies have a legacy linking them to older or ancient groups or teachings, thus demonstrating an inherited lineage, an unbroken stream of esoteric knowledge, and a link to an established authority. This was especially important in the late nineteenth century. Westcott undoubtedly felt a need to produce an ancient legacy, knowing that serious Kabbalists, Rosicrucians and Masons would not otherwise be attracted to the new organization. So, he fabricated a legacy: the Cipher Manuscript, a mysterious document that served as the basis for Golden Dawn rituals and teachings.

Westcott claimed that in 1887, he acquired part of an old manuscript written in brown ink cipher that contained fragments of rituals. The manuscript had been found in a London bookstall in 1884. He said that thanks to his Hermetic knowledge, he was able to decipher the manuscript. He discovered that it concerned fragments of rituals for the "Golden Dawn," an unknown organization that admitted both men and women. Inserted in the manuscript was another document, also written in cipher, which provided the name, address, and credentials of a woman in Germany, "Fraulein Sprengel" (Anna Sprengel), whose magical motto was Soror Sapiens Dominabitur Astris, or "the wise person shall be ruled by the stars." Westcott said he wrote to Sprengel and was informed that she was an adept of an occult order called Die Goldene Dammerung, or The Golden Dawn. Sprengel advised Westcott that he and his associates could establish "an elementary Branch of the Rosicrucian Order in England." In so doing, the Golden Dawn claimed to be directly descended from Christian Rosencreutz, the legendary founder of Rosicrucianism. Westcott said that Sprengel authorized him to sign her name to any documents.

In 1887, Westcott contacted Mathers, an occultist, who, with the help of his clairvoyant wife, Moina, determined that the manuscript concerned the Kabbalah and the Tarot.

The true authorship of the Cipher Manuscript has never been disclosed. Westcott is believed by many to be the author, though other occultists have been put forward as candidates.

In the spring of 1888, Westcott created a Charter of Warrant for the Isis-Urania Temple No. 3 of the Order of the Golden Dawn in London, with himself, Mathers, and Woodman as the three Chiefs. Westcott asked Mathers to flesh out the fragments of the Cipher Manuscript into full-scale rituals.

The secret society quickly caught on. By the end of 1888, the temple had thirty-two members, nine of whom were women. Three more temples were established. Membership grew rapidly, reaching a peak of 315 by 1896.

From 1888 to 1891, the Golden Dawn taught Outer Order theoretical magic. One advanced through the ranks of the Outer Order by examination. Initially, Westcott, Mathers, and Woodman were the only members of the Second Order, and they claimed to be under the direction of the Secret Chiefs of the Third Order, who were beings which manifested only on the astral plane. Mathers's rituals were based largely on Freemasonry.

After Woodman's death in 1891, Mathers became the primary Chief and created an initiation ritual based on the legend of Christian Rosenkreutz for a fully functional Second Order, open by examination and invitation. He revised the curriculum, and added practical magic. Second Order studies centered on the Kabbalistic Tree of Life. Three magical systems were taught: the Key of Solomon, magical grimoire supposedly derived from the magic possessed by King Solomon, who had control of all spirits, including Djinn; Abra-Melin magic, based on a magical grimoire attributed to a Jewish kabbalist, and derived from The Key of Solomon; and Enochian magic, based on the "angel" channelings of John Dee and Edward Kelly.

Materials also were incorporated from the Egyptian Book of the Dead, William Blake's Prophetic Books, and the Chaldean Oracles, which were surviving fragments of ancient Greek magical texts. Teachings were given on ritual magic, the Kabbalah, the Tarot, astral travel, scrying, alchemy, geomancy, and astrology. Mathers adopted "Qabalah" as the spelling for Kabbalah, stating that it was closer to the original Hebrew term.

Mathers' curriculum was so rigorous that few people could complete it.

Almost as soon as The Golden Dawn reached its peak, it began faltering in a series of personal disputes, schisms, and rivalries. Mathers fell on hard times and he and Moina moved to Paris, losing control over the order. In 1900 he exposed the Sprengel letters as fakes, which rocked the Order. Wescott, who was still alive, declined comment.

More trouble came from Aleister Crowley, who had been initiated in 1898 and had risen rapidly up the ranks. Initially he was an ally of Mathers, and in 1899 unsuccessfully attempted to help Mathers regain control of the Second Order in London. Crowley, wearing a black mask and Highland dress and wielding a gilt dagger, stormed the Second Order's headquarters. He staged a dramatic attempt, but was rebuffed.

Crowley then turned on Mathers, and the two engaged in a famous magical battle, hurling astral vampires and demons at each other. Outraged at these antics, the London Lodge, under the leadership of Florence Farr, expelled both of them.

Crowley retaliated by publishing the Golden Dawn's secret rituals. In 1910, Mathers went to court and obtained an order to stop Crowley, but Crowley won on appeal, claiming he used magic to do so.

William Butler Yeats then took over the Second Order. He attempted to restore unity by restructuring the Order, but the Golden Dawn broke into independent groups. By 1901, Yeats gave up and resigned.

Followers of Mathers left and formed the Alpha et Omega Temple. In 1903, Arthur Edward Waite and others left, forming a group with the name Golden Dawn, but with more of an emphasis on mysticism than magic. In 1905, another splinter group was formed, the Stella Matutina, or "Order of the Companions of the Rising Light in the Morning," which absorbed the Alpha et Omega Lodge. The original Isis-Urania Temple No. 3 became defunct. In 1917, it was resurrected as the Merlin Temple of the Stella Matutina. The Stella Matutina went into decline in the 1940s, following the publication of its secret rituals by a former member, Israel Regardie (1907-1983), Crowley's one-time secretary and a member of the Stella Matutina offshoot lodge.

Waite's group, which retained the Golden Dawn name and some of its rituals, declined after 1915 with Waite's departure.

Some distant offshoots of the Golden Dawn continue in existence. Golden Dawn rituals and teachings continue to be widely used and adapted.

Magical work with the Tree of Life

The Tree of Life served as the major tool for spiritual exploration and ceremonial magic, as well as a model for the Golden Dawn itself. Dion Fortune (1891-1946), a Golden Dawn initiate who then joined the Alpha et Omega Lodge, called the Kabbalah the "Yoga of the West." In spiritual and magical study done then and now, the Tree of Life is used to achieve union with God. The pathways between the *sephirot* are avenues of navigation on the astral plane. The occultist William G. Gray (1913-1995) described the Tree of life as a living entity that changes in accordance to use. The Tree is an "alphabet of symbols" for constructing a spiritual language that can be understood on both sides of the veil, by humans, gods, and angels alike.

In magical training, the occultist must learn the associations of each *sephirah* and path, such as magical tools, colors, planets, chakras, virtues, vices, sounds, perfumes, and Tarot cards, in addition to the associations given above. Symbols are used as magical images for constructing specific visions. The symbols are not understood consciously, but are used to evoke images from the subconscious. Communication with the Tree is accomplished through prayer, meditation, contemplation and ritual magic. Some traditional meditations of arrays of numbers and Hebrew letters take days to complete.

The *sephirot* are contemplated by visualizing them vibrating with color (which represent various qualities), together with images of their corresponding Hebrew letters of the divine names of God, and the planets, angels, metals, parts of the body, and energy centers. Breath and sound also are utilized to raise consciousness. Mantras of arrays of Hebrew letters, having specific numerical properties, are employed.

The Tarot in the Golden Dawn

Also of great importance in the Golden Dawn curriculum was a set of Tarot papers called Book T, which was given to initiates. Book T set forth the Tarot as the key to the Qabalah and all Western esotericism, and corresponded the Major Arcana to the Hebrew alphabet. According to Rosicrucian legend—an account that mirrors the legend of Hermes Trismegistus and the Emerald Tablet—Book T was found clutched in the hand of the perfectly preserved corpse of Christian Rosencreutz when his secret burial vault was discovered in 1604. He supposedly had died in 1484 at 106 years of age.

Golden Dawn Tarot teachings corresponded the Major Arcana to the paths connecting the sephirot of the Tree of Life. Tarot visualizations and meditations were part of the practical magic taught to initiates. The Tarot became increasingly important as the initiate advanced in rank. It served as a visual representation of the initiate's progress on the Tree of Life, and thus through the Order itself. The Tarot also was an important tool for uniting astrology and the Qabalah, and played a role in ceremonial magic and the energies of the four Kabbalistic worlds.

The Golden Dawn Tarot deck

Mathers, who claimed prodigious feats with the help of occult powers, designed a Tarot deck for the Golden Dawn, and Moina painted the finished product. Members copied the original. Decades later in the twentieth century, the Golden Dawn Tarot was reconstructed by artist Robert Wang, working under the direction of Israel Regardie. It was published in 1978, marking the first time the deck was made public.

The Golden Dawn Tarot is widely regarded as one of the most, if not the most, "Qabalistically" correct Tarot decks created.

The Waite-Smith Tarot revolution

The greatest advancement to the Tarot was made by Arthur Edward Waite, working in partnership with another Golden Dawn member, Pamela Colman Smith (1878-1951), an artist with psychic ability and a Bohemian bent. Waite, also a Freemason, reinterpreted the Tarot cards according to what he believed were their original and lost mystical meanings. The spurious history and theories ascribed to the Tarot by earlier occultists, and the bad designs given the cards such as by Etteilla, prompted Waite to "restore and rectify" the cards, he said. He thought the cards themselves were no older than the fourteenth century, but they portrayed much older, even ancient, esoteric symbols.

Waite drew upon his own extensive esoteric knowledge, including magic, the Qabalah, alchemy, and Book T to design his own Tarot deck. His stated purpose was to "produce a Tarot with an appeal in the world of art and a suggestion of significance beyond the Symbols which would put on them another construction than had ever been dreamed by those who, through many generations, had produced and used them for mere divinatory purposes." The card symbols, he said, were "gates which opened on realms of vision beyond occult dreams."

As for fortune-telling, Waite said, the Tarot was never intended for such purpose, he said, but was adapted to it. The fact that nothing but divinatory meanings had ever been assigned the Minor Arcana indicated that the Tarot was a merger of two independently evolved decks. In his book *The Pictorial Key to the Tarot* (1910), written to accompany the deck, he said:

> The true Tarot is symbolism; it speaks no other language and offers no other signs. Given the inward meaning of its emblems, they do become a kind of alphabet which is capable of indefinite combinations and makes true sense in all. On the highest plane it offers a key to the Mysteries, in a manner which is not arbitrary and has not been read in. But the wrong symbolical stories have been told concerning it, and the wrong history has been given in every published work which so far has dealt with the subject....
>
> [The Tarot] is not, by attribution or otherwise, a derivative of any one school of literature of occultism; it is not of Alchemy or Kabalism [sic] or Astrology or Ceremonial Magic; ...it is a presentation of universal ideas by means of universal types, and it is in the combination of these types—if anywhere—that it presents Secret Doctrine.

In redesigning the cards, Waite said that he drew upon the "Secret Doctrine" (the Golden Dawn teachings) as much as he could within the confines of restrictions against revealing too much to non-initiates. He accepted sole responsibility for the variations in symbols from the Marseilles deck, the standard up to that time.

Waite and Smith named the allegorical trumps the "Major Arcana" (major secrets), and the four suits the "Minor Arcana." They dramatically changed the Tarot forever by giving each card in the Minor Arcana its own pictorial image instead of just repetitions of suit symbols. This made the pip cards much more suggestive to divination and contemplation with the help of pictures.

It is sometimes erroneously reported in Tarot literature that Waite moved The Fool to the beginning of the pack. On the contrary, he left The Fool, numbered 0, between XX and XXI, where Levi had placed it. He did so despite the fact that he believed that Court de Gebelin's placement of The Fool at the beginning of the pack made more sense, and that the efforts to correspond the cards to the Hebrew alphabet remained unsatisfactory. "The truth is that the real arrangement of the cards has never transpired," Waite said. The placement of The Fool was a source of disagreement between Waite and Smith; significantly, it is the only design she did not sign. [Much later, The Fool became 0 at the beginning of the deck.]

Waite also transposed two cards in the Major Arcana, Justice and Strength (or Fortitude), but gave no explanation for his reasons in doing so. In the Marseilles deck. Justice and Strength are VIII and XI, respectively. In Waite's deck, they trade places. The transposition is still debated. An argument is made on the one hand that Waite rectified a blind used to veil the true meaning of the cards, and an argument is made on the other hand that he deliberately created a blind. Another theory, advanced by Paul Foster Case, was that Waite had changed the cards to fit astrological associations: the number VIII card should correspond to Leo, and thus Strength, the woman subduing the lion, is appropriate; the number XI card should correspond to Libra, and thus Justice, holding the scales, provides a match. Because Waite never made public his reasoning, this may or may not have been the case.

In the court cards, Waite replaced the Knave with the Page, a youth who is in servitude to the Knight, who in turn is the son of the Queen and King.

Waite and Smith placed no Hebrew letters on the cards, but the cards do bear Kabbalistic symbols, and Waite did make references to the Kabbalah in the guide book to the deck. He apparently did correspond the cards to Hebrew letters—something the adepts would know and recognize secretly—though he publicly stated that he saw no association between the two: "I am not to be included among those who are satisfied that there is a valid correspondence between Hebrew letters and Tarot Trump symbols," he said. This would have been a typical practice of the times to cloak the secret mysteries from all but the adepts. In fact, the deck has been criticized for its many blinds intended to obscure secrets from casual users.

Even without the Hebrew letters, the result was a revolutionary Tarot. All the new images contained numerous occult symbolisms and provided rich terrain for advanced uses of the Tarot. The entire deck was useful for occult meditation, visualization, and high magic. Only persons with sufficient esoteric knowledge would be able to read the true visionary secrets of the cards. The Tarot images could be employed in magical meditations and contemplations as gateways and guides to various levels in astral projection. Use of the images helped to avoid wandering along the astral byways, and kept the initiate on track. Meditating on the Tarot also served to develop the important faculty of imagination.

The deck was published alone in 1909 by the Rider publishing house in London, and was called simply Tarot Cards. In 1910 Waite brought out the deck's guide book, *The Pictorial Key to the Tarot*, which included Smith's black-and-white drawings of the cards. In 1971, U.S. Games systems, a major publisher of Tarot decks, bought rights to publish the deck.

The deck was called the Rider Tarot and the Rider-Waite Tarot, both of which slighted Smith. More recently, her name has been restored to references to the deck, as the Waite-Smith Tarot.

Nearly a century after its creation, the Waite-Smith is still considered one of the best renditions of the Tarot and is the universal standard by which many other decks have been designed.

In subsequent decades, the majority of new Tarot decks have taken their cue from Waite-Smith, or at least used the deck as a springboard. Many modern decks have Minor Arcana with pictures, follow similar suit designations, and have the transposed Strength and Justice. The Fool, however, most commonly—and most sensibly—is placed at the beginning of the deck.

Crowley's Thoth Tarot

Aleister Crowley's Thoth Tarot was the last great deck to come out of the original Golden Dawn. Crowley was indisputably the most colorful and notorious of the Golden Dawn initiates, the self-proclaimed "Beast of the Apocalypse" and "Lord of the New Aeon" whose ritual magic rites involving sex (much of it abusive), blood sacrifice, and the conjuring of demons earned him the media label of "The Wickedest Man in the World." There seems to be no middle ground when it comes to Crowley: he is either despised as a charlatan or revered as one of the most brilliant ritual magicians of modern times. He destroyed himself with dissipation and drugs, yet his writings of magical and mystical instruction survive with an ever-changing audience of formidable size.

Crowley referred to the Tarot as "the Book of Thoth," and he gave his own interpretation of the Major Arcana—which he called the Atus of Tahuti—as a formula for initiation. "I have satisfied myself that these twenty-two cards compose a complete system of hieroglyphs representing the total energies of the universe," he said. He saw the cards as living entities that could only be understood by living and interacting with them daily over a long period of time.

He also used the Tarot for divination, and recorded at least one incident in which the Tarot passed "a very remarkable test" for that purpose. While in Shanghai, Crowley's hostess was visited by the postmaster, who was distraught over the loss of a packet of a large sum of money that had been mailed by a bank in Peking to its head office in Shanghai. The postmaster had placed the packet in a safe and found it missing less than an hour later. Crowley offered to investigate the situation via the Tarot. Laying out the cards, he was able to accurately describe two postal clerks who had access to the safe. One was reliable and conscientious, and the other, a junior clerk, was careless, a gambler who had an unsavory reputation. Naturally, the junior clerk was the likely suspect, which Crowley said was confirmed by the cards.

Then, however, the cards "went crazy," saying first that the junior clerk should not suffer for his act, and then saying that the postmaster's reputation would not suffer. To Crowley, it made no sense, in light of the loss of a large sum of money, for which the postmaster ultimately would be held responsible. The turn in the reading annoyed Crowley, and he wound up apologizing to the postmaster, saying, "Well, they [the cards] insist that it is all right for you."

Several days later, the reading bore out. The junior clerk had accidentally placed the parcel in the return mail pouch to Peking, and the bank eventually received it. It was all a mistake, and no one suffered any consequences.

Crowley applied the Trumps to astrology, Qabalistic letter and numerical correspondences, and the Tree of Life, and drew a relationship between the Tarot and Enochian magic, a system of magic developed in the sixteenth century by John Dee, the royal astrologer to Queen Elizabeth I, and his associate, Edward Kelly, for communicating with alleged angels and spirits and traveling through various planes, or aethyrs, of consciousness.

Like Waite, Crowley set out to restore the cards to their "original form" and give complete explanations of their meanings. He admitted once in print that although he succeeded in doing so with some of the trumps, "others, however, I understand imperfectly, and of some few I have at present obtained no more than a general idea."

He renamed four of the Major Arcana: Justice became Adjustment, Strength became Lust, Temperance became Art, and Judgement became The Aeon. The suits of the Minor Arcana are associated with the four elements: Swords with air, Wands with fire, Cups with water, and Disks with earth. He named the court cards the Knight (father), Queen (mother), Prince (Son), and Princess (Daughter), based on the Hebrew concept of the Mother and Father, who issue the Son and Daughter.

In 1938, Crowley was asked by Lady Frieda Harris to work with her in painting a new deck. Harris's interest in the Tarot had been stimulated by P. D. Ouspensky's book, *The Model of the Universe*. The collaboration spanned five years, during which Harris and Crowley "endeavored to reinstate the cards in their original sacred, simple forms and, in addition, indicate the New Aeon of Horus, a terrifying apparition," according to Harris. Symbols were drawn from Freemasonry, alchemy, Rosicrucianism, Kabbalism, magic, geometry, *gematria*, mathematics, divination, numerology, the Druids, Spiritualism, psychology, philology, Buddhism, astrology, and heraldry, among others.

The images also are erotic in nature, which is not surprising, considering Crowley's sexual proclivities. The deck also departs dramatically from the French and Waite-Smith traditions.

The first printing in 1944 consisted of only 200 copies. A complete, color edition was not issued until 1969, and an improved edition appeared in 1979. Despite the unsettling, almost disturbed nature of the images, the Thoth deck is one of the most popular decks among the Tarot practitioners.

The BOTA deck

Another, later Golden Dawn initiate who left a major influence on the Tarot was Paul Foster Case (1884-1954). Case served as Praemonstrator General (Supreme Chief) of the Order of the Golden Dawn for United States and Canada. He became fascinated by the Tarot in 1901, and devoted many years to its study.

Case resigned from the Golden Dawn in order to found his own esoteric organization, the Builders of the Adytum, a Los Angeles-based organization devoted to the study of practical occultism. Case made his own interpretation of the Tarot, drawn by Jesse Bums Parker in the 1920s or 1930s. The deck is published by the Builders of the Adytum and is known as the BOTA deck. Some of the images are similar to those of Waite-Smith, but bear more and significantly different occult symbols; other images are very different altogether. Case's intent was to create cards that were explicit in their symbolism and not obscure, as he felt was the case with the Waite-Smith cards. Case placed The Fool at the beginning and accepted Waite's transposition of Strength and Justice. His pip cards are not illustrated with pictures.

Case promoted the link between the Tarot and the Qabalah, and his cards are inscribed with a corresponding letter of the Hebrew alphabet. He composed a thoughtful and detailed analysis of the Tarot-Hebrew alphabet correspondences in his work. *The Tarot: A Key to the Wisdom of the Ages* (1947). His correspondences included not only the letters but the accompanying colors and musical tones associated with each letter, and the astrological signs that fit each Arcanum. With the letter correspondences, Case probed the hidden, occult meanings of Hebrew words by spelling them out with the Tarot, with the greatest yield coming from many words in the Old Testament, divine and angelic names, and the names of the twelve tribes of Israel.

Although Case appreciated Levi's efforts to associate The Fool with the Holy Spirit, he criticized Levi's overall approach. "The attribution of the major trumps to the Hebrew alphabet is the crux in

Tarot study," Case stated. "Eliphas Levi knew it but could not give it, because he received it from a secret order. He did, however, announce the fact that the major trumps correspond to the Hebrew letters, and then proceeded to give an attribution so patently absurd that one wonders how it ever gained credence."

In placing The Fool at the beginning of the Major Arcana, Case assigned it to the letter Aleph, which has the numerical value of 1 and represents Breath, the Life-Breath or Spirit. This is substantially different than Shin, the Life-Breath of the Holy Ones or Holy Spirit, but does give The Fool, as 0, the symbolism of formless spirit, or that which precedes creative activities. Case observed that all the other trumps then logically fell into place.

Case argued that Waite's interpretation of the Tarot, showed that he (Waite) agreed with the correspondence of cards to the Hebrew alphabet. "In his [Waite's] later writings he endeavored to throw dust in the eyes of the uninitiated by pretending to believe that the attribution of the cards to the letters… was not the true arrangement," Case stated. "Yet his own rectifications of the symbolism and numbering of earlier exoteric versions of this picture-book of Ageless Wisdom are sufficient evidence that he understood and accepted the validity of this attribution."

The BOTA cards are drawn in black and white, to be colored by the Tarot student according to instructions given, on the theory that the act of coloring imbues the cards with particular and personal energies. This is similar to the ceremonial magician's act of making his or her own magical tools, which imbues the items with the practitioner's energy.

Tarot today

Tarot decks proliferate with all kinds of themes. The structure of the deck remains consistent, but after that, any artistic interpretation can be applied. Many decks are designed more for art collectors than readers.

The Waite-Smith deck still remains the most popular, and is considered one of the best decks for learning the Tarot. While some Tarot practitioners move on to other decks and leave Waite-Smith behind, many more stay with it as the deck of choice. Still others make Waite-Smith their primary deck, and use other decks for occasional variation.

From a Qabalistic perspective, the Tarot is still used for pathworking on the Tree of Life. Pathworking is a magical imagery technique of following inner pathways of consciousness to experience archetypical visions. The Major Arcana of the Tarot can facilitate a personal experience of the divine, or, in the case of the Tree of Life, a deep insight involving the *sephirot* and the paths that link them.

4

The Return of Alchemy

The next great advancement in the Tarot was made by artist Robert Michael Place, who recognized the complex relationship between the cards and alchemy. Working under inspiration from the spirit of Arthur Edward Waite, Place restored more alchemical content of the cards in The Alchemical Tarot, published in 1995. I was pleased to join Bob as collaborator on this ground-breaking deck and book set.

Bob's journey to the Tarot was nothing short of an alchemical journey in itself, unfolding in stages. In the early 1980s, Bob and his wife, Rose Ann, were living in upstate New York, where Bob pursued his art and original jewelry designs with mythological and magical motifs.

At various points in life, our dreams steer us in new and meaningful directions. These "turning point" dreams are intense, often lucid, and have a huge impact. In 1982, Bob had such a dream. He described it, and the results that followed, in his introduction to the guide book for The Alchemical Tarot:

> On a summer night in 1982, I had a dream in which I was walking through a room when the phone rang. The phone

was also part of the dream, but its ringing woke me into lucidness while I continued dreaming.

With a feeling of utter amazement—that another being could actually call me in a dream—I picked up the phone. On the other end an international operator informed me that she had a person to person call for me from a law firm in England. I accepted the call, and then a secretary from the firm came on the line. She told me that she was sending me my ancestral inheritance. She could not tell me what it was, but only that it would come from England, it is kept in a box, and that it is sometimes called the key. She added that I would know it when I saw it. Then she ended the conversation with some precautions on its use and misuse.

I awoke that morning with a feeling of excitement and expectation. All through the week I eagerly anticipated receiving my inheritance. At the end of that week a friend came over with his new deck of Tarot cards. It was the deck designed in England in 1910, by Arthur Edward Waite and Pamela Colman Smith. Although I was not unfamiliar with this deck, I now saw it in a new light—I knew that this was it.

Within a few days another friend gave me a deck called the Tarot of Marseilles. That was my own first deck, but soon I went into Manhattan to buy the Waite-Smith cards that I had seen.

I began experimenting with the cards. At first I resolved not to read any books on the Tarot. I wanted to communicate directly with the images unhindered by preconceptions. I did remember being shown the Celtic cross spread in college. So I decided to begin with that combined with Jungian techniques of dream interpretation.

In 1987, I was sitting in the living room reading a book on alchemy while a commentator on the radio was talking about the Harmonic Convergence. I had been hearing about this for a few weeks, but thought of it as just another new-age curiosity. However, this time it was different, the commentator said that during this period of spiritual transformation sensitive individuals all over the Earth would be experiencing a flood of information on spiritual subjects. Finally, someone had an explanation for what was happening to me.

The Tarot had taught me a great deal directly, but eventually I realized that to unlock its secrets further I had to gather more information. I began reading everything that I could find on the Tarot, Gnosticism, alchemy, and related subjects. I soon filled a large hardbound note book with charts, lists, and notes—this was odd because at that time I was not a writer, and had no plan to become a writer. My reading had become noticeably excessive to my wife and friends, and at last someone was able to explain that this intensity was a product of the time, that in some way the spirit of the Earth demanded it.

Shortly after August 16th I was reading the *Picture Museum of Sorcery, Magic, & Alchemy*, by Emile Grillot de Givry, when I became fascinated by an alchemical hieroglyph representing the Philosopher's Stone. In a flash, I realized that the symbolism in the design was entirely interchangeable with that of the World card. This realization was like a key opening a lock. I sat mesmerized as it became obvious that the Tarot trumps are alchemical, and that the series of trumps outlines the alchemical opus.

This insight happened in seconds, but it began a long journey that led to these Tarot designs and this book. It led me back into illustration work, and caused me to start writing. It helped me to experience the Western tradition of meditation, and spiritual transformation.

From the beginning the journey was marked by synchronistic events that brought information to me and led me on the right path. Synchronicity led to my first article on The Alchemical Tarot that was published in *Gnosis*, and it led me team up with Rosemary Ellen Guiley.

At the time, I was living in Westchester County, New York, where I worked full-time as an author. I was a subscriber to *Gnosis*, and I was at work on a Tarot book. I was also studying alchemy.

When I read Bob's article and saw some of his prototype drawings for The Alchemical Tarot, I was electrified. I knew Bob had hit the heart of the mysteries of the Tarot, and I knew I had to meet him.

That connection led to our collaboration on the deck and book set for The Alchemical Tarot, and to a life-long friendship. We also collaborated on a second set, The Angels Tarot. Bob went on to develop several more Tarots and oracle decks, and become one of the leading Tarot and alchemy experts in the world. He has done ground-breaking research unearthing little-known historical information about the Tarot. More recently, he began collaborating with another Tarot authority, Rachel Pollack.

For The Alchemical Tarot, both of us embarked on an intense spiritual journey of meditation, research, and contemplation of alchemical images. Bob experienced direct inspiration from Waite, who, he felt, wanted to see the true alchemical secrets of the cards brought out—something that was not possible in Waite's day, where there was a separation between the exoteric teachings for the masses and the esoteric secrets reserved for initiates.

We did many comparisons of Tarot images and alchemical images. The Alchemical Tarot bears a strong resemblance to the Waite-Smith cards, yet many of the new images are complete departures into alchemy.

The Tarot is an excellent alchemical textbook. Its Major Arcana is Jung's path of individuation and the alchemists' Great Work of transmutation, starting with the "base metal" of The Fool and ending in the Philosopher's Stone or World Soul of The World card. The Major Arcana represent stages of consciousness and awareness. The Minor Arcana are a supporting cast of influences, representing people, emotions, actions, thoughts, and elemental associations that act upon the forces and direction of life.

The twenty-third trump

After The Alchemical Tarot was published, I had an unusual, lucid dream in which I was given the key to a twenty-third Major Arcana card. In the dream, a white-bearded man dressed in the robed clothing of antiquity and wearing a triangular aura crown of gold held up an oversized card bearing an image and told me it was the twenty-third trump. The card was named Truth.

Truth, the Twenty-third Trump, © Robert Michael Place. Used with permission.

The image was a seven-layered pyramid with a flame coming out of the apex. The layers were three solid bars separated by spaces and a triangular apex. I knew it was a pyramid, even though the image showed only one triangular-shaped side of it.

I described the image and the figure to Bob, who drew it as a Major Arcana Tarot card. The triangular aura crown was known to us both as a symbol of God the Father, who is Truth. Bob realized that my flame-capped pyramid strongly resembled an alchemical woodcut of the Emerald Tablet, depicted as a triangular-shape stone or mountain with flames at the top. The figure holding the card is thus revealed as Hermes Trismegistus, the original alchemist and guardian of the Emerald Tablet, the central teaching of the Corpus Hermeticum, the foundation of Western esotericism, magic and alchemy.

The Emerald Tablet by Heinrich Khunrath, 1606.

No original text of the Emerald Tablet survives, only translations. According to one translation, the text states:

> True, without falsehood, certain, most certain. What is above is like that which is below, and what is below, like that which is above, to make the miracle of One Thing.

And as all things were made from contemplation of One, so all things were born from one adaptation. The father is the Sun, its mother is the Moon. The wind carried it in its womb, the earth breast fed it. It is the father of all works of wonder in the world. Its power is complete if turned towards earth, it will separate earth from fire, the subtle from the gross. With great capacity (Wisdom) it ascends from earth to heaven. Again it descends to earth, and takes back the power of the above and the below. Thus you will receive the glory of the distinctiveness of the world. All obscurity will flee from you. This is the most strong strength of all strength, for it overcomes all subtle things, and penetrates all solid things. Thus was the world created. From this comes marvelous adaptations of which this is the procedure. Therefore I am called Hermes Thrice-Crowned because I have three parts of the Wisdom of the whole world. And complete is what I had to say about the work of the Sun.

Numerous analyses of these statements have been made by scholars. Some interpretations are as follows:

1. *True, without falsehood, certain, most certain.* The Emerald Tablet speaks a universal truth on many levels. If the text cannot be perceived as truth, the fault lies with the individual, not with the text.

2. *What is above is like that which is below, and what is below, like that which is above, to make the miracle of One Thing.* The One Thing is an infinite continuum of upwardness and downwardness. Since the continuum is infinite, any point along it is at the center. The One Thing symbolizes the Self.

3. *And as all things were made from contemplation of One, so all things were born from one adaptation.* The One is the Universal Mind, which contemplates or meditates all things into being. All things mirror its power, and can create by adapting the creative process of the One.

4-6. *The father is the Sun, its mother is the Moon. The wind carried it in its womb, the earth breast fed it. It is the father of all works of wonder in the world.* The father/sun is the archetype of light/fire and downward creative process of light piercing darkness. The mother/moon is the archetype of informing/water, taking the light of the father/sun and reflecting it to the earth. The wind/womb is air, which mediates between fire and water. The earth/breast fed is the archetype of form. It is the element of earth, created by the combination of the other three elements. The father of all works of wonder in the world is the four elements combined with the fifth element of the Quintessence, the conscious awareness of the One or creator, which is independent life.

7. *Its power is complete if turned towards earth, it will separate earth from fire, the subtle from the gross.* The Quintessence is clothed in physical form, and is divine conscious awareness as expressed through human beings.

8. *With great capacity (Wisdom) it ascends from earth to heaven.* Again it descends to earth, and takes back the power of the above and the below. Conscious awareness rises and falls through the continuum in a constant process of integration and unison.

9. *Thus you will receive the glory of the distinctiveness of the world.* All obscurity will flee from you. The constant process of integration creates a new level of enlightenment.

10. *This is the most strong strength of all strength, for it overcomes all subtle things, and penetrates all solid things.* The new Father/Light, or new level of enlightenment, is completely realized Self-awareness. There is a constant cycle of recreation, where each level of Father/Light creates a new level of Father/Light.

11. *Thus was the world created.* Everything in the world is imbued with the power of Father/Light.

12. *From this comes marvelous adaptations of which this is the procedure.* Everything in the world is the seed of its future self.

13-14. *Therefore I am called Hermes Thrice-Crowned because I have three parts of the Wisdom of the whole world. And complete is what I had to say about the work of the Sun.* There is personal knowledge and experience of the process of enlightenment, which is to be done physically, mentally and astrally. The triple crown expresses the power of the center within the infinite continuum, for it can be anywhere and everywhere; it is the sun and moon and everything that lies between. Thus, the Emerald Tablet describes the process of enlightenment as force into form.

All of this is contained within the multi-faceted dream image of the Truth trump, demonstrating the power of image and symbol to convey knowledge. To contemplate the image is to come into contact with, and absorb, this Truth.

Bob related the image to other aspects of alchemy. The seven-layered pyramid has a correspondence to the sevenfold journey of the Anima Mundi or World Soul. The World Soul, of which all individual souls are part, descends to the world of physical matter via a ladder formed by the seven known planets of the ancients. In turn, mystical ascent is made via the same ladder.

The Truth card moves beyond the last trump of the World Soul to Nous, or unchanging Truth, the pattern behind the world of matter. In addition, Bob said, the structure of the pyramid has a relation to the Tetractys, a sacred Pythagorean symbol that expressed the numerical value of the intelligent Cosmos. This symbol consisted of ten dots arranged in four layers to create a triangle.

There are many more correspondences as well, as I discovered. The four solid layers represent foundation, and the three spaces between are levels of spiritual awareness. The flame at the top is the solar flame of Truth and Enlightenment, which in turn has associations to the archangel Uriel, the keeper of the flame of Truth.

The number of the twenty-third trump is XXII, twenty-two, a master number which is the Spiritual Master Builder. Characteristics associated with twenty-two are manifestation of dreams, intuition, power, accomplishment, visionary capabilities, universal love, and transformation. Twenty-two and repetitions of two, such as 222, also have connections to the angelic realm.

The dream image of the twenty-third trump had a powerful effect on me. Like all symbols, it conveys far more than can be put into words. I had the seven-layered, flame-topped triangle turned into the logo of my publishing and media company, Visionary Living, Inc. My art director,

Raúl daSilva, designed it with the flame internalized as a starburst—the light of enlightenment that shines within. The logo is on the spine and back cover of this book and all books published by Visionary Living, Inc.

Logo of Visionary Living, Inc.

In summary, you can see the far-reaching effects and benefits of working with the Tarot. The cards are much more than a divination system—they connect us to the highest Truth of all.

5

Symbols in the Tarot

The key to the metaphysical meanings of the Tarot lies in understanding symbols. Before language came symbols—pictures and designs that communicate thoughts, objects, concepts, and information. As written language developed, letters and words also became symbols.

Symbols speak directly to us. They imply something greater than their obvious, surface meaning, and thus elude precise description. In fact, a true symbol cannot be taken literally, but remains beyond rational comprehension, just out of reach. Symbols, said Jung, take the mind "to ideas beyond the grasp of reason."

Symbols take on a cosmological importance, and act upon our subconscious, and our collective unconscious, in ways that unlock powerful energies and creativity. Jung, who spent much of his life studying symbols, saw them as messengers to the psyche that connect us to the archetypes in the collective unconscious. William Butler Yeats termed symbols "the greatest of all powers," whether used consciously, such as in ceremonial magic, or drawn upon "half unconsciously" by those in the creative and performing arts.

Symbols fuel the vitality of culture. Whether we realize it or not, we react to and interact with symbols every day, either consciously or unconsciously. Everything around us—our art, architecture, ways of communication, and our mundane and sacred rites—make use of symbols. Without symbols, a culture is spiritually bereft, perhaps even dead.

It is impossible to pinpoint a time when symbols originated for they are as old as mankind. They are evident in pictorial remains of the late Paleolithic Age, a time when humankind lived in caves and subsisted by hunting and gathering. These hunters and gatherers recorded their symbolic language on the walls of their caves. Cave paintings were discovered in France and Spain at the end of the nineteenth century, but it was not until later in the twentieth century that archaeologists began to comprehend the full, symbolic meanings of the pictures. Many of them depict wounded or dying animals, indicating belief in sympathetic magic for hunting. The most dramatic example is the cave at Trois Freres, France, which depicts scenes of successful hunting and perhaps some sort of shamanistic or magical rites, the focus of which is a dancing human figure with a stag head and bear paws.

The most universal and enduring symbols are man, stones, animals, and circles, all of which the ancients saw in terms of their relationship to the divine. Man was seen as the symbol of the universe, the microcosm that represents the macrocosm. Stones were animated with divine or supernatural spirits. The characteristics of animals were projected onto deities, who sometimes took animal forms. Animals also became culture heroes. The circle, perhaps one of the most powerful symbols of all, came to represent the sun, the source of all light and life; the continuity of life through rebirth; and the totality of being.

Virtually anything can become a symbol. Besides man, animals, stones, and circles, there are symbols that are natural and manmade objects, numbers, shapes, the elements, the earth, the sky, the heavenly objects, and deities. Words and entire myths and folk tales can become symbols. A symbol's creation and its power depend upon the psychic energy invested in it, both at the moment of creation and over time. In some cases, symbols can arise quickly. Within a few years, the Nazis turned the swastika into the symbol of their ideology, probably destroying forever its original, pagan meaning of a solar symbol. The swastika resides now in the collective unconscious as a symbol of bigotry, hatred, greed, and abuse of power. Generally, however, symbols emerge over a long period of time as they are used over and over again in rites and customs. Not all symbols last—as civilizations rise and fall, their symbols perish if they are not absorbed into a succeeding society. Even within a culture, symbols can lose their potency over time, as beliefs and customs change.

In esoteric philosophy, symbols have the dual role of concealing information from the neophyte while revealing it to the initiate. Symbols are found in all esoteric philosophies and religions. In the East, the supreme symbol is the mandala. Symbolical devices are present in the Bible and in other scriptures. According to ancient scholars, the priests of the day devised a symbolic language called sacerdotal (which now means "priestly"), which they used to conceal information from the uninitiated masses. This language was made up of signs and symbols used in the everyday world, but which to the priests had entirely different meanings. The ancient Egyptians exhibited a wide use of symbols for philosophical purposes. Symbols became art under the Roman Empire, when numerous religious cults flourished, but had to conceal their true purposes with secular fronts as guilds, burial unions, literary societies, and the like. The cults, which included the early Christians, were forced to develop systems of symbols to communicate with members and spread their teachings. The symbolisms included images and signs borrowed from the building guilds, and sacred numbers borrowed from the Pythagoreans.

Symbols in alchemy

Symbols formed the vital, secret language of alchemy and secret societies. The alchemists, who were engrossed in the mysteries of matter and spirit, created dreamlike symbols to express the process by which man could become whole in mind and body, or by which base metals could be transmuted to silver and gold.

The *Mutus Liber* (Wordless Book), mentioned earlier, is one of the best examples of a text consisting only of symbolic images. It is an anonymous text of unknown origin for creating the Philosopher's Stone. It was first printed in France in 1677, and was reissued in 1702. The book has fifteen plates showing different stages of the Great Work, with no accompanying explanation. In true alchemical tradition, the images are meant to be interpreted and understood intuitively.

The French alchemist Nicholas Flamel (1330-1416) was led by a dream to a mysterious alchemical text bearing strange images. According to legend, he became one of the most successful alchemists ever.

Flamel was a bookseller who became intrigued by alchemy, and began a search for the secret of transmutation. He was convinced he would find it in a book. One night he dreamed that an angel stood before him and held out an old, strange and beautiful book. The angel said, "Look well at this book, Nicholas. At first you will understand nothing in it—neither you nor any other man. But one day you will see in it that which no other man will be able to see." When Flamel stretched out his hand to take the book, the angel disappeared in a golden cloud.

In 1357, a man desperate for money came to Flamel's bookstall and offered to sell a rare book for two florins. Flamel was shocked to recognize the book from his dream, and he quickly paid the man his price without quibbling.

The book did not have parchment pages but instead had leaves made of tree bark that had been inscribed with a steel point. The binding was quite old and made of copper that was covered with strange symbols. There were only twenty-one pages, divided into three sets of seven. The seventh page of each set contained no writing, only pictures that Flamel could not understand. The first drawing showed a caduceus with intertwined serpents, the second a serpent crucified on a cross, and the third a desert covered with snakes and a beautiful mountain in the middle. The first page of the book identified the author as Abraham Eleazar (the Jew): "prince, priest, Levite, astrologer and philosopher," and described the curses that would befall anyone who tried to read the book who was not a priest or scribe. The word "Maranatha" appeared throughout the manuscript, adding to its mystery. Other drawings illustrated winged Hermes with Saturn holding an hourglass and scythe, and a rose with a blue stem and red and white flowers blowing in the winds on a mountain.

Flamel decided that as a scribe, he was immune from the curses. He tried to decipher the images but could not. He and his wife, Pernelle, studied it for twenty-one years. Finally, Flamel found a Jewish adept who told him enough to decipher the images. Supposedly, Flamel and Pernelle began producing heaps of gold.

Tarot symbols

To the initiate, symbols are the means by which he or she can acquire or express the abilities or qualities embodied in the symbols. That is why it is so important to become thoroughly familiar with Tarot images, for they speak through symbols. Everything in the image, each element—including objects, people, animals, structures, nature, numbers, colors, and shapes—has a possible symbolic meaning. By understanding symbols, you can quickly comprehend the deeper meanings of the cards. The information conveyed by symbols will be received not as part of your rational thought process, but on an intuitive, knowing level. Deep within you, the messages will be absorbed; you will understand on a higher level of consciousness, without the need to put it into words.

Different interpretations of the Tarot use symbols to give unique and subtle shadings to the card meanings. For example, compare The Hermit from two different decks, and you will see that the essential meanings of the cards are the same, but are approached differently through use of symbols. Knowing symbols will help you gain a better intuitive feel for the overall interpretation of a particular deck.

Not all decks follow the same traditions of symbols. The notable exceptions are some decks designed as art objects, or which use photo or drawing collages, or which are oriented to specific cultures or themes.

Jung said that symbols are capable of unleashing great redemptive power. The Tarot, then, offers an excellent opportunity to tap into powerful energies that can help one to heal and to grow. Jung also believed that modern Western society has lost touch with its own symbols. It is a mistake, he said, for Westerners to look to the East for meaningful symbols, for to do so is to take them out of context from the culture and way of life in which they arose. Appropriately, there has been a resurgence of interest in the Western occult tradition, with an accompanying rediscovery of the rich symbolisms it contains. The Tarot is a product of the Western tradition, and it contains symbols that are very old and that still have the ability to impact our psyches in profound ways.

The following sections discuss major symbolisms of numbers, colors, and shapes as they apply to the Tarot. In the Appendix, I have provided a glossary of additional symbols that are frequently used in the Tarot.

Numbers

In occult philosophies, numbers are not quantities, but ideas or forms that constitute the building blocks of all things in the universe. Each number has its own character and attributes, which in turn influence all things physical that are associated with that number.

The mysticism of numbers appears in both Western and Eastern occultism and is of ancient origin. The Greeks placed great importance on the significance of numbers. "The world is built upon the power of numbers," said Pythagoras, who believed that the entire universe could be expressed in combinations of the primary numbers one through ten. This stemmed from his discovery that the musical intervals known in his time could be expressed in ratios between the numbers one, two, three, and four which, when added together, total ten. Ten then returns to one, because its digits of one and zero, when added together, equal one. Odd numbers were considered to be definite, masculine, and positive. Even numbers were indefinite, feminine, and negative.

The Hebrews, Gnostics, and early Christians applied numerical values to letters, which enabled them to calculate the numerical value of words. The tallied numbers yielded secret meanings. For example, the number 888 represented the "Higher Mind" in the Greek Mysteries, because Iesous ("Jesus") adds up to 888. Both the Greeks and the Hebrews considered ten the perfect number. As mentioned earlier, correspondences between numbers and letters of the Hebrew alphabet played an important role in the development of Kabbalism.

Numbers also were important in alchemy. One through four have primacy as the foundation of all things, for all of them added together equals ten, which reduces back to one. In alchemical literature, the Hebrew prophetess, called Maria Prophetissa, states, "One becomes two, two becomes three, and out of the third comes the One as the fourth." Four is the number of the elements, which through a symbolic circular process of distillation and sublimation, could be broken down and recombined in the higher unity of one.

In occult tradition, the system of ascertaining the numerical values of words works only when a word is spelled in its original Hebrew or Greek form; English does not agree closely enough with the Greek and Hebrew alphabets to work. Nonetheless, numerology—the reduction of names, words, and birth dates to their base numerical values—has become a popular modern form of this ancient practice. The letters in the English alphabet are assigned values of one through nine. The base numerical values are obtained by adding together all digits assigned each letter until a single digit remains. It is believed that one's fortunes may be changed by altering numerical values in names, although the original Pythagorean philosophy offers nothing to substantiate this practice.

Numbers achieved a new significance in the psychology of Jung, who considered the importance of numbers and their unconscious roots in dreams. Jung attempted to find personal meanings behind numbers in dreams, yet recognized that their appearance also sometimes represented the presence of archetypal forces or qualities.

A grasp of number symbolism is essential in working with the Tarot. It is employed in the construction of images for the Major Arcana in many decks, especially the newer ones. This is expressed especially in backgrounds and objects, such as a pair of birds in the sky. All elements in a Major Arcana image should be examined with numerical considerations in mind. They should be interpreted in light of the essence of the card and its position, if applicable, in a spread.

Number symbolism also is of primary importance in deriving meaning from the Minor Arcana pip cards. The symbolism of the number of the card, plus the suit sign, determine the fundamental meaning of the card. Images, if they are used for the pip cards, give further shadings to the meaning, as does the placement of each card in a spread.

The following are the essential meanings of the ten primary numbers, plus zero and a few others that are likely to appear in Tarot images. Keep in mind that odd numbers (except the number one) have masculine properties such as activity, logic, reason, communication, and left-brain functions. Even numbers have feminine properties, which embody passivity, intuition, emotions, inspiration, creativity, fertility, and right-brain functions.

Zero

Before numbers, which represent creation and order, comes zero, the unmanifest, the nothingness that precedes all things. Zero also represents the Cosmic Egg, the container of all life. Symbols related to zero include the egg and the circle.

One

The Pythagoreans called one the Monad and equated it with God, the beginning and end of all things, and the Source. One is the Mystic Center. It is the spiritual unity that unites all beings. It is mind, which gives it stability, for mind is stable. Unlike other odd numbers, one is not masculine, but is hermaphroditic in nature, comprising both male and female principles, because one added to an even number makes an odd, and added to an odd number makes an even one. From one issues all other numbers; no number can exist without it.

The Pythagoreans associated one with the names of various deities, whose attributes reflected the qualities of one. Among them were Phoebus Apollo, the brilliant and shining god of the sun and the Python-slaying god consulted at the Oracle at Delphi; Prometheus, who brought man fire and light (illumination and creativity); Zeus, the primary father god; and Hestia (Vesta), goddess of the hearth and home fires.

Symbols related to one include the ship and the chariot.

One points to beginnings, creation, unity, divinity, light, and matters of spirit and mind. It is an auspicious number, holding promise and optimism.

Two

From one issues two, the number of duality. Plato said the number had no significance, since it implied the existence of a relationship, which introduces a third factor. In alchemy, two is the number of opposites, which must dissolve and recombine to form the Philosopher's Stone. Two is the number of balance. It is sometimes regarded as weak and sometimes evil, because of its associations with duality, opposition, and polarity, and therefore illusion. In fact, the Pythagoreans, who considered two the number of the divided terrestrial being, despised the number.

Two has passive, female properties. Its duality is symbolized by horns, which have associations with the crescent moon and with Mother Goddess, a symbol of fertility, She who brings forth all life, which cannot prosper without Her blessing. In mythology, She appears often in a triple aspect representing maiden, mother and crone, with such correspondences as youth, adulthood, and old age, and virgin, nurturer, and destroyer. In her many roles, Goddess rules over wisdom, truth, magical powers, nature, fate, the home, healing, justice, love, birth, death, time, and eternity. She also rules the inner self—one's emotion, intuition, psychic forces, and mysteries. In mythology, her consort, and thus another symbol of her, is the bull—again, the horns. She is also represented by the crescent moon, the source of magical, psychic, and fertilizing powers.

Two also represents ignorance, but even this cloud has a silver lining, for out of ignorance emerges wisdom. Two is the darkness before the light. In mythology, two often signifies the emergence of something into the consciousness.

In Christian symbolism two represents the dual nature of Christ (God and human). In Kabbalistic symbolism, it represents wisdom and self-consciousness.

Three

As the product of one and two, three symbolizes the generative force, creative power, multiplicity, and forward movement. It is spiritual synthesis, harmony, and sufficiency; also prudence, friendship, justice, peace, virtue, and temperance. Anatolius observed that three, "the first odd number, is called perfect by some, because it is the first number to signify the totality—beginning, middle, and end." Thus, we find in mythology, folklore, and fairy tales the recurrent motif of the triad: three wishes, three sisters, three brothers, three chances, blessings done in threes, and spells and charms done in threes.

Three is an important number in mysticism. It is expressed in the threefold nature of man: body, mind, and spirit. The name of the mythical author of the Hermetica, Hermes Trismegistus, means "Thrice-greatest Hermes." In Christianity, three is expressed in the Trinity. In the Sefer Yetzirah (Book of Formation) of the Kabbalah, three is expressed in the Three Mothers, Aleph, Mem, and Shin, which form the foundation of "all others." Aleph, Mem, and Shin are letters of the Hebrew alphabet which mean, respectively, "breath" or vital spirit; "seas," or water; and "life-breath of the Divine Ones" or "Holy Spirit." The Three Mothers resemble a balance, the guilty on one side, the purified on the other, and the tongue of the balance standing between them. The Sefer Yetzirah states:

> The Three Mothers Aleph, Mem and Shin are a great Mystery very admirable and most recondite, and sealed with six rings; and from them proceed Air, Fire, and Water,

which divide into male and female forces. The Three Mothers Aleph, Mem and Shin are the foundation, from them spring three Fathers, and from these have proceeded all things that are in the world.

The Three Mothers in the world are Aleph, Mem and Shin: the heavens were produced from Fire; the earth from Water; and the Air from the Spirit is as a reconciler between the Fire and the Water.

The Three Mothers Aleph, Mem and Shin, Fire, Water and Air are shown in the Year; from the fire was made heat, from the waters was made cold, and from the air was produced the temperate state, again the mediator between them. The Three Mothers, Aleph, Mem and Shin, Fire, Water and Air are found in Man: from the fire was formed the head; from the water the belly; and from the air was formed the chest, again placed as a mediator between the two.

In Wicca, three is expressed in the threefold aspect of Goddess as Virgin, Matron, and Crone, and in the waxing, full, and waning phases of the moon.

Three is also the number of wisdom and knowledge in its association with the Three Fates and the past, present, and future, and the ancient sciences of music, geometry, and arithmetic.

Among the shapes symbolized by three are the triangle, trident, and tripod. According to Pythagoras, Apollo gave his oracles from a tripod.

Four

Four is the number of solidity, stability, foundations, hard work and toil, and tangible achievement. It also is the number of the earth, and of rational and logical thought and intellectualism. Pythagoras considered four the perfect number, the foundation of all things, connecting beings, elements, numbers, and seasons. To the Pythagoreans, four also symbolized God, because when added to the first three numbers, the total is ten, which returns to one. In addition, they believed that four represented the soul of man, which had the four powers of mind, science, opinion, and sense.

Many things can be associated with four: the four seasons, the four elements, the four cardinal points, the four basic functions of Jungian types (thinking, feeling, sensation, and intuition), the four suits of the Tarot, the four limbs of the human body, the four rivers that flow from the Garden of Eden.

When the number four occurs, it often indicates a stabilizing or ordering process taking place. In matters of hard work and toil, four can signify dullness.

Four is represented by the square and the cross (especially the equilateral cross); it also has associations with the cube. In alchemical symbolism, the element earth, which is associated with four, often takes the form of a dragon.

Five

Five is the microcosm. This number symbolizes the physical man and his five senses, and thus connotes sensuality and pleasure. It also resonates with higher qualities: it is man with his four limbs plus a head, the four cardinal points with the Center, the four elements plus a fifth element of ether, the universal vitalizing substance that permeates all things. In this respect, five is the number of the hierophant (appropriately, this is the number of The Hierophant of the Major Arcana).

Five is the number of upset and change, which often involves both gains and losses. Change can be painful, but necessary for something new and good to enter.

Five is symbolized by the five-pointed star, the pentacle or pentagram, considered by the ancient Greeks to symbolize light, health, and vitality. In occultism, the pentacle is a powerful symbol of divine power, and represents the dominion of mind over the lower nature. Like the circle, the pentacle also symbolizes wholeness. Another symbol for five is the pentagon, which also has associations with the circle.

The number five is often represented by five-leaved plants, such as the rose, lily, or vine.

The Kabbalistic meaning of five is fear.

Six

Six is also a number of equilibrium, as well as balance (as seen in scales), harmony, health, and time. The six-sided figure, the hexad, is formed by the union of two triangles. In addition, this union represents marriage and the hermaphrodite, both of which are the result of the union of the male and female. The Pythagoreans considered six the form of forms, the perfection of all the parts, and associated it with immortality. In Christian symbolism, six also is the number of perfection, because God created the world in six days. In Kabbahsm, six represents beauty and creation. In shapes, six is represented by the hexagram, the symbol of the union of opposites.

Seven

Seven is almost universally a sacred number, and the number of mystical man, for it is the sum of three (spirit) and four (material), thus making the perfect order (remember the seven layers of Truth, the twenty-third trump). Seven, then, represents the macrocosm. In alchemy, seven metals make up the Work, the alchemical transformation to the Philosopher's Stone. Seven also is the number of religion, the psychic, magic, and luck. It is associated with clairvoyance and healing powers. In initiation, seven is the highest stage of illumination. In Hebrew symbolism, it is the number of occult intelligence.

The ancient Greeks associated seven with the seven known planets and their corresponding deities. There are seven notes in the musical scale, and seven colors in the spectrum (which in turn corresponds to a rainbow, the bridge between earth and heaven).

When the number seven occurs, it often indicates the search for wisdom, the growth of spirit, the need to rely upon intuition, or to meditate on what has been learned. It also indicates a fondness for, and harmony with, nature.

Eight

Eight is the number of regeneration and the spiritual goal of the initiate. Because of its association with regeneration, eight symbolized the waters of baptism during the Middle Ages.

On its side, the figure eight resembles an ellipse, which is the lemniscate, the symbol of eternity, infinity, the Alpha and Omega, infinite wisdom, and higher consciousness. Right side up, the eight is associated with the spiral, a shape representing evolution, growth, and flexibility. The serpents entwined in a spiral on the caduceus of Hermes represent transformed consciousness: spiritual illumination. Thus, it is not surprising that the number eight was important in the Eleusinian mysteries.

In the Hermetica, eight is the magical number of Hermes Trismegistus. In Kabbalism, it is the number of perfect intelligence, for eight is the numerical value of YHVH, Yahweh, the Tetragrammaton.

The octagon, the eight-sided figure, represents a transition between the square and the circle.

Eight also has strong associations with four, because it is comprised equally of two fours.

Nine

The number nine has polarized positive and negative associations. In its positive aspects, nine is the number of spiritual and mental achievement. The Hebrews considered it to be the number of truth, because when multiplied, it reproduces itself. In Kabbalism, it represents the foundation. As the Triple Triad, it is the incorruptible number of fulfillment and attainment. In the Eleusinian mysteries, there were nine spheres through which the consciousness had to pass before it could be born anew. It is also a number of man, symbolizing the nine months of gestation before physical birth. Because of its composition of equal threes, nine has associations with the triangle.

The Pythagoreans regarded nine as an evil number because it is an inverted six, and also regarded it as the number of imperfection and failure, because it falls one short of the perfect ten. Within this context, nine is the number of limitations.

Ten

To the Pythagoreans, as well as other Greeks and the Hebrews, ten was the number of perfection. The Pythagoreans said it was the greatest number, the number of both heaven and earth, and associated it with memory, age, faith, power, and necessity. Ten also is a number of completion and wholeness, for it returns again to one. It is the number of the law.

In Christianity, it is the number of the Commandments. In Kabbalism, it is the number of the *sephirot* of the Tree of Life and the ten names of God.

Eleven

Because it exceeds ten, eleven is an unstable and imperfect number, and represents sin and transgression.

Twelve
Twelve represents the cosmic order and is expressed in many ways: the apostles of Christ, the months of the year, the hours of the day and night, the fruits of the Tree of Life, the signs of the Zodiac, the Tribes of Israel.

Thirteen
Thirteen is traditionally an unlucky number, also unstable because it exceeds twelve by one. In Christianity, it is associated with the betrayal of Christ, who had twelve disciples (himself making thirteen), one of whom betrayed him to the Romans. In some magical traditions, however, thirteen is a lucky number, representing the number of full moons in a year and, in modern Wicca, the traditional number of the witches' coven.

Forty
There are numerous Biblical references to forty, which is the number of trial and initiation: the days Jesus spent in the wilderness, the elapsed time of the resurrection, the Deluge, the wandering of the Jews, the reign of David, the days Moses spent on Mt. Sinai.

Colors

Colors are one of the most universal of symbols and have had esoteric significance since ancient times. In religion, heraldry, rank, occultism, alchemy, high magic, folklore, art, and architecture, colors are ascribed specific properties, attributes, symbolisms, or effects. Color lore was developed by the ancient Indians, Chinese, Tibetans, Egyptians, Greeks, Persians, and Babylonians. The occult, healing, and protective powers of gems and stones were evaluated based on their colors and the associations made with them. Blue, for example, the color of the sky, naturally became associated with spirit and spiritual properties.

The ancients corresponded colors to the planets, musical notes, the seven major chakras, the seven virtues and vices, the days of the week, and the seven faculties of the soul. In the early Christian Church, colors were used carefully in the garments and implements of religious service. For example, the color of a saint's robe, and the ornaments upon it, indicated whether he had been martyred, and for what.

Colors are vibrations of light. White light—the Godhead in Pythagorean thought—can be broken down into the seven basic colors of the spectrum: red, orange, yellow, green, blue, indigo, and violet. The basic colors can be combined to create secondary colors, shades, and hues. Edgar Cayce (1877-1945), the American psychic who gave medical diagnoses in trance, once noted that vibration is movement, and movement is activity that is either positive or negative. Thus, colors have an impact upon us emotionally, intellectually, physically, and intuitively.

In the Tarot, colors are one of the elements used to express hidden symbolic meanings. The color of an item of clothing, a flower, jewelry, a tool, or an object in the background adds meaning to the card. This applies primarily to modern decks. Even the early Waite-Smith deck was not colored as vibrantly as it is now. The earliest known Tarot cards were created more as objects of art and were gilded. The Marseilles, for example, deck is colored entirely in the primary colors of red, yellow, and blue. You will have to examine your cards and determine the extent of the role played by colors.

The following is a color symbol guide to help you interpret the Tarot.

Red

As the color of blood, red has obvious associations with life, the life-force, the body, wounds, and death. It is also the color of animal life, and animal nature in man. It is the color of lust, passion, and materialism, and by extension, with evil, the Devil, and base energies.

Red is associated with fire. It is the color of activity, energy, courage, and willpower. It also is the color of creation, which links it to the Mother Goddess, who brings forth all life. The Empress, a pregnant woman, often wears a gown of white (the traditional feminine color) decorated with red and green fruit, the colors of life and fertility.

In medieval Christian art, red represents love and charity.

Red with white appears in mystical teachings. Red and white in alchemy represent the conjunction of opposites, symbolized by white lilies together with red roses, or red roses and white roses. Two-headed eagles and the Rebis, a two-headed hermaphrodite, are colored often red and white to signify the sublimation of polarities. The Magician card may feature red and white to demonstrate that The Magician is the bridge uniting the macrocosm and microcosm.

Also in alchemy, red is the color of the third and next-to-last stage in the creation of the Philosopher's Stone, which is the culmination of spiritual ascension, and represents sublimation, suffering, and love.

In Kabbalistic symbolism, red represents severity.

Orange

Orange often symbolizes pride, ambition, flames, egoism, cruelty, ferocity, and luxury. These traits are represented by The Devil card. Orange-colored animals, such as portrayed in some Strength cards, represent the animal nature in humankind. The Fool may sport orange, revealing his pride, ambition, and egoism, which can lead him in the wrong direction.

Orange also signifies health and vitality, and thus the ability to weather trials ahead. It also represents the positive side of ambition and drive that result in accomplishments.

In Kabbalistic symbolism, orange is splendor.

Yellow

Yellow is the color of the sun, illumination, light, intellect, and generosity. The Fool often wears yellow boots that ground the intellect and that will take him on the path of illumination. Death, the card of endings and transition, often bears a yellow sunrise or yellow-clad figures in the background, indicating that transition ends with the dawning of new light.

Yellow is the *citrinitas*, the third stage in the Philosopher's Stone, which is the emergence of a new and higher consciousness.

In Kabbalistic symbolism, yellow is beauty.

Gold

Closely associated with yellow, gold in alchemy represents the attainment of the Philosopher's Stone— spiritual illumination—and glory. It also symbolizes the celestial.

Green

As the color of vegetation, green naturally symbolizes life, fertility, abundance, growing things, prosperity, youthfulness, and the earth. It also symbolizes sensation. Blue-green represents water. Spiritually, green is an intermediate, transitional color, the halfway point on the spectrum. Green symbols often decorate the Pentacles (Coins) suit to signify material abundance and prosperity.

Green also has associations with death: all growing things eventually die, but are reborn in another cycle of change and the budding of new growth. The Egyptians used green for Osiris, the god of both vegetation and the dead, and king of the underworld. Thus green can symbolize rebirth, regeneration, and renewal.

In Kabbalistic symbolism, green represents victory.

Blue

Blue is the color of the heavens, and therefore carries a heavenly quality. Blue represents godliness, spiritual qualities, contemplation, inspiration, devotion, and truth. Water, the symbol of emotions and the unconscious, is blue. Mountains, the abodes of the gods, and the symbols of the spiritual ascent, often are blue. Blue figures that are prominent in cards portray our connection to the intuition/psychic faculty, Higher Self, and spirit, such as in some renditions of The Priestess and The Star.

In Kabbalistic symbolism, blue represents mercy.

Indigo

Indigo is another color that represents advanced spiritual qualities or wisdom, psychic faculties, and the intuition.

Purple

Royalty, imperial power, pomp, pride, justice, and truth are symbolized by purple. In Christian symbolism, purple represents God, humility, and penitence. In pagan symbolism, it is the color of rites of chthonic deities.

Violet

Violet symbolizes sanctity, religious devotion, knowledge, sorrow, temperance, grief, old age, and mourning. In Christian symbolism, it represents love and truth, passion and suffering, sacerdotal rule, and authority.

In Kabbalistic symbolism, purple symbolizes foundation.

White

White symbolizes purity, holiness, sacredness, redemption, mystical illumination, timelessness, ecstasy, innocence, joy, light, and life. White is sometimes regarded as a purified yellow.

The combination of all colors, white is the opposite of black, the absence of color. White and black represent polarities of positive/negative, light/dark and feminine/masculine forces. This juxtaposition is often portrayed in the Tarot, such as the pillars of Boaz and Jachin in The Hierophant, the sphinxes in The Chariot, and the twin duality of Gemini.

In the alchemical process of the Philosopher's Stone, white marks the third stage, the beginning of the ascent up from darkness. In Kabbalistic symbolism, white represents the crown, a symbol of proximity to God and the highest spiritual attainment.

White with red and black symbolizes the three stages of initiation.

Black

Black is the symbol of death, destruction, negation, and deterioration. It represents the underworld, and thus presages transition and resurrection. In alchemy, the process of the Philosopher's Stone begins with a stage of blackness, the necessary dissolution before the new and better can be created. The Death card represents transition from the old to the new.

As the absence of color, black is the opposite of white, and is negativity, inertia, and lack of spiritual light.

In Christianity, black is the symbol of the Devil, and thus sin, materialism, and ignorance. The Devil card is black, symbolizing being chained to materialism, or the lower nature.

Black also represents the unknown, mystery, and spiritual mysteries.

Brown

Brown symbolizes renunciation of the world, spiritual death, and degradation. It also symbolizes the earth, and thus foundation, solidity, and grounding.

Gray

Gray is the color of mourning, humility, neutrality, and penitence. In Christian symbolism, gray is the death of the body and immortality of the spirit—the transformation from material to spiritual.

In Kabbalistic symbolism, gray is wisdom.

Silver

Silver is the color of the moon, which gives it associations with magic,

Goddess, psychic nature, emotions, and intuition. Paired with gold, silver is the feminine aspect of duality of the cosmic reality. In alchemy, silver is Luna, "the affections purified."

Pink
Pink is often associated with love and the heart center. It is more likely to be found in newer Tarot decks.

Shapes

Knowing the symbolisms of shapes will also help you plumb the deep meanings in Tarot images. The more you use the cards, the more you will become aware of symbols on both conscious and intuitive levels.

Circle
One of the oldest and most universal of symbols, the circle represents wholeness, completion, perfection, unity, totality, eternity, and world without end. It is the wheel of life, the continuing renewal of life in cycles of birth-death-rebirth. The circle is the sun (intellect, light, and spiritual illumination) rolling through the heavens. It is also the psyche and the whole Self, a symbolism that dates back to the time of Plato, who described the psyche as a sphere.

A circle with a dot in the center is an alchemical symbol for the sun or gold, and corresponds to the divine circle of celestial unity of all.

Semicircle
The semicircle represents borrowed light. It is the spark, the hidden fire, which resides in the soul of man, waiting to be awakened.

Mandorla
A symbol of the divine and the holy, of Spirit and the soul, the mandorla resembles an oval with pointed ends and is formed by the intersection of two equal circles, the circumference of which goes through the center of the other. It also represents virginity; the vulva; a gateway; the interpenetration of heaven and earth and spirit and matter; and the perfect equilibrium between equal forces. Thus, it has associations with duality and the number two. It is also known as the *vesica piscis*, or "vessel of the

fish," and *ichthus* ("fish") because of its shape. The mandorla appears often in sacred geometry, architecture, and art.

Mandala

"Mandala" is Sanskrit for "circle," a shaped used extensively in rituals of worship and contemplation. Mandalas have appeared universally since the Paleolithic Age, in the circular spiral and the sun wheel. Mandalas appear in Gnosticism, Christianity, and other religions, and in alchemy (such as the Ouroboros, the dragon or serpent that bites its own tail, forming a circle), mythology, healing practices, art, and architecture.

The association of the mandala with wholeness, individuation, and the structure of the psyche (a circle or sphere) has made it a useful therapeutic tool for integration in modern psychotherapies. Jung found that patients could work out their inner chaos by drawing mandalas of their dreams.

The mandala is itself a symbol with form and meaning, but it symbolizes the formless: it is an expression of, and a means of communication with, the unknowable and the ineffable. It reaches a level of consciousness much deeper than conceptual thought.

A mandala has three main features of construction: a center, symmetry, and four cardinal points. All mandalas have a center, whereas their symmetries and orientation to the cardinal points vary considerably according to design.

The center of a mandala represents the Godhead, the Beginning and the Eternal Now, or the Self, which is the total psyche.

Symmetry is expressed in concentric and counterbalanced geometric figures, with polarities often represented in terms of sexual tension. The mandala harmonizes those polarities to make order out of chaos.

The circle may be oriented to the cardinal points, and this is done in several ways. The circle is squared—that is, placed within a square—or it contains squares within its design. This orientation harkens back to Hindu and Buddhist creation myths. Before the Hindu god Brahma began creation, he stood on a thousand-petaled lotus (a mandala in itself) and looked to the four points of the compass. Similarly, Buddha, after being born, stepped onto an eight-rayed lotus flower that rose up from the earth, and looked into ten directions of space, one for each ray of the lotus, plus up and down.

Jung associated the cardinal points with the four types that humans need to orient themselves to the world: thinking, feeling, intuiting, and sensing.

In studying the symbols of Tarot cards, virtually anything round can be viewed as a potential mandala or component of a mandala: the sun, the moon, the earth itself, an equilateral cross (which can be contained within a circle), the Zodiac, the wheel, a rotunda, a halo, a flower, a maze, a labyrinth, a rose window of a cathedral, or an octagon. Squares and triangles suggest mandalas, since circles may be drawn within squares and vice versa. Triangles appear often in circular mandalas.

Triangle

In its position with point up, the triangle represents the aspiration of all things toward a higher unity. It is a symbol of fire and the masculine, creative principle. It also represents the penetration of the spiritual realms and the ascent of consciousness.

In Christian symbolism, the equilateral triangle is a symbol of the Trinity.

When two opposing triangles are joined together to form a hexagram, they represent the union of opposites, and also the human soul.

With its tip cut off, the triangle represents earth. Inverted, it is a symbol of water and the feminine, receptive principle.

An inverted triangle contained within an upright triangle is a symbol for the number nine.

Square

The square, and sometimes the rectangle, represents earthbound matter and earthly existence, the body, the physical plane, the limited space of the terrestrial world. The square gives the impression of solidity and firmness—it is a foundation, an anchor. It also indicates the process of becoming stabilized and secure. When squares are present, organization and cohesion are taking place, and scattered pieces are coming together.

Squares also indicate organization in terms of fours, as in the four seasons, the four quarters and the four elements, all of which are part of the foundation of the natural world. In alchemy, the square represents salt, itself a symbol of the earth and of earthly matter.

The squared circle—a circle inside a square with its perimeter touching the sides—is one of the most important of alchemical symbols, and represents the transition from the material to wholeness.

In Freemasonry, the square or rectangle represents the lodge and the sacred temple.

Cube

Like the square, the cube represents earth, salt, and the fraternal lodge. In Kabbalistic teachings, the cube represents the manifest universe, with specific meanings ascribed to the six faces and the interior. In Masonic thought, the cube is analogous to the building block; each person should build a temple of the soul comparable to the physical temple of learning and worship. In another respect, the cube represents one's fundamental faith. Thrones and seats of power often are represented as cubes. The High Priestess often sits on a cube, and The Hierophant often rests his feet on a cube.

Cross

Like the circle, the cross is an ancient and universal symbol that appears in many different shapes. In general, it represents the world axis that unites heaven, earth, and the underworld and provides a means by which the human soul can access the upper and lower spheres.

As an early pagan symbol, an equilateral cross represents the sun. The cross with feet—a swastika—was a solar wheel. The Greek cross (equilateral) was a dominant shape until Carolingian times, and then was replaced by the Latin cross, a stake and crossbeam, which represents the elevation of man from earth to the heavens. The Latin cross is the central symbol of Christianity, representing the crucifixion of Christ and thus is the symbol of salvation and redemption.

A cross with a serpent entwined upon it is a symbol of Christ. In Rosicrucianism, the cross represents the human body and spirit. Crosses are related to the number four.

Pentacle and Pentagram

A pentacle is a five-pointed star with tip upright, and a pentacle inscribed within a circle is a pentagram. The pentacle was used as an esoteric symbol by followers of Pythagoras. It is an important symbol in the magical arts, and represents the five senses of man, the five elements (the fifth being spirit), and the five extremities of the human body (head plus limbs).

"By means of the pentagram within his own soul, man not only may master and govern all creatures inferior to himself, but may demand consideration at the hands of those superior to himself," observed philosopher Manly P. Hall. The pentacle also symbolizes the dominion of mind over the lower forces.

Inverted, the pentacle and pentagram represent the infernal.

Pentagon
A pentagon is a five-sided figure that is associated with the pentacle, and also with the circle as a symbol of wholeness.

Hexagram
A hexagram is a star formed by the interpenetration of upright and inverted triangles, which symbolizes the union of opposites, the Philosopher's Stone, and the attainment of spiritual wisdom. It also represents the human soul.

Hexagon
A hexagon is a six-sided figure associated with the hexagram and the circle.

Octagon
The eight-sided octagon carries the numerical meaning of eight, which is regeneration, renewal, and transition. It symbolizes the four cardinal points (the square) plus four intermediate points. In architecture, the octagon supports a dome, thus representing the squaring of the circle. Christian fonts, the receptacles for baptism, often are octagonal in shape.

Spiral
The spiral is an ancient, widespread, and complex symbol that denotes emanation and the creative/destructive powers of the universe. It represents waxing or waning, life or death, expansion or contraction, masculine or feminine, and solar or lunar powers. In its perpetual unwinding, the spiral also represents the cyclic nature of the seasons and the cosmos.

In yoga, the spiral is the coil of the kundalini force, a powerful, primal force that resides dormant at the box of the spine. When aroused through yoga practice, the kundalini energy spirals up the spine to the brain in a burst of enlightenment.

As a whorl, the spiral is a symbol of Goddess, who weaves the web of life and controls all destiny. Lightning and spirals of air are associated with fertility and generative forces, as in the rainstorms that help to bring forth life on the earth. The spiral also signifies change in an upward or downward direction.

Exercise

To learn the language of symbols, spend time studying them in your Tarot deck. Examine each card individually for colors, numbers, and shapes. In addition, look for other symbols represented by birds, animals, plants, tools, clothing, celestial objects, suit signs, shapes, and such. Look at the cards and repeat the meanings out loud. Making verbal statements will help impress the information in your memory.

After you have gone through an examination of each card, then go back through the deck and look each card in a holistic fashion. What do all these symbolic elements say together? Each symbol is like an instrument in an orchestra: each has its individual part, and together they create beautiful music.

Say whatever comes into your mind. Talk out loud. You may feel awkward at first, but you will find yourself getting into a stimulating, creative flow. Suddenly you will see the images in an entirely new way, like fuzzy pictures that abruptly snap into a crystal-clear focus. Small, seemingly insignificant symbols will emerge into the forefront. Keep in mind that many symbols have multiple meanings, depending on the context in which they appear. As you practice, you will intuitively find the correct frames of reference. Discard whatever does not fit.

Here is a sample stream-of-consciousness look at The Magician from the Waite-Smith deck:

> The Magician stands with one arm raised toward heaven and one hand pointing to earth... he is a channel of energy from heaven to earth, spirit to matter... on an even greater scale, the macrocosm to microcosm... the lemniscate over his head represents eternity, infinity... better still, infinite wisdom and higher consciousness, the attainment of Spirit... the lemniscate has associations with the number eight, spirals and octagons: regeneration, alternating

currents of opposites, transformation of consciousness... the table bears the objects that represent the suit signs of the Tarot... also the four elements, without which magic and transformation are not possible... four, the number of the square, the earth, matter, the building blocks of the spirit... the background is yellow, the color of the sun, intellect, spiritual wisdom.

The Magician wears red and white... red, the color of materialism, passions, life... white, the color of spirit and purity... red and white together represent the union of opposites in alchemical transformation to achieve Unity and wholeness, the Philosopher's Stone... in his upraised hand he holds a white wand... wand, the conductor of supernatural force and power... drawing down Spirit into Matter, the macrocosm into the microcosm... around the Magician's waist is an Ouroboros, symbol of regeneration, immortality, the self-contained alchemical process... he stands framed in flowers, lilies and red roses... lilies, purity... roses, the mystic heart Center, the union of spirit and matter... the red-white theme again: the conjunction of opposites, the joining of the macrocosm and microcosm.

You can now see in a dramatic way how everything in the card's image works to reinforce the meaning of The Magician. You may know on an intellectual level that The Magician is the transformer, the interface between Spirit and Matter and macrocosm and microcosm. Now you see also see The Magician on a richer, intuitive level.

This exercise is important because it teaches you to listen to your intuition, a psychic skill you will need in reading the cards. The exercise works best if you limit yourself to a few cards at a time. Move on when you feel you have fully absorbed each card (pip cards without images can be studied fairly quickly). Do the exercise daily. When you have gone through the entire pack, go through it again.

6

The Major Arcana

The Major Arcana are the portion of the Tarot deck that offer the greatest depth of meaning and the most profound mysteries. Taken in sequence from The Fool to The World, the cards represent the journey through life, the spiritual Quest that begins in the Nothingness, the unmanifest, and the Cosmic Egg, and moves through the trials and learning of the initiate to culminate in wholeness—the ultimate Oneness that is ever the striving of the human soul. The cards mirror different stages along the way. Each of the cards offers insights into a person's growth and development as the Wheel of Life turns.

The interpretations of the cards presented here, and in the following chapter on the Minor Arcana, are intended as a guide to prompt your own discoveries. As you gain familiarity with the cards and increase your experience in readings, you will find that they convey far more than their "book" meanings, especially when laid out in spreads.

How to use the interpretations

I have written the interpretations to fit virtually any deck. Take each card and study it to see how it expresses the interpretation. From there, example the details of symbols, colors, and supporting images that the artist has employed, and incorporate those nuances into your understanding of the cards.

I have included reversed meanings. In general, reversed positions indicate that circumstances are not well positioned, being impeded or blocked, or need further attention.

0 The Fool

Who but a fool would leap headlong into the void, seemingly uncaring about the potential dangers, trials, and challenges that lie ahead? The Fool's innocence is also his charm and what makes him so attractive. The Fool is untouched by life, but ready for the experience. He represents purity of action. There is no time for analysis or strategy. He does not look behind him. He only looks forward. The Fool needs no encouragement to begin the journey. He does not need to test the water. He will find out when he steps in it whether it is warm or cold.

What about the rest of us? We all can think of thousands of reasons in any given situation why we should not take action or commit ourselves. Not The Fool. He stands poised on the precipice ready to jump without hesitation. He lives for the future—nothing holds him to the present.

His motives are pure. He seeks to discover. His quest is for life—and he is willing to give it a chance, come what may. The Fool lives to live.

Life has not left its marks or scars on The Fool. He is not yet connected to anything in this world. His few possessions are in a bag, tied to a wand, which rests against his shoulder. They do not weigh him down; they are behind him.

Unlike those of us who have been tested—and think we possess great wisdom from our experiences—The Fool cares not to hear the warnings. ("Don't be a fool.") The Fool frightens us a little because nothing frightens him. He is a liberated spirit.

The Fool is a believer in all things, especially the potential that life holds. But ask him to be elaborate, and he will smile and say, "Find out for yourself."

His source of knowledge comes from inside. He trusts his instincts—he instinctively "knows."

The card tells us to take the plunge, follow our heart, and listen to the inner call. We are being told to face the risks, even tempt fate. The card also reminds us of the power of our imagination and our dreams. The message is simple: all things are possible.

Reversed: A thin line divides risk-taking from foolishness and impulsiveness. Perhaps you need to exercise caution and not to charge ahead foolishly. Have you thought things through carefully? Is the timing good? Are you overlooking warning signs? It also could mean that you are holding yourself back, not paying attention to your instincts. You say to yourself, "If in doubt, don't do it."

I The Magician

The Magician is one of the most practical of the Tarot symbols. He represents the powers we each possess to create meaning and purpose in our lives. With one hand pointed to the heavens, the other pointing downward, The Magician tells us that this creative power resides both within and outside ourselves—but always within reach.

The Magician seems to be saying, "Open yourself to the forces surrounding you, the life-giving powers, the powers of creation—draw them to yourself, transform yourself into whatever you wish to be."

Unlike The Fool, who lives without order and approaches life with a randomness, the Magician represents a more structured way of life. He believes there is a formula for every given situation. He understands that the secrets of manifestation begin with thought and a connection to the spiritual realms, and are followed through with action in the material world.

Although The Magician already possesses a great deal of knowledge, most of which he has learned through trial and error, he seeks to learn more. He relies especially on his powers of observation to expand his awareness of how things work in the world. He is acutely interested in learning the basic structure underlying all things as well as the patterns, cycles, and rhythms that exist in the world.

The Magician believes in experimenting until he gets things right. For The Magician, failure means either the wrong formula was used or something was done incorrectly. Either way, there is always something to be learned, a piece of knowledge that can be used again later.

Not surprisingly. The Magician also is extremely self-reliant and self-confident. There's a bit of a showman in him as well. Notice in the card how he appears to be onstage, working his magic—he likes to show off what he has learned. He is not a teacher, however. He does not share his secrets, but he makes it clear that all of us can learn to do the same things.

Reversed: You are not recognizing or are blocking your creative energies, and as a result, things are not happening as you would like. Or, you are afraid to experiment and try new things. Your self-confidence is lacking because you are unsure of yourself. At the same time, the card could be telling you not to be so self-assured, that what worked once may not be right this time around, but may need a different approach.

II The High Priestess

The High Priestess symbolizes the power of unconscious forces in the world—the unseen powers that give the earth its form and purpose; the invisible thread that binds us together. She reveals little about herself. Her source of knowledge is kept hidden, yet she appears to know all. It is a depth we can hope to achieve during our lifetime or as we try to come to grips with a problem we face.

Her tranquility is also representative of her great powers. She is like a giant tree that stands tall but silent—or like still waters that run deep. The High Priestess also represents the invisible powers in nature that give life to all things. She is our link to the energy that turns a seed into a flowering plant, a sapling into a towering tree. In life, it is this same power that can nourish us on our journey.

The High Priestess is deeply connected to her intuition, dreams, and spiritual guidance, which she knows beyond a doubt are accurate and will always help her steer a clear course. She goes about her affairs quietly and in a self-assured manner. She does not perform or ply her craft out in the open like The Magician, and does not jump from one place to the other like The Fool. Her silence exudes confidence.

The High Priestess signals us to seek the answers from within—to look inside ourselves, to listen for the guidance and to follow the prompting of our heart. From reflection and meditation, the answers will come. The High Priestess tells us to use our intuition as a guide.

Because The High Priestess does not reveal all to us, it is an indication that we must continue the journey for answers. Things will come if we are patient. What we do not know now will be revealed to us later. We should be open to the possibilities, especially things we have not even considered. Life is a mystery. But it is with purpose. The High Priestess knows the secrets, and she lets us know that we can someday know those secrets ourselves. They could come to us in a flash, or after a lifetime of searching.

Reversed: You are ignoring your intuition and guidance. Things do not feel right to you and you are afraid to follow your hunches. You keep looking for more and more external validation. Your feelings are strong, but you are afraid or unwilling to act. You are distant from, and not a part of the life process, still sitting on the sidelines watching. You want things revealed to you in advance before you will commit. Pay attention to the inner voice or the voice of spirit, and then formulate plan of action.

III The Empress

If The High Priestess represents the unseen forces in nature, then The Empress represents the visible manifestation of those forces. She is the fulfillment of the feminine or life-giving power in nature—she is the Earth Mother or Mother Nature. On one hand she represents fertility, creativity, and growth. She also symbolizes the passage from one stage to the next. She is the reason a seed planted in the soil will germinate and grow and why it will eventually wither away and die. She is the manifestation of the evolutionary process. She governs the eternal cycle of birth, death, and rebirth.

The Empress is tangible power—something we can reach out and feel. We can sense The Empress in our daily lives when we look at the natural world that surrounds us. Although she is a material presence, she enriches our soul. Her presence fills our heart with joy when we watch a tree unfurl its blossoms in the spring. She also reminds us of the eternal process at work when we return in the fall to watch the leaves fall from the same tree.

In her dual roles as Earth Mother and Mother Nature, The Empress gives and she takes. She does so without prejudice or judgement. She is the ebb and the flow. She stands for the process of life and its cyclical pattern.

The Empress makes our lives fertile so we can grow, in mind as well as body. As the symbol of motherhood, The Empress also stands for compassion and caring. When we welcome The Empress in our lives, she mothers us and looks out for us.

Because she represents growth, The Empress also reminds us that not all things stay the same, that the process of life is constant—that it is about growing and changing. The Empress is telling us either to plant a seed or harvest the yield. She can also be a sign of harmony and material satisfaction in our lives that comes from a good solid grounding in the process of life itself.

Reversed: You are refusing to accept change or move to the next stage. You may be overly satisfied with the present, blind to the opportunities ahead. Or, you are seeing your material possessions as ends to themselves instead of momentary rewards. Also: you are not applying yourself to productive tasks, no growth, just stagnation. You need to get in touch with your creative forces.

IV The Emperor

The Emperor represents the external world that exists outside of the natural world. He stands for ties that bind us together as a society and civilization. He is the unity and order in our lives, the laws that guide us as well as the logic that dictates our actions. He represents the different controlling forces in our lives: "father," "ruler," "supreme being."

The Emperor lays it out straight for us, articulating the difference between right and wrong. He lets us know there will be consequences from deviating from the correct path. In The Emperor's world *A* leads to *B* and *B* leads to *C*. There is little room for deviation from the norm. Also in The Emperor's world—the secular side of our life—everything we need to know, every answer to every question is written down somewhere. All we have to do is research and look it up. No one is going to do it for us—we have to do the work ourselves to gain the authority and power.

The Emperor and The High Priestess can sometimes symbolize the tension that exists between following the dictates of the heart and doing what logic says is right. Even so, The Emperor can only speak for what is right according to the external rules that govern our lives in general or the choices we face in every given situation. He cannot punish, only warn.

The Emperor can be a stabilizing influence as well. His firmness gives us something to hold on to in times of turbulence and change. His course of action is spelled out ahead of time, eliminating any ambiguity or decision about the correct actions to follow. His is the path of preservation, of protecting the status quo.

At the other end of the spectrum, The Emperor can represent the restraining influences in our lives—and the need for change. Instead of a path that leads to growth and fulfillment, the old, orderly ways can be restraining and stagnating. The Emperor could be telling us to turn our back on the comfortable and the known and that it is time to strike out into unfamiliar territory so that we can experience new growth and make new rules as we go along. We can always return to the comfortable path—and we may eventually do so—wiser from the experiences of having tried something new.

Reversed: Your focus is too narrow. You use the rule of law to shield yourself from the truth. You say, "I know it is wrong, but it is the *law*." Or, "I agree with you, but my hands are tied." You may need to listen more to your internal voice. Logic speaks only for the head, not the heart.

V The Hierophant

There are many ways of regarding The Hierophant, depending on your personal view of religion and its role in your life. According to classical interpretation, The Hierophant is the link between God and man— the high priest on earth. His are the ways of tradition.

Perhaps a more fitting interpretation for our modern age is to see him as the channel between divine or esoteric knowledge and ourselves. He is our spiritual guide who transcends the material world. He is our teacher. He can unlock the doors of hidden knowledge. He can help us get closer to the truth. He can help us see meaning in life. He can help us discover the God that exists within each of us.

The Hierophant can be an important element in our lives, particularly as a reminder that we cannot grow if we limit our pursuits to material satisfaction alone. Our spiritual side needs nurturing, too. The Hierophant will help us in this quest.

The path we choose on this quest is personal. It can be through avenues that traditional religion provides, such as prayer and following the tenets of our personal faith. For others, meditation and contemplation may be the better way.

The Hierophant can also serve as a beacon in the night, guiding us toward the next level of evolution of our own consciousness.

On another level, The Hierophant represents our moral growth and development—the knowledge of true right and wrong, not that imposed by the rule of external law and order. But, like The Emperor, The Hierophant reminds us that there are consequences from deviating from the "true" path. He suggests that there is a higher authority to whom we must answer.

The card may be a signal that we should take account of our spiritual stock. Or perhaps, it is a reminder that we need to recognize the limitations when we are too grounded in the material world.

In his guise as the keeper of the old ways, The Hierophant could be telling us we would be wiser to follow a more "orthodox" approach to a problem at hand or a question we are trying to answer.

Reversed: You are too dogmatic in your interpretation of events, allowing faith to be your guide instead of questioning and seeking the answers. There is a higher truth to be discovered. You must open yourself up to new ways of thinking.

VI The Lovers

On its simplest level, The Lovers represents the act of union between the male and female. Man and woman together are a potent creative force. On another level, the card speaks to the next stage of a development—the point at which we move forward to begin building for the future with another. A third meaning relates the male and female sides to a personality that exists within each of us—men and women alike. The male side represents the intellect, which is linked to the outer world, through conscious thought and reason, whereas the female is our connection to our unconscious self and also our psychic side.

The Lovers acknowledges the emergence of sexuality within each of us—a change in our physical bodies and emotional and intellectual framework that both separates man from woman and at the same time creates the dynamic tension that draws us together. Similar tensions exist within ourselves as we try to live in both the external and unconscious worlds simultaneously.

When man and woman unite, there is harmony and balance. This could symbolize the harmony within ourselves, with both our emotions and intellect in balance, or a balanced relationship with a partner.

Even with these different meanings, there is a thread that binds them all together, and that is the power of love in our lives, both to create and destroy the love of ourselves and the love for another.

The card also speaks to the dichotomy that exists in our lives on different levels—and the constant choices we make. Do we follow our intellect or be guided by our inner thoughts? Is one side of our personality more dominant than the other and, if so, how do we find balance?

The card may be a recognition of the absence of love or another person in your life. Or, that you need to turn to the person you love for help in resolving a problem. It can also be a sense of peace and harmony that reigns in your life. Or, the need to put things in balance, with yourself or with another.

Reversed: Love can be blind. A relationship could be out of balance. You are not looking at both sides of an issue. You cannot or should not go it alone. The answers cannot be found by looking on the outside alone.

VII The Chariot

A quick glance at this card reveals all: we can read the power, ambition, and determination of the charioteer. But notice, too, that he is youthful—a young and possibly immature man driven by a burning desire to win, dominate, and succeed.

The Chariot card reflects the innocent desire to charge ahead into the world when we are young. This is not the naivete of The Fool. The Fool is just beginning his journey. He does not know what he wants. He is a free spirit who dashes to and fro, hither and yon. The charioteer has chosen his purpose. He has chosen his battlefield. He will emerge from the battlefield the victor. His successes will be a measure of how much he accumulates. It is only later in life that the charioteer—like the rest of us—recognizes that these possessions only bring limited happiness.

Clearly, there is nothing wrong with the drive for success, especially in the early stages of our lives. Ambition can serve us well. It can help us build the material foundation we all need. Our society depends on the charioteers who blaze new trails into the future.

On another level, the card reveals that there need to be no limits on our drive for success, no matter what our age. Of course, this is a particularly important strength to possess when we are young. If we feel we can conquer all, no task is too difficult. Only later when the stresses of life begin to take their toll, words like *burn-out* creep into our vocabulary. If we can remember our past successes as we get older, we can rise above these stresses to confront new challenges. This is especially true when we begin new ventures, for we need the determination of the charioteer to propel us forward and to prevent us from looking backwards.

This is also a card of discipline and control. The charioteer has his mind fixed on a single purpose. His emotions are under control. His path is laid out clearly and he has no desire to deviate. He feels he is the master of his fate. He represents the power of the will. Too often in life, we allow ourselves to get distracted. We lose sight of our goals. Not the charioteer. He charges ahead—and so should we.

Reversed: You are too focused on material gain. Perhaps you are moving too fast and need to slow down. ("Pull back on the reins.") You need to temper your ambition. It is time to take account of your success, or broaden your worldview. You are charging off without knowing where you are going, or why.

VIII Strength

Just as The Chariot represents the outward manifestation of power and drive, the Strength card symbolizes the inner forces that help carry us forward throughout life. From the outset we learn that life will be filled with difficulties. Experience quickly teaches us that we must develop an inner strength if we are to persevere and enjoy life. It is also what helps define our personalities—distinguishing a strong person from a weak person. With this inner strength we are able to face up to the questions in our lives and cope with the changes, both positive and negative.

Strength is the belief we have in ourselves—it is a different kind of self-confidence than what The Chariot driver exudes. His is raw courage and might. This is the strength of wisdom and belief, the strength that comes from learning about ourselves and learning to trust ourselves. The more we believe in ourselves and our abilities, the more barriers that will fall.

A strong person also keeps his emotions in balance or—in the extreme—in check. Inner strength can be a calming influence. Think of the archetypal images of the strong, silent hero. You can read the strength in his face. He has proven himself to himself. He does not have to prove anything to anyone else. The same sense of serenity and strength combined is reflected on the Strength card. The woman silently strokes the lion. This is a representation that she has tamed the beast inside. Instead of fighting it, she draws from it. It is her source of inner power.

Strength also implies wisdom. A strong person believes in life. He recognizes that there is a reason for everything and from everything he can learn. He regards adversity and trouble as a test of will. He believes he can overcome. With this as his foundation he can never lose. Even in defeat, he can feel proud he stood his ground. By turning and running, we lose more than the battle. We lose confidence in ourselves. We lay the foundation for defeat.

A strong person has hope. He faces life eagerly: "I am ready, willing and able."

Reversed: You are lacking self-confidence, questioning your abilities. ("Am I up for this?) It is time to believe more in yourself. Do not look outside yourself for what exists within. Silence your fears and pull yourself up to a higher spiritual perspective.

IX The Hermit

As much as we need the company and counsel of others, there are times in life when we have to withdraw into ourselves and meditate upon the important questions we face. The Hermit, sometimes called the Wise Man, reflects this need.

On a simpler, more practical level, The Hermit underscores the need for peace and quiet, contemplation, and meditation in our lives. Our minds are subjected to so much, especially in today's information age. We are bombarded with news, opinion, distractions, and the stresses of daily life.

We need to become like The Hermit: enter a contemplative or meditative state, withdrawn momentarily from the world, deep in thought and reflection. We need to seek the light of inner wisdom.

The act of gazing inward can accomplish many things. It can bring order to the chaos in our lives, helping us sift through the different signals we are receiving so we can put each in its proper place.

Meditation can also help us remove ourselves from our problems, look at them objectively, and weigh different solutions. The answers may not come immediately, but having prepared ourselves for this discovery, the answers will eventually come.

Also, we occasionally need to look deep inside ourselves with no set purpose in mind other than to open our mind to new thoughts, discoveries, and truths that reside in our unconscious self. We need to develop this link to our unconscious self and build bridges to the higher reality, those hidden forces that help determine our destiny. By spending this time alone, deep in thought and contemplation, we come to realize that we are not alone. All of us are here for a purpose, and we are united in spirit. We all have access to the same truths. The Hermit lights the way for us to make these discoveries about the mysteries and meaning of life.

Meditation also allows us to learn from our many past experiences. It provides the opportunity to glean the deeper lessons about what we have accomplished and how it relates to our true task. Time spent alone gives us also a sense of peace. The memory of that serene feeling can be helpful in times of turbulence. It can help ease our anxieties.

Reversed: You are closed off from others, too self-absorbed. You need to connect with reality. The card also may mean you are too externally focused, and the answers you seek are within yourself. In addition, it can pint to excessive withdrawal to avoid action, decisions and moving forward.

X The Wheel of Fortune

The Wheel of Fortune card is a self-assessment tool—it can help you take account of where you are in your life. Use it to get a fix on where you are coming from as well as where you are going, and even why you might not be making any progress. The card represents the Wheel of Life, the coming and going of all things. What is here today is gone tomorrow. Today's challenges are tomorrow's opportunities. Adversity may be followed by triumph or vice versa. ("Relax, you are just going through a bad phase. Things will be looking up soon.")

The card reminds us that although we may not always be in control of our destinies, we are not locked into any particular place or stage in our life. We can stand still and wait for changes as the Wheel continues to spin, or we can initiate those changes ourselves and move forward. In other words, we can color the outcome of our destiny. New doors are always opening in our lives. We can choose which ones to go through. The process never stops.

The card also tells us that the Wheel spins with or without us. If we go with the flow, we grow. If we resist, we stagnate. We can either be a part of the process or watch life pass us by. Greater satisfaction, growth, and fulfillment come from living a life that is in tune with the cycles and rhythms.

The Wheel also underscores the cyclical nature of our personal growth and development. We frequently relive the past by looking back over all the major changes in our lives as a way of measuring progress. The past is a part of our future. The Wheel card also warns that we are condemned to repeat the mistakes of the past if we do not learn from them. That is one reason why we often compare decisions we made in our youth with decisions we make years later. ("If I would have known what I know today, I never would have done that.") Just as important, the card tells us that what we are today is because of what we did yesterday, and what we do tomorrow will depend on what we do today. At the same time, we must take responsibility for whatever comes around.

Reversed: You are stuck in a rut, spinning your wheels, or running on a treadmill. You know what happened the last time you did that. Things may take a turn for the worse before they get better. You are only in a phase, it will not last forever.

XI Justice

The Justice card is about bringing balance and harmony into our lives and what happens when we do not. The scales of Justice remain balanced as long as we maintain this proper equilibrium or harmony. When we tip the scales we pay the price. The cosmos operates on the principle of cause and effect, the law of karma, punishment and reward.

By placing too much emphasis on work, we can damage our family relationships. By finding balance, we enjoy the fruits of both worlds.

By placing too much focus on the secular side of our lives, we leave ourselves spiritually deficient. By making time for material and spiritual pursuits, we feel wholesome and see purpose in everything we do.

By being too self-centered, we live life alone. By finding time for others, we benefit from their companionship, counsel, and friendship.

By pushing ourselves too hard, we can damage our health. By knowing where to draw the line, we perform at peak capacity in all pursuits.

The list goes on and on. The choice is always ours.

Justice is nonjudgmental. When we are fair to ourselves and fair to others, we are rewarded. When we are out of balance, in our lives, in our relationships, in our pursuits, we are doing an injustice to ourselves, our friends, families, and associates. But because we are doing the injustice, we pay the price.

Life is give and take. We have to find that proper balance if we are to live life to its fullest. We must learn to compromise. We must learn to find where to draw the line between work and home, between the material and spiritual worlds, between drive and pleasure.

Justice also implies living in harmony with nature.

An appreciation for justice also is a measure of our personal development. The more we understand the principle of justice, the more we practice it in our daily lives, the more we grow, share in rewards, and the more fulfilled we are. The more we as individuals believe in justice, the more it is practiced by our society, the more humankind will evolve.

Reversed: You are being unfair to yourself. You need to bring balance back into your life. You are not looking at both sides of an issue. Weigh the pros and cons carefully before deciding what to do. You are getting what you "deserve," not what you want. An issue is not going your way, or will not be decided in your favor. Also, sometimes life is unfair. Do not get stuck—move ahead.

XII The Hanged Man

It takes a brave soul to hang upside down suspended from a tree—and by choice. Someone who has enough confidence in himself to risk injury, even scorn from others. But that is the essence of The Hanged Man card. It is a transitory card that represents a break with the past, a willingness to turn the world over, to take a fresh look at things from a new angle or vantage point. The card implies nonconformity.

The mere fact the card depicts someone hanging shows that things are in suspension, and that perhaps we are between stages in life—the known and the unknown—and ready to face what awaits us. In other words, we are willing to give up what we have because we believe we will either grow or benefit in some important way by taking this dramatic step. Once suspended from the tree, there is no turning back.

The card also reminds us of the experience of the great mystics who plunge themselves into a spiritual crisis, hanging between reality and the unknown, hoping to emerge enlightened. Sometimes we must be willing to give up everything we know, cut ourselves off from our comforts and roots, and open ourselves up to the mysteries of the world.

Above all, The Hanged Man does what he thinks is right, not what others tell him. The Hanged Man represents a stage in our development when we have grown more certain of ourselves than ever before, when we know we can overcome the challenges we face and we willingly put ourselves to the test.

There is a strong link between this card and The Fool, who stands ready to jump headlong into the void. The difference is, The Fool does so out of innocence at the start of his journey and without any idea of what awaits him. The Hanged Man has the experience of hindsight to guide his action.

This is also a card of faith and destiny, and a strong belief in both. The Hanged Man believes in the forces that rule our lives and because of his deep faith he has no fear about the eventual outcome. He believes he is fulfilling another step on the road to his eventual destiny. He is so immersed in the life process himself that he is giving himself to it entirely.

Reversed: You are not willing or able to break with the past. You may be too comfortable with the way things are, and prefer the status quo over change. You might think you are the master of your fate, but the longer you delay getting out of suspension (limbo), the more you stand to lose.

XIII Death

The Death card strikes fear in the hearts of most people when actually it should be welcomed. It is not an evil card, but a card of change and transformation. It is the darkness that precedes the light, the death that is necessary for rebirth to take place. It is another turn on the Wheel of Life.

Death and life go hand in hand. Both are linked as part of the eternal process. Life ends in death, and from death comes new beginnings. Where The Hanged Man represents a suspension between two states, Death symbolizes the end of the old and the start of something new.

Death takes many forms on the physical and mental planes. In nature, the four seasons are a graphic representation of the life-death process that we know well. From the end of winter comes the birth of spring, which leads to summer, then to fall, and back again to winter. Over and over and over again. For eternity.

Our lives are like that, too. From the moment of birth to our eventual death, we pass through different life stages. Each new stage follows from the death of the other. From childhood we grow to adolescence. From our teens we enter adulthood. Our middle age passes to our later years. The passage of each stage brings new beginnings, new challenges. Without the force of death, we would stagnate. The Wheel would stop turning. And then we might truly be dead.

Death is a revitalizing force. It is a cleansing, a clearing away of the old to make way for the new. Just as gardens have to be pruned of their dead growth, so do our lives. We have to cast off old ideas and old ways of doing things that are no longer valid or useful. We have to embrace the new challenges and opportunities, and cut our ties to the past.

The Death card symbolizes mortality of things, relationships, and phases in life. We should take solace in the fact that nothing is forever, that new doors will always open. We are not locked in place. We can grow in new directions once we are liberated from our past selves.

We should welcome the Death card and look forward to the changes in our lives. Death tells us to be open to new adventures about to begin.

Reversed: You have a fear of change and the future. You are clinging to old ideas or values that are no longer relevant. This may not be a good time to make the break. Stop grieving for the old ways or what you have lost. Also, you may need to let go of something that has become a "dead" part of life.

XIV Temperance

The Justice card tells us of the consequences of not living life in perfect harmony or balance; the Temperance card is a guide to living that harmony.

We know that life itself is a neutral process. The ebb and flow only lead to more of the same. How we live within the process—preferably in balance—is the key to fulfillment and happiness. The Temperance card suggests we recognize the need for limitations, know how far to go, and when to pull back on the reins. It is not a denial or sacrifice, but rather mixing or matching or weaving together what is right for you. Just as you have to keep mixing hot and cold water until the temperature feels right, you have to select the path that feels the best for you.

The Temperance card implies great self-knowledge. The more you know about yourself, the better able you are to find the balance between your wants and needs, strengths and weaknesses, and likes and dislikes, as well as finding balance in how you function in different situations. After all, we are not the same all the time. Our behavior changes as circumstances and environment changes.

The Temperance card also reminds us that to pursue anything in the extreme is a bad tactic. We would be wiser to choose the middle path and put together a plan that leaves room for accommodation, flexibility, and change along the way. By tilting too far in one direction, we might topple over. Or by turning the flames up too high, we might get burned.

The Temperance card is a moderating force between the raw determination ("full speed ahead") of the chariot driver and the sword-wielding force of justice. Why live life on the edge when you do not have to? Draw from all that life has to offer. Compromise, accommodate, and be happy. Remember, you are in control and calling the shots. You can choose what is best for you.

Temperance is also about timing and patience—knowing when to push ahead and when to wait.

By pursuing the path of Temperance, you will also live a more fulfilling and enriching life in company with others. Your personality, strengths, and weaknesses will be balanced against theirs. You will draw what you need for yourself and share from yourself what they need.

Reversed: There is a lack of control in your life. You are being close-minded. You may be uncomfortable with what is facing you. ("It doesn't feel right.") You are impatient—pull back.

XV The Devil

The Devil is a card of darkness—the kind that limits our vision and blocks reality from our view. In the dark, it is hard to find the path to happiness. The real evil that The Devil represents is being unable to enjoy life for what it is, and being misled by false notions, usually because of an attachment to material things.

The Devil also symbolizes the limitations we place on ourselves. Instead of facing challenges, we are urged by The Devil to turn and run, and seek the path of lowest resistance. The Devil tells us to give in to our temptations, do what we know is wrong, and be weak instead of strong.

In our modern age, The Devil is synonymous with the trap many of us build for ourselves, in the belief that we cannot make changes or better ourselves, and that our world is cold, cruel, and uncaring. The Devil makes us believe it is our fate to suffer. The Devil would have us believe we cannot break free of a confining job or a stifling relationship. The Devil also would like us to believe that the Wheel of Fortune crushes us as it turns instead of carrying us to a higher plane.

In the same vein, when we feel so down, depressed, and mired in a sense of hopelessness, we are easy prey for The Devil. The key is not to give in but to plunge headlong into life's experiences with the innocence of The Fool and ambition of The Chariot driver, and draw on all our internal strength so that we can face the future with fearlessness of The Hanged Man.

The Devil also represents the fears we carry around and which limit our growth because we are afraid to confront them. For most of us, fear of change is the strongest and most crippling. Fear of making a commitment can grip us in an equally strong stranglehold. The fear that The Devil card represents is paralyzing. The Devil would like us to think we cannot do anything about it and that we have no control over our lives.

We know the opposite is true. We did not have this fear when we began the journey as The Fool, and we should not succumb to it now, not after we have grown so much and learned to trust ourselves. We should recognize our fears, confront them, and get on with our lives. We must be strong and chase The Devil from our lives.

Reversed: Let go of what is chaining you or weighing you down, including your fears. Examine your priorities—it is time to shift.

XVI The Tower

The Tower card is about breaking free and knocking down the walls that imprison us. It is not a subtle change, but a major, and sometimes sudden and even severe transformation in our lives. It is appropriate that it follows The Devil card. If The Devil card represents the darkness in our lives, The Tower card means we are ready to welcome some light in our lives—even if it descends upon us with the fury of a lightning bolt.

The Tower is the process of transformation itself, not the steps leading up to it. This card says change is happening *now*. A new door has opened in your life and you are going through it.

The walls of The Tower can symbolize many things: a relationship that has trapped you, a job that stifles you, a family relation that you cannot get close to, ideas or fears that imprison you, and so on. You are ready to break free.

The Tower card also reminds us that sometimes change is unexpected—even when we hope for it. Often this can be the best kind of change because we do not have to debate with ourselves about whether we should do something now or later. Like it or not, ready or not, change is happening right before your eyes. The outcome is likely to be good because it is something you want.

The Tower can also be a final message that you cannot hide from yourself or from life forever. No matter how thick the walls or how tall The Tower stands, it can be blown apart without warning. Maybe you would be wiser to act first. It could be less traumatic or tumultuous that way.

The Tower may signify sudden, traumatic change in life that shakes your very foundation and makes you concerned about your ability to get through it, or even survive it. Though the Tower image is cracked, it does not fall. It—and you—will survive.

The Tower card is also about inspiration that hits like a bolt, the way answers to tough questions that have eluded us suddenly break through our consciousness, usually when we least expect it, and sometimes after we have given up on finding those answers.

On yet another level, The Tower card represents sudden spiritual enlightenment—knowledge that comes to us from deep within, without warning, and opens our eyes to the wonders and mysteries of the world.

Reversed: The change is over and you had better get used to doing things a new way. You are out in the open now, so do not try to hide. The old ways are gone forever. Brace yourself for a bumpy ride.

XVII The Star

The Star is another card of balance and harmony—the kind that comes after a storm, a violent eruption or a major change, all the things represented by The Tower. The Star is a card of calm and peacefulness; hope and joy; comforts and pleasure; and things feel good. There is order in nature once again.

We can rest and reflect and turn our gaze to the heavens. The Star will guide us to our destination when we are ready to begin journeying again. The Star will illuminate the path for us. It will also protect us under the night sky.

When we look up to the starlit heavens, we are filled with awe and wonder. For a moment, we feel small in relation to the grand scheme of the cosmos. At the same time, we feel a part of this master plan. We recognize that all things have their purpose, all things their place. On the earthly plane, we are like the stars above. We light the path for our own lives and for others.

The Star's light is a soft light, not a blinding flash like the lightning that strikes The Tower. We want to look at it, not away from it. Although liberating, the lightning terrifies us. In contrast, The Star, which represents the light from the heavens, warms the soul and the inner self the way the sun warms the body. It nourishes our minds, and helps us think of the infinite possibilities—like the countless stars above—that life offers us. It is a card of inspiration.

The Star is another card of personal reflection, meditation, and contemplation. It is a reminder to turn our gaze inward and be guided by an inner light; to trust ourselves and our intuition. We have come so far, learned so much, at last we are becoming enlightened. We are reminded of our connection to spirit and the divine.

The card also tells us to be at peace with ourselves, be true to ourselves, and bring love into our lives. The card encourages us to feel good about ourselves.

On a spiritual level, The Star is our link to the higher plane and to our Higher Self. It tells us to open our minds and let the light shine in. To grow in spirit, awareness, and knowledge, and to apply all we learn in pursuit of even higher knowledge.

Reversed: Your eyes are closed to future possibilities. Your gaze is focused downward instead of up to the heavens. You have feelings of insecurity and disquiet. You need to latch onto your dreams again. Set your sights high.

XVIII The Moon

The Moon glows, but it does not illuminate the earth below. It is not a guide like The Star and it does not warm or brighten. The light The Moon casts is not even its own—it is a reflection of The Sun. The reality we know by day is now cloaked in an illusion.

When The Moon is high in the night, we enter the dreamworld. In this netherworld, things are not as they always seem. The familiar shapes of the daytime hours take on different meanings. We must be on guard.

Even the Moon does not reveal all of itself to us. It shows only one side. It grows from a little sliver to a full moon—another reminder that not everything has been revealed to us.

The Moon card suggests we are being tested. Can we remain true to the path, or will we be distracted by the shadows, illusions, and mysteries of the night? Will we be able to tell our dreams from reality? Will we be able to glean from our dreams what we need to apply to our waking hours?

Because we have only ourselves to rely on until morning comes, we must trust our instinct, follow our hunches, and create an inner light. The night, ruled by The Moon, will teach us to trust our unconscious self.

The Moon also is a symbol of madness and lunacy. Think of how often people's strange behavior is attributed to a full moon. The Moon is an unsettling influence. It looms overhead, appearing to threaten. The night of The Moon is an uneasy time. While it may be quiet outside and seem peaceful, that is just another illusion. Inside we are churning. We are so close to completing our journey, so eager to reach the end of the path, yet we must muster the courage to trudge onward in the dimly-lit night.

We must tread carefully during this period. We do not know what awaits us. But we have to have faith that we are up to the task. Our dreams will guide us.

The Moon card warns us of the unknown, yet at the same time it beckons to us. It is that fear of the unknown that attracts. We do not know where the journey will lead and yet we are willing to take the risks andventure out into the darkness. The Moon tugs on us, just as it pulls the tides.

Reversed: This is not a time to venture out. Stay with the path you know best. You are lacking in faith and in nerve. You are going through an uncertain phase. You are in the dark about things. Be careful that you are not under illusions about the reality of your situation.

XIX The Sun

The Sun is the source of life. Its rays nourish our bodies as well as our minds. Without it, existence would cease. When we see The Sun card, we should take a moment to reflect on all that is good in our lives.

In symbolic terms, a life without sun would be a life of total darkness. There would be no growth, no happiness. We would exist in limbo. Thankfully, The Sun shines brightly. Our time in The Sun is our reward for passing through the trial of the night and the shadows cast by The Moon. We emerge into the warm rays of golden sunshine feeling reborn, renewed, and energized.

The Sun card exudes a satisfying, happy, and wholesome feeling. Contentment reigns in our lives again. Optimism is the word of the day. We are triumphant.

The Sun also means enlightenment and empowerment. With things so brightly lit, we can see clearly, which makes us feel positive about the future. We feel our creative juices at their highest. Because warmth is also synonymous with feeling secure, we feel more than able to tackle any and all challenges.

The Sun, which sits at the center of the solar system, means our lives are centered.

The Sun card often depicts children at play. In the sunlight we are children of the earth—innocent and happy, full of hope and promise, trusting in both life and in ourselves, and filled with a desire to live life to its fullest.

The Sun means a new day is dawning. The air is fresh, the sky blue, all is right and well. We are the masters of our fate.

In The Sun we are free—free of our burdens, our material concerns. We have traveled far since beginning the journey as The Fool, and yet we come to this stop along the way even younger than when we began. That is because we are young in mind and spirit.

Enriched by the past experiences of our lives, we begin a new stage in life on a higher plane, wiser and more confident. We have been reborn many times on this journey, and we will be reborn many times more.

Reversed: There is unhappiness and emptiness. You feel a lack of purpose. You are in the dark about things, or your mind is unclear. Clouds loom on the horizon. You are too set in old ways. You need to let some light and warmth into your life.

XX Judgement

Made pure by The Sun, we are now ready to face the challenges, tackle our problems, and get on with new chapters in our lives. If the Death card meant the clearing away of the old to make way for the new, the Judgement card calls us to action. It tells us the time has come.

We are ready to assume a more meaningful existence, to live life on the higher plane, not just as individuals, but united with all others. We have an appreciation of our role in the world. On our journey we have been seeking truth, enlightenment, hidden knowledge, self-awareness, and trying to bring balance, harmony, and a sense of peace and contentment to our lives. We now possess those things—and we can use them during the adventures to come.

Judgement tells us to look no further, wait no longer. New paths are opening. As we travel along these new paths, we may be starting once again the cycle that brought us here in the first place. But as we have learned from The Wheel of Fortune, when we return again next time, we will be wiser.

Judgement means we are being awakened from the dead of inaction, hesitation, and withdrawal, and pulled into a resurrection. We are emerging from dormancy, lifting the obstacles that block our growth and development. We can also see ourselves rising above our problems, the mundane concerns that restrict us from achieving our potential and that leave us locked inside ourselves. We have been released.

By the time we reach this stage, we have changed, and we recognize the change. We now fully understand that our life's work is a combination of personal fulfillment and achieving some higher destiny. We understand our purpose for being here and how to integrate that purpose in everything we do.

The time for questioning is over. The real work—our life's work—is just beginning. The next time we pass this point, we will be able to show real progress.

Reversed: You are unable to see the purpose in your life. The shackles have been broken, but you will not let go. You are closing your mind to new possibilities, or shunning responsibilities, or turning a deaf ear to a call to action.

XXI The World

The World card signals arrival--the journey's end, a coming together of all things, the joining of all the forces in the world, and a wholeness or oneness.

All is in balance. All is in motion. We have completed the cycle. We are ready to move again, to dance the dance of life and go in any direction we choose. It has been the journey of a lifetime—or the journey of an instant. Time is not the issue here, just what we have learned.

We have arrived at that stage in life when we have an appreciation for life and the world that comes from deep inside. The wisdom of the ages is now ours.

The card is also a reminder that life is infinite, not finite—that the world spins forever, and we with it. We must accept constant change in our lives, for that is the only constant of life. We must recognize this change as the life force itself. From change comes growth. From this growth we ascend to new heights. And someday, we will start at the bottom all over again.

The World card is the ultimate goal for all of us. Total enlightenment. To see ourselves as part of the cosmic order. Not separate and distinct, and with our own value judgments about what is right and wrong with the world, but as one piece of the puzzle that makes up the whole. In other words, we see our place in the universe.

The World card explains that there is a purpose for all things. We do not need to understand this process intellectually. We should not stand at the sidelines and observe, or put the world under a microscope. We only learn by being part of the process and by experiencing its wholeness. A Zen expression says that the danger of pointing your finger at the moon is that you might mistake your finger for the moon. We must not make the same mistake by thinking we know all there is because we have watched the world in motion. Rather, we would be wiser to experience the truths for ourselves.

The World card is an affirmation of the life process itself—both its good and bad. It is nonjudgmental about either. The good and the bad are just elements of life. The card tells us to accept both and to recognize that they have a place in the grand scheme. The ups and downs, the wins and losses, the joys and sorrows—they are just different sides of the coin. They are part of life and they help us grow in equal measure.

The World card is also about having it all and getting what you want.

Reversed: You are not there yet. Goals still elude you. You are not committing yourself, but running in place, not moving forward. You have unrealistic expectations about how something will work out.

7

The Minor Arcana

The meanings of the Minor Arcana are presented here with the same approach as that used with the Major Arcana: interpretations that can be applied to almost any deck. Please note that suit names and court card names vary in accordance to the theme of a deck. I have used traditional names here.

The four suits of the Minor Arcana correspond to the four basic elements of the universe:

> Wands to fire
> Cups to water
> Swords to Air
> Pentacles to Earth

Each suit has fourteen cards: ace to ten are the numbered (pip) cards; Page, Knight, Queen, and King are the court cards.

Numbered cards represent events in our lives, their different stages of development, and possible courses of action open to us:

Ace: Beginning
Two: Formation, coming together of opposites
Three: Growth
Four: Practical attainment, tangible achievement
Five: New cycle, change, stability upset
Six: Finding equilibrium, harmony in the face of constant change
Seven: Facing complex choices, development of the soul
Eight: Setting priorities, putting things where they belong, balancing
Nine: Bringing things to an end, completion, conclusion
Ten: Over but not finished and about to begin again

Court cards reflect the influence of aspects of personality in our lives, from ourselves or other people:

Page: Youthful innocence, learning
Knight: Energy, drive, risk-taking
Queen: Understanding, awareness, discernment
King: Strength of will, authority, dominion

The suits represent different aspects of life and the forces surrounding them:

Wands (Fire)

The Wands suit stands for fire and the spark of life. It reflects enterprise, energy, activity, doing, and the constant renewal of all things. It is linked to our positive feelings about the future: hopeful, forward looking, and ambitious. Wands capture our desire for growth, how we strive for achievement and success, and the inspiration that fuels us.

Cups (Water)

The Cups suit is about love, happiness, the emotional pleasures of life, and the function of intuition. Cups go with the flow and relate to how we respond to emotional influences, impulses, and inspiration. Cups put the romances, relationships, and ups and downs of our lives into perspective, and also address how well we are paying attention to our spiritual guidance and intuition.

Swords (Air)
Life is a constant struggle, and the Swords suit represents the qualities necessary to survive: boldness and courage. It also is a suit of mental energies, reason, logic, judgement—all the things that stand separate and distinct from our emotions. Swords allow us to observe scenes from our life without emotion and somewhat detached. The suit also addresses our communication with others.

Pentacles (Earth)
Pentacles is the suit of the material world. Its images deal with attainment and the things you can feel and hold, the material aspects of life: money, wealth, and the acquisition of fortune. Pentacles represent the value of physical experience. They also address other personal assets of time, energy, and health—they reveal how we are "spending" ourselves. In addition, Pentacles address our connection to earth and nature.

The interpretations that follow are designed to guide you in your search for answers. They are not absolute. Use the deck of your choice and study each card in relation to the interpretations. Note symbolic details in the images. As always when using the cards, allow your intuition to suggest fresh interpretations and new insights. The Tarot is your tool to help you make important discoveries about yourself, about life.

Wands

Ace of Wands
A fresh start in a new direction with activity, projects, a path in life, a job or career change. The birth of an idea that leads to action. The start of an enterprise or new challenges. You are filled with a sense of optimism, eagerness, enthusiasm, excitement, and boundless energy. You sense the potential. You are looking forward to what's ahead.

Reversed: Difficulty in getting something started. False hopes. Misdirected energy. You are lacking motivation, ambition, or drive to face the challenges. You do not want to attempt anything new.

Two of Wands
You have a grasp of what you are capable of accomplishing and know what needs to be done. You know your investments will pay off if you follow the plan you have laid out. You sense success, feel proud, and are looking forward to the outcome. You are moving in the right direction. You may be in a productive partnership, or receive important support from someone.

Reversed: Going in the wrong direction. Not paying proper attention to details. Receiving mixed signals. Tasks seem overwhelming, and you cannot get a grip on what you must do. You are not in touch with your energies. Look for something out of kilter with someone who is important to the situation.

Three of Wands
You are reaping success from your efforts. Your ship comes in to safe harbor. Now that you have proven what you can do on your own, it is time to form partnerships and alliances with others so that you can seek their advice and work together as a team.

Reversed: Achievements may not last. Your alliances are not proving to be productive. Goals seem elusive. Control is slipping away. Best to take time to reassess and regroup. Be wary of advice from others.

Four of Wands
Your accomplishments leave you feeling satisfied. Because your goals have been achieved, you feel a sense of peace, security, and happiness. You can take time to rest, relax, enjoy, and count your blessings. There is a feeling of harmony in the air. You have productive relationships with others.

Reversed: Goals fall short of the mark, or you are unsatisfied with the results. Insufficient results.

Five of Wands
The calm is shattered. You face competition from others for the same thing.

There are distractions, disagreements, and confusion. The outcome could be in your favor if you are careful, act forcefully, and do not give in. You may have to change your game plan. Be firm and stand your ground. Do not let anyone get the advantage over you.

Reversed: The conflict and disharmony are passing. New opportunities will be forthcoming. Positive change is in the air. Be ready for it. Also, the card can indicate healthy competition.

Six of Wands

Through hard work, intelligence, and a clear understanding of the objectives, you achieve your goals. Victory, recognition, and congratulations are yours. You have the drive, ambition, and desire—and a belief in your abilities—that lead to success. But even though you have earned your place, you will have to work to keep it or someone might take it from you. Victory cannot last forever.

Reversed: Victory eludes you. You do not get the recognition you feel you deserve. You are not strong enough for the challenge, and are letting others beat you. Keep trying, you may be successful yet. You need to develop faith in yourself and a desire to win.

Seven of Wands

You are facing adversity and challenge— and still holding your ground. You are able to rise above obstacles. You must draw on your inner strength and personal faith to deal with this latest challenge. Something is coming to a head. An unexpected confrontation looms on the horizon, yet you are not afraid.

Reversed: You are not willing to confront your problems. You would prefer to turn and run. You are feeling a sense of anxiety, or are uncomfortable about what is ahead. You are disturbed by choices facing you. You lack willpower. You must focus on priorities.

Eight of Wands

Things are moving fast and bringing you closer to your goal in a satisfying way. Results are coming in quickly—and you must keep things in order. Sometimes the card indicates a journey.

Reversed: You cannot handle the pace and feel overwhelmed. Things are stacking up against you. Events may overtake you. Life is passing you by while you stand still.

Nine of Wands
One last test will require you to draw on all your abilities; for which you are prepared. You are at or near the culmination of your efforts, project, or goal. If you face adversity, the fight is on familiar turf and you will win out in the end, arriving at your destination with your achievement intact.

Reversed: You are being made to deal with something that you are not yet ready to face. Your path is blocked. You are uncertain which way to turn next. Adversity lies ahead.

Ten of Wands
You are carrying a heavy load, more than you can handle, more than you really want. Things weigh you down. You must share responsibility with others before continuing. Get rid of what you no longer need.

Reversed: Someone has made you responsible for their problems, or led you astray. You are near collapse. Take stock of what you can manage, and let go of the rest.

Page of Wands
You get or are about to get good news. You get a signal to proceed with something new and exciting. It is time to tell the world about your plans, share your news with others. You are learning new skills.

Reversed: You do not know how to interpret the news. You receive information that upsets you. You need to learn new skills and finesse.

Knight of Wands
A time of movement and journey. You are on your way to meet something or it is coming into your life. You are taking reasonable risks, experimenting, testing new ideas. Things are in a state of transition. There may be a stirring or turbulence in the air.

Reversed: Frustration. You are knocked off track, derailed. There is disruption in your life, movement without purpose, no sense of destination. You are running in place or moving in circles. You have lost sight of your path or goals.

Queen of Wands
You have an appreciation for life, relationships, friendships and family. Your work and home life are in harmony. All pursuits are surrounded by a positive force. You are confident in your ability to make good decisions.

Reversed: You are under the influence of someone (probably female) who is narrow-minded, self-centered, and domineering. You must guard against feelings of jealousy. You falter in decision-making.

King of Wands
You are looking forward to challenges, new pursuits, or healthy competition. You give to others and reap the rewards of self-fulfillment. Take the lead and others will follow. You are in a position of strength and authority. Delegate where necessary. You are running your empire.

Reversed: You have a lack of tolerance and let your ego get in the way of what is required for the best and highest good. Opposition looms. It may be necessary to bend to a stronger point of view.

Cups

Ace of Cups
A new outpouring of emotions: first love, new appreciation for life, a spiritual awakening. A journey that begins with special blessings. Good fortune shines on you. An acceptance of life and all the joys it brings. A sign of fertility.

Reversed: Emphasis on material over spiritual. You are closed off from nurturing love or from your true feelings, or denying the wonders of life. You are not ready for emotional involvement. You are in a state of neither giving nor receiving love.

Two of cups
The start of a relationship or love affair, or a budding romance. A sharing of love, good feelings, ideas. A sense of harmony. The beginning of a partnership. Emotional balance. Give and take. You are entering or enjoying a harmonious relationship.

Reversed: Arguments, disputes, distrust. A relationship out of balance. Inequality among partners—one is putting in more than is being received. A relationship is in danger of coming undone.

Three of Cups
Time to celebrate your accomplishments, reap the happiness you have achieved in family relationships, friendships, and work. You are supported. A sense of joy envelops all you do. The cup of life tastes sweet.

Reversed: Anything enjoyed to excess can lose its value or worth. There is a price to pay for overindulgence. Happiness turns to sadness, joy to sorrow, pleasure to pain. Emphasis is on the sensual instead of the spiritual. You lack key support from others.

Four of Cups
Material pursuits no longer satisfy. You are uninterested in what is offered to you, or unable to recognize it. Past endeavors go unattended. It is time to reassess, reevaluate, and turn inward for answers. Look for new, more fulfilling, and satisfying challenges and pursuits. What do you need to regain your stability and foundation? Answers to your questions are within reach.

Reversed: You are ready for new challenges, relationships. A sense of excitement is in the air. You are feeling revitalized, refreshed, and invigorated. Ready to resume past relationships and renew friendships.

Five of Cups
Unhappy endings, broken relationships. Time to pick up the pieces and start building again. Painful emotional change with some gain and some loss. See what you can learn from your losses. Turn your back on the past and look to the future. What is gone is gone. Do not turn your back on

what you still have. Hold on. No matter how little it seems, it can always be nurtured and made to increase.

Reversed: Although a loss has been suffered, there is no reason to feel hopeless about the future. Things will start looking up again. Pull yourself up out of focusing on what has been lost and pay attention to what you still have. An old friend may hold the key.

Six of Cups
Memories of good times fill you with happiness. The past is not lost--it can always be remembered. Also, past events can figure favorably in the present. Old friends may serve you well at this stage, sharing generously of their resources.

Reversed: Do not allow the past to cloud your emotions. It is time to open yourself to the present. You need to find new friends and share new experiences. Leave the past in the past. Others may not come through for you.

Seven of Cups
Feelings of indecision swirl around you. There are many choices and they all look good. Nonetheless, choices must be made, but you are not giving yourself fully to the task at hand. You are spending too much time dreaming about the future when you should be acting on those dreams instead. Draw on those inner energies and begin moving from thought to action.

Reversed: You have allowed indecision to stall you, and at the risk of losing opportunity. It is time to pursue that dream, see where it leads.

Eight of Cups
The time has come to seek higher meaning and purpose from life. It is also time to say goodbye to friendships and relationships you have outgrown. Or, you must get out of your comfort zone in order to move ahead. You may also want to follow the path of The Hermit and look inward for answers.

Reversed: Putting emotional pleasures ahead of spiritual needs. Hanging on to what no longer serves you or suits your needs. Not making an effort to grow or expand. Also, the card could mean that it is better for you to stay, not move on.

Nine of Cups
The culmination of material and emotional satisfaction. You are enjoying the pleasures of life. You are enjoying your work, friends, and family.

Reversed: What at first seemed like happiness leaves you feeling empty and unfulfilled. You are spending too much time enjoying the sensual pleasures at the expense of spiritual growth and development. You are living life in the shadow of false values.

Ten of Cups
Tranquility reigns. Family relationships, friendships, home, and work are all under the sign of protection. Life itself means happiness. You have achieved what you have been seeking on both the material and spiritual planes. You feel complete—comfortable with yourself.

Reversed: Relationships are in disharmony. Family quarrels. Loss of satisfaction. You are unhappy, depressed, sad, and wondering what went wrong. Also, you may be blind to the many wonders that surround you. The card can also mean you have no reason to be unhappy, so stop looking for one.

Page of Cups
A new idea will break through the surface. It may be delivered by a friend. This is a good time to apply your creativity to something--try new methods, initiate new projects. Be playful and have a beginner's mind. The card can also signal development of psychic ability. Pay attention.

Reversed: You are acting on impulse that could lead to trouble. You need to mature and become more thoughtful. You must learn to accept responsibility for yourself and your actions. You are ignoring ideas, guidance, or intuition that may be beneficial.

Knight of Cups
You are following your dreams or traveling down your intuitive path,

which will lead to fulfillment and satisfaction. This is a time for mental stimulation. Live your vision. Be bold and take prudent risks.

Reversed: You are lost in a world of fantasy, cut off from reality. Your motives are insincere. Be on guard against duplicity, fraud, or trickery from those around you. Someone may tell you what you want to hear just to get the better of you.

Queen of Cups
You are protected by love, warmth, and caring. You are able to express yourself emotionally and be generous with your affection. This is a good time to pursue the creative arts—poetry, music, literature. Open yourself up to new visions and possibilities. Follow the prompting of your heart.

Reversed: Your emotions are out of control, leading to self-deception and false hopes. Confusion reigns. You are caught between the worlds of reality and illusion without knowing which way to turn. Be careful not to fall victim to deception by someone who plays upon your emotions, and who you think shares your best interests, but who is really trying to manipulate you.

King of Cups
Seek out advice and counsel from trusted friend, a wise person. Follow your head and keep your emotions under control. Probe for the meaning in what you plan to do. Stay in control.

Reversed: Look beyond the façade. You or someone around you may be putting up a false front to hide insecurity and immaturity. Be careful of judgements rendered, or advice offered from someone you do not know well. You are at risk of losing control over an emotional issue.

Swords

Ace of Swords
The unleashing of great mental energy, dissemination of information, and new communication. You must put this power to work to vanquish obstacles facing you. You have new clarity of mind. It may mean that you

will be able to think through a problem that has been troubling you. Set your mind to accomplishing your goals.

Reversed: Think carefully before taking action. Instead of seeing reality clearly, your vision is clouded with illusions. Sort out all your options and consider each one carefully. See everything in clear light as it is, not as you wish it to be. Focus on the truth.

Two of Swords

You cannot decide. Instead, you close your eyes to what faces you. You need to step back from the situation, taking time to get your emotions in check, to ponder things in silence. You cannot remain aloof forever; soon you will have to decide. The card can also indicate being at odds with someone in terms of not agreeing, or not being able to persuade them to your point of view.

Reversed: Uncertainty over a decision. Inability to work through an impasse. Failure of communication or diplomacy or negotiation. You need to take action to break stalled energy. Stop being blind to the reality of a situation.

Three of Swords

You have been deeply wounded—something has gone dreadfully wrong, or someone has let you down, disappointed you, or betrayed you. Life has become full of stormy conditions. You may even feel you cannot go on. You must realize that wounds can heal. Use your clarity of mind to take a realistic look around you, and formulate a plan to move on.

Reversed: Your pain will remain with you until you acknowledge the reason for it, and make the decision to heal and put it all behind you. You must get on with your life. The card may also point to painful discord created by different points of view, and the inability to reach consensus with others.

Four of Swords

It is time to back away from your troubles, and to make time for quiet contemplation. Your problems will still be there when you return, but you will be energized and able to approach things with a clearer head, wiser from your rest. The card may also indicate that you have already pulled back and put yourself on hold. Is this what you want to do?

Reversed: It is time to end your retreat—action is needed. You are being called back. Make sure you are ready. Use caution.

Five of Swords
All your emphasis is on winning, but look around you at the wreckage you have created. Victory, winning at all costs and taking all the spoils may not be much of a reward. It could even be a loss in the long run. You must think of all the consequences that may arise—especially those who might get hurt, including yourself— before you come out swinging.

Reversed: You have won a hollow victory, or are heading in that direction. You are experiencing defeat and feelings of pain, loss, and despair.

Six of Swords
You are able to navigate through your problems. Even though your difficulties still face you, you are learning how to deal with them and how to live your life with their presence. You are trying to look at things with a more open mind by putting distance between yourself and the past.

Reversed: You do not feel like you are making any progress. You are trying to paddle against the current. You are not able to look at your problems afresh or put them behind you. You feel weighed down by others or by responsibilities.

Seven of Swords
Your attempts to deal with your problems are incomplete and not well-planned. In the process, you are hurting yourself. Trying to solve things alone may not be a wise decision. It may be more than you can handle by yourself.

Reversed: It is a good time to seek advice from someone else, to learn what you need to know. Do a little listening and seek constructive criticism. Good results may follow. Do not be afraid to ask others for help.

Eight of Swords

You have boxed yourself in and not allowed yourself any options. You are holding yourself back—and for no good reason. Liberate yourself.

Reversed: It is time to see, think, and act without restriction. You can put your fears behind you and start moving forward again. You feel a great sense of release and relief.

Nine of Swords

The world is filled with pain and sorrow, and somehow you must find a way to make peace with it. You feel overwhelmed by negative conditions, sorrow, and depression. Or, you feel as though you want to take on the pain of the world yourself, to protect others from it. Pain and sorrow are only the other side of joy and happiness.

Reversed: You are moving out of hopelessness, and now a sense of hope fills you. The doom and gloom of the past are fading. The pain will be replaced with joy. You must have faith. Time will heal all wounds.

Ten of Swords

You have suffered and great and unexpected loss, or the end to something on which you had been counting. The defeat could have been of your making or the result of circumstances beyond your control. As gloomy as things look, this too shall pass. The card can also signify a cycle of pain and defeat that keeps recurring, and you feel unable to get out of it.

Reversed: Problems are on the wane. Blue skies appear on the horizon, signaling a change for the better. It is up to you to take advantage of this opportunity and move on before new problems crop up again, or before an old one reasserts itself. It is time to break the cycle.

Page of Swords

You are making a halfhearted approach to solving the problems facing you. You are not taking things seriously enough, or having a full understanding of the problem and what it means to you. It is not enough to brandish your sword.

Reversed: Unexpected problems lurk in the distance.

Knight of Swords
This is a good time to apply your mental energies to solving problems, seeking solutions, and developing plans. Time to evaluate, results will come later. Put your mental powers to work and develop a plan of action.

Reversed: Your thoughts are too scattered, coming too quickly. You need to slow down and focus. Be wary of anyone who suddenly presents you with unsolicited ideas for consideration.

Queen of Swords
Hone your intellectual abilities. Learn to see both sides of an issue and analyze carefully, free from emotions, before deciding what action to take. Do not allow your emotions to play on you.

Reversed: Do not look at things from a narrow perspective, or shut yourself off from the truth by closing your ears to other points of view. Keep a balanced perspective.

King of Swords
Hear everything out. Use your experiences of the past to guide your thinking. Be fair in making decisions that affect other people. Make your thought processes and decisions clear to all.

Reversed: Your lack of compassion can hurt other people. Do not be so strict that you border on cruelty in your dealings with others. Also, do not allow prejudice to cloud your vision.

Pentacles

Ace of Pentacles
Something new brings an increase in prosperity and well-being. You have a good foundation for increasing money, perhaps through a new venture or enterprise. There is fertile soil in which to plant your ideas and come back later to harvest what grows. A chance to better your financial situation through promotion, career change. Improvements in health.

Reversed: Move with caution before making major investments. Plan carefully, weigh the risks. Do not succumb to greed. There is a possible loss on the horizon. Material gain may not provide the answers you are seeking. Be cautious of new enterprises requiring investments of time and energy as well.

Two of Pentacles
What comes in goes out as well. New ventures may require you to adapt to changing circumstances. Check pros and cons before initiating new project. Keep home and work in proper balance. You are in a juggling act managing money, time, and personal resources.

Reversed: You have more than you can handle, and you may not be able to hold things together. Something is out of balance. Things are up in the air. You are misleading yourself into thinking you are happy in your pursuits.

Three of Pentacles
You can apply your knowledge, skills, and abilities to great advantage. A time of positive, measurable achievement that will win you reward and notice. Others will be happy to assist you and also will respond to your lead. Keep your link to spiritual guidance strong.

Reversed: Less than satisfactory efforts produce poor results and disappointment. There is no gain. This is not a good time to enlist others in your project or undertaking, because there is still much for you to learn. You are missing what you need to finish task.

Four of Pentacles
You have worked very hard to achieve a solid foundation of resources, but are you seeking happiness exclusively from money? Do not put material gain above all else. The card also indicates that positive rewards are yours to enjoy.

Reversed: Rewards are less than expected or less than fulfilling. You are unable to hold on to your money. Your health is suffering from an over expenditure of time and energy. Your goals are being blocked. You are stressed because you do not have the power or influence you require. You are holding on to something when you should let go.

Five of Pentacles

There is sudden misfortune, loss, or failure. You are lacking faith in your abilities. If you hold on, your fortunes could reverse. Time to take care of yourself, and especially pay attention to your health. Ask others for help. You are so focused on your loss that you cannot see the help that is available around you. Do not neglect your spiritual side.

Reversed: A situation has turned around for the better. Things are beginning to look up. You are feeling better about yourself and future prospects. You recognize the need to balance material interests with spiritual development.

Six of Pentacles

Your hard work pays you dividends. A bonus is coming. Business pursuits prosper. You feel generous and want to share. There is plenty for everyone. You are feeling satisfied, in harmony with everything. Others around you appreciate what you do for them.

Reversed: You are not getting your fair share. Someone is holding out on you. You are not satisfied with the return on your investment. There are possible debts. You are not sharing with others, thinking only of yourself.

Seven of Pentacles

You have a lot to show for your efforts, but you are not sure if your achievements are what you want. You are weighing your options about the future. Also, this is time to take a moment to reflect on your gains.

Reversed: Difficult choices are facing you about finances and your personal resources. You are in doubt about which way to turn, and are afraid that bad choices could lead to loss or debts. Be careful not to make rash decisions. You want to abandon a project or undertaking after investing a lot of effort in it.

Eight of Pentacles

By applying yourself, you can build great success. You are willing to learn new skills and trade to help improve your situation. This is a good time to commit to a project, venture, or investment of money, time, effort and energy. You take great pride in what you do, and your care shows. You are happy and satisfied with your work and projects.

Reversed: You are interested only in short-term gains and are not willing to commit for the duration. You are impatient and mistakenly think shortcuts will produce desired results. Your heart is not in your work. Lack of quality shows. You are no longer challenged or stimulated and need to find something new.

Nine of Pentacles
You have earned great success and have much to enjoy. You are at the pinnacle of achievement, and your hard work has paid off. Skills honed in business world can help you manage your life overall. Your abilities can take you wherever you want to go; you are not dependent on others for success.

Reversed: Gains have been, or could be, lost. Bad decisions may be at fault. You did not pay attention to what others were telling you. Expected yields are not forthcoming and you will need to work harder.

Ten of Pentacles
You have achieved much of what you want, but you do not know if it is enough and you should seek more, or if it is as satisfying as you hoped it would be. At a minimum you are secure, have comfortable home, and sufficient wealth. The card also indicates an obsession with piling up money.

Reversed: Your financial security in jeopardy. This is not a good time to invest in new projects, or make a big gamble on possible returns. You are facing a multitude of financial problems. You feel constrained, unable to do anything to improve your lot.

Page of Pentacles
Approach new projects with a schoolboy's wonder and enthusiasm. Study hard, apply what you learn and you will reap positive rewards. Seek out solid, well- researched information before making any moves.

Reversed: You are not using your intelligence to guide you. Your actions bespeak of ignorance and closed-mindedness. Listen to the advice of others and learn from their experience. Do not allow your nonconformity to lead to difficulties and losses.

Knight of Pentacles
Hard work produces desired results. Persist in your efforts. Outline your goals ahead of time, then make a plan for achieving them. Do not leave things up to chance. Choose tasks in keeping with your abilities. Keep an eye out for new opportunities and explore them.

Reversed: Impatience will lead to failure. Be careful not to go in too many directions at the same time. You are not applying yourself as you should. Do not narrow your pursuits so that you exclude opportunities as they arise.

Queen of Pentacles
It is time to enjoy what you have earned. Rest secure in the knowledge that your wealth and material comforts will continue to flower as long as you stay at it and apply your creative powers to tasks at hand. You have everything you need to make good decisions.

Reversed: You are not taking care of business or acting responsibly where your financial affairs, time, energy, and health are concerned. You depend too much on others to help you. Your security and independence are at risk.

King of Pentacles
You have reached the pinnacle. Your efforts have paid off and you have much to show for it. People know you as a reliable, hard-working person. It is no longer necessary to take risks. You concentrate on projects with reliable outcomes. You are the master of your world.

Reversed: Money is an all-consuming passion, and you are willing to do anything you can to accumulate more. Out of this stubbornness and your passion for gain, you put work ahead of everything else in your life, including family.

8

Tarot Rituals

Working with the Tarot is richer, more powerful, and more productive when it is structured around ritual. In the modem West, the term *ritual* usually is associated with church worship or with the elaborate social and sacred ceremonies of tribal societies. Ritual, however, is much broader—it is any prescribed ceremony that is performed in order to accomplish a certain goal. Ritual is the means to come into contact with divine or supernatural will or forces. It helps the individual relate to the cosmos and mark progress through life and spiritual unfoldment.

Ritual raises energy. Even the smallest of daily routines is a ritual that puts in motion certain mental, psychic, and physical energies. When you work with the Tarot, you raise psychic energy, expand your consciousness, and heighten your intuitive ability. Ritual can help you do that most effectively.

Ritual is symbolic behavior, consciously performed to discipline the mind, body, and spirit. Jung said that rituals "are an answer and reaction to the action of God upon man, and perhaps they are not only that, but are also intended to be 'activating,' a form of magic coercion."

Hsun Tzu, a Chinese philosopher of the third century BC, said rituals create harmony in the universe and bring out the best in human beings—they are the culmination of culture.

Mythologist Joseph Campbell once stated that the function of ritual "is to give form to human life, not in the way of a mere surface arrangement, but in depth." Ritual serves as a bridge between the conscious and the unconscious: it releases psychic energies, opens psychic gateways, and allows the power of the inner world—where your intuition and psychic power reside—to manifest in the physical. Ritual also works inward, causing changes to take place deep within the unconscious where attitudes and values are born and nurtured. The more a ritual is performed, the stronger it becomes, and the greater effect it has on consciousness.

Ritual has formed the backbone and structure of sacred and social occasions since the dawn of history. As mentioned earlier, the Paleolithic cave paintings in Trois Freres, France, depict rituals that appear to be aimed at ensuring successful hunts. A man with a stag's head, perhaps a shaman wearing an animal headdress, dances. Animals are shown bleeding and dying from spear wounds. Early man prepared for hunts by performing various rituals, which either were recorded by the cave artists, or which included the painting of such scenes as part of the rituals. The rituals helped the hunters visualize and expect a successful outcome. If the ritual was performed well, and energies raised were high, the outcome of the hunt undoubtedly was influenced in a positive way.

Throughout history, rituals have been central to all religions and all spiritual, mystical, and magical traditions. There are many types of rituals, such as worship or appeasement of divine or supernatural forces, or marking the transition from one major stage of life to another, such as puberty or marriage. Rituals performed over a long period of time accumulate great psychic power.

Rituals can lose their potency, however, when the institution they serve deteriorates, or when the people performing the ritual lose sight of its original meaning. Unfortunately, most rituals in the modern West—the few that still exist—have lost much of their power. Campbell pinpoints the beginning of the decline of ritual in the West at 1914, the start of World War I, which profoundly changed European society. Since then, there has been an increasing disregard and even disdain for ritual, as though it has no place in a high-tech world but belongs to the outdated past or to less developed civilizations. People now attend church and go through the motions of moribund rituals without knowing their origins or true meanings, and without making any emotional connection to them, and thus receive little or no benefit from them. The machine has become a dominant god, replacing the need to propitiate the supernatural forces to aid us in our lives.

When we lose meaningful ritual, we cut ourselves off from our psychic roots, the archetypal realm, the *mundus imaginalis*, and our deep connectedness to each other, all life forms, the planet, and the cosmos. A strong sense of connectedness and harmony with the flow and flux of the universal energies is essential to good Tarot work.

There are no hard and fast rules or rituals for working with the Tarot, although there are some widely used practices. The beauty of the Tarot is that it is wonderfully adaptable to innovation. You decide what works best for you. This chapter will help you design your own rituals.

Tarot rituals need not be elaborate to be effective. Tarot rituals that are short and simple can be just as productive as more elaborate ones. In fact, sometimes the most powerful rituals are those that are simple.

Keep a Tarot journal

Before you begin Tarot study, get a notebook to serve as a journal of your progress. Use this notebook to record your rituals, the spreads you use, meditations, thoughts, dreams, and inspirations related to your readings. As your study progresses, you will get many ideas for creative ways to use the cards, as well as important insights for daily life, goals, and aspirations. Jot them down and allow them to grow.

When to do Tarot rituals

You should have a ritual to open your work session and one to close it. The opening ritual preps you, raises the energy, and opens you up psychically. The closing ritual helps you ground yourself and disconnect.

One opening and closing is sufficient and can serve as a general purpose for all kinds of Tarot work. You might wish to add new ones as you expand your work, however, so that you have different rituals for meditation, reading for yourself, reading for others, and such. The advantage of variety is that each ritual becomes a shorthand setup for work of a specific nature. The additional rituals need not be markedly different from your original ones—you can simply make small variations. The laying out of a spread is a ritual in itself, each unique unto itself, and so contributes to the overall procedure.

You also should have a ritual for breaking in and energizing a new pack of cards.

Is it necessary to do rituals every time you work with the Tarot? No—but it is a good idea to do them periodically to energize the spiritual connections formed by them.

The structure of ritual

Ritual is composed of four primary elements: concentration, intent and commitment, movement, and sound.

Concentration
The mind is stilled, focused, and relaxed—extraneous thoughts and mental chatter are pushed away. If you meditate, you will find it easy to center yourself quickly. Use the techniques described in the chapters on psychic power and meditations.

Intent and Commitment
Your intent and degree of commitment to the work influence the productivity of the ritual, and in turn the work. You will attract what you focus upon and project. A sincere desire to learn, grow, and help others attracts the appropriate energies.

Movement
Each time a ritual is performed, the same things are done in the same way and in the same order. This establishes a pattern and rhythm, which help raise energy and add to the ritual's cumulative power.

Sound
Parts of a ritual are spoken. Many Tarot users say their words silently, particularly if they are reading for others, but it is a good idea to include at least a few words that are spoken out loud. Sound carries power and contributes a great deal to the accumulation of the psychic power of a ritual.

Sound in a ritual also includes background music or chanting, which many individuals find conducive to achieving an open, psychic awareness in working with the cards. Others, however, find they work best in a quiet environment. Experiment with and without background sound. Choose something soothing and nonintrusive, just as meditation music. I like to use a continuous Om chant that has been embedded with a binaural beat, which balances the right and left hemispheres of the brain.

Ritual objects and tools

Ritual involves ceremonial objects, the use of which fosters physical and psychological changes intended to help achieve the goal of the ritual. The more that objects are used in ritual, the more they become imbued with psychic power. Your own energy will become embedded in the objects and in the cards that you use.

These items are good for Tarot rituals:

- A box or pouch for storage of your cards
- A wrap cloth
- A reading cloth or a Tarot table
- A candle or candles
- Personal objects of significance

Storage box or pouch

Your primary tool, of course, is your deck, and it should be well cared for. It is all right to keep the cards in the cardboard box they were purchased in, but they will be better protected and will acquire greater ritual significance if you store them in a special box or pouch. Many greeting card, occult, and import shops carry inexpensive, hand-carved wooden boxes that are perfect for Tarot cards. Avoid used boxes and pouches because they contain the imprints of their previous owners, which might interfere with the cards. Objects pick up the energies of those who handle them, as your cards will of you. If they remain in a used box, they will absorb unwanted energies, which could interfere with your psychic attunement to the cards and, in some cases, bring in unwanted energies to readings, perhaps without you being aware of it.

Alternatively, you can cleanse an old or previously owned container by smudging it, placing it in sea salt, exposing it to sunlight, and using energy healing techniques to send cleansing light into it.

Objects can yield amazing information to a psychically sensitive person merely through handling. Object reading is called psychometry, a term coined in 1840 by Joseph R. Buchanan, an American professor of physiology, from the Greek terms *psyche*, meaning "the soul," and *metron*, meaning "measure." Psychometry, said Buchanan, is a means to measure the soul of objects. He conducted experiments with students by having them hold vials of drugs to see if they could correctly name the contents. Buchanan's successful research interested others, most notably William F. Denton, a contemporary of Buchanan's and an American professor of geology. Denton conducted his own experiments and recorded his results in his now-classic book *The Soul of Things*. Today, psychometry is used by many psychics, especially those involved in crime detection and missing persons work.

I use psychometry in my Tarot readings if the client is physically present. While they are shuffling the cards, I hold a personal item of theirs, preferably metal. Jewelry and watches are ideal. If they have neither of those, then I ask for car keys. Cars are extensions of our lives and personalities. The objects should be originally theirs and not inherited or acquired second-hand, otherwise impressions will be muddy and possibly inaccurate pertaining to the client. Metal holds personal energy the best, followed by stone and crystal, and then wood.

The longer an object is owned and the more it is handled, the stronger and more precise are the psychic impressions contained within it. If an object changes ownership or is handled by many people, it absorbs different impressions and will give a psychic an unclear or confusing picture.

Wrap cloth

In occult lore, colors have their own energies, too, and different colors have different effects and symbolisms, as noted in an earlier chapter. Your deck will benefit from being wrapped in a colored cloth while it is stored in the box or pouch. Many Tarot users prefer natural fibers such as silk or cotton. More important are the cloth's newness—again for the absence of the impressions of others—and its color. You should steer clear of red, for example, because that is the color of the base passions, anger, sensuality, and materialism. Purple, gold (or yellow), and blue are best for the Tarot. Purple symbolizes the higher mind, deep affection, and spiritual power. It is the color of royalty and is associated with the crown chakra. Gold (or yellow) is the color of the sun's rays, the symbol of spiritual illumination, wisdom, intellect, and goodness. Blue represents spiritual qualities, such as inspiration, contemplation, and divinity.

Reading Cloth

Some Tarot practitioners like to lay their spreads out on a cloth placed over a table instead of directly onto a table top. The purpose of the cloth is to protect the cards against unknown impressions stored within the table. This might be a concern for you if you travel with your cards and give readings in different locations, but if you always use your own table, a reading cloth is not essential. An attractive cloth, however, does have a pleasing effect and is a nice touch if you read for others. If you decide to use one, make sure it is big enough to contain the largest of your spreads, and choose the color as you would for the storage box cloth. Large square scarves are a good choice.

Tarot table

In lieu of a cloth or the bare kitchen table, consider purchasing or making a special Tarot table, which in effect becomes an altar. We generally think of altars only in connection with religious worship, but an altar also is a special table used as the center of a ritual, which is exactly what Tarot work is. If you have a table reserved only for Tarot work, it is transformed into a sacred space, a place where you connect with higher energies. Nothing else occurs in this space. If you are fortunate enough to be able to work in a space like this, you will find that the psychic atmosphere of it increases rapidly, because nothing from daily life will intrude upon it or diminish it.

If you are able to make the table yourself, you imbue your own energies into the very substance of the table much more strongly than if you merely purchase it and use it. This is a traditional fundamental of ritual magic, which is why all magical textbooks advise the personal construction of ritual tools.

If you choose not to make a table, a purchased table will still serve the purpose quite adequately, however. You can personalize it with decoration.

Candles

Candles should never be omitted from ritual work, for according to lore, their light illuminates the spiritual darkness, purifies the air, and attracts benevolent energy while repelling negative energy. Candles have a long history of use in religious, magical, and other types of ritual. Their origin is not known, but they appeared as early as 3000 BC in Egypt and Crete. By the fourth century, they were part of early Christian ritual, and by the twelfth century they were given a place on Christian church altars.

White candles are customarily used in sacred ritual, because white symbolizes the spirit, purity, and protection. Both white and colored candles are used in magical work; the colors are selected for their specific occult meanings. Colored candles certainly are appropriate when working with the Tarot. Purple, gold, and blue are the best all-round choices, but choose according to your intuition and needs.

I often use flameless candles in a decorative holder. Sometimes this is of necessity, if I am reading in a hotel or event location where open flames are prohibited. A flameless candle still conveys the spirit of candle flame.

Personal objects

If you wish, you can enhance your Tarot working space by putting out objects that have special significance to you, such as crystals, stones, good luck pieces, jewelry, or symbols of the four elements. The latter can be represented by small bits of wood or clay (earth); feathers (air); water in a small cup; and incense (fire). Incense is a staple in religious ritual because of old and widespread beliefs that it purifies the air of negativity. For travel and space-saving purposes, small tea light holders are excellent containers for water and earth elements.

Personal objects can act as triggers to release creative energies at the conscious and subconscious levels, and help to put into motion the powers of thought, imagination, and will.

Breaking in a new deck

A new pack of Tarot cards is fresh and virgin. With repeated handling, the cards absorb your personal energies. Therefore, it is important that you be the first person to handle the cards, and that you be the only one to handle them during the break-in. This will ensure that the cards absorb the unique energies that constitute you.

After you have purchased your new cards, take them out of the box when you can set aside a time to work with them free from distraction and pressure. It is important that you be able to concentrate your full attention on the task at hand.

Unwrap your new pack and go through the cards, handling each one individually. Look at the images. Even if you have used the same style of deck before and are thoroughly familiar with the designs, absorb them anew into your consciousness. Notice the feel, shape, size and texture of the cards. Observe the design on the backs of the cards.

Shuffle the cards and notice how they feel in your hands. Mix up the positions by turning some upside down, and continue shuffling. Draw cards and do spreads. When you are done, wrap the cards and place them in their storage box.

Many Tarot users like to place new packs under their pillow for a night or two, because they feel it quickens and improves the seasoning process. If you would like to try this, keep the deck wrapped in its cloth, and hold the cards in your thoughts as you fall asleep.

Get the cards out daily and handle and work with them. You will know when they feel "broken in." I like to shuffle and then draw a card for the day.

Some readers do not like their decks to be handled by others at any time. In readings, I feel it is useful to have the client shuffle the cards to put their energy into the reading. I shuffle first and then have them shuffle. While they are doing that, I hold an object of theirs for psychometry impressions.

I give my reading deck a periodic cleansing of healing energy and suffusion of light.

Opening and closing rituals

Performing a brief opening and closing ritual in Tarot work sets sacred space, defines boundaries, and focuses your concentration. The following is an example of an opening and closing:

> Spread and smooth the Tarot work cloth. Place other working tools in their appropriate positions: candle(s),

symbols of the elements, crystals, and so on. Light the candle. Have a moment of quiet. Visualize your psychic protection.

Say: "All the Powers around me, I give thanks for your assistance. Protect me from all negative energies. Only the positive may enter my presence."

Take out your cards and shuffle them, then place them on the table and tap them.

Say: "All the Powers around me, I ask for your guidance. Let the Truth be revealed in the cards."

Begin working with the deck. When you are finished, wrap the cards and return them to their box.

Say: "All the Powers around me, I give thanks for the wisdom revealed."

Snuff out the candle and put away all tools.

Exercise

Compose your own Tarot ritual. Write down the spoken parts, which will reinforce the ritual in your consciousness. Visualize the ritual, which will do the same.

Practice it. The more you practice and perform your ritual, the more it becomes part of you and unlocks creative energy. You can say the words silently to yourself or speak them out loud. However you perform it, do it with concentration and mindfulness. The ritual will accumulate power over time.

Add and discard elements to suit. Especially discard anything that feels devoid of energy.

Sigils

You can augment ritual with sigils. A sigil is a shape, symbol, or mental image that is linked to a particular idea or set of ideas. Concentrating on them can invoke higher energies. They are like a form of shorthand.

For example, instead of going step-by-step through a visualization of protection, you can create a sigil that represents that protection, and accomplish the same thing by concentrating on the sigil. For example, use a crystalline egg as a symbol of the ideal protection. You visualize the egg, and in so doing you will automatically call upon whatever higher assistance you have chosen to work with. Another sigil can open the gates to the revelation of Truth in the cards. An example might be a mental image of gates with divine light shining through them. Still another sigil can close the work.

The effective use of sigils requires skill in mental imagery. If you are a beginner, work through each step in your ritual first, then add sigils.

9

Reading the Cards

The Tarot is a powerful tool for helping us answer life's questions and learn more about ourselves. Some Tarot practitioners believe that you should not read for yourself—only for others—and that you should have your own questions read by someone else. This is treated like a truism, but there is no reason why it should be so, nor is there any basis for believing that self-readings are going to be wrong or inadvisable. You can read for yourself just as well as for others. In fact, self-reading is one of the great benefits and joys of learning the Tarot. You do have to be willing to be unbiased and accept difficult answers that may run contrary to your hopes. Truth is always for your highest good.

Here are some general guidelines to keep in mind for your readings.

Setting up a reading
For most readings—thirty to sixty minutes in length—I use a large spread such as the Celtic Cross (different spreads are discussed in the next chapter). If a reading is short, such as the fifteen-minute ones I do at expos

and fairs, I may use fewer cards. For short readings, I will ask the client if they want to state their questions up front. It helps the reading cut to the chase in a limited amount of time. Otherwise, I prefer not to know much, if anything, about what the client wants to know, and let Spirit set the tone of the reading through the spread.

I shuffle the cards and then ask the client to shuffle them. Since I use psychometry, I will hold an object of their while they shuffle. I focus on attuning to the client in order to receive impressions and information that will be helpful to them.

When the client is done shuffling, I take the deck and cut it into thirds right to left, and then restack the deck right to left. Then I lay the cards down in the spread, moving according to the flow of the pattern. As I lay down every card, more impressions come. I take a moment to survey the spread, and start talking. Inevitably, the cards plus the psychic impressions will address whatever reasons the client has for coming to the reading.

In interpreting the cards, bear in mind that the Tarot is consulted for insight, not to dictate. I do not recommend making any decision solely upon the Tarot—or upon any other divination method, for that matter. Tarot readings should be done with the intent of helping the client see a situation in a new light, or get validation for something they already realize. If there are obstacles, the reading should help the seeker get fresh ideas for solutions. If a projected path appears clear, the reading should help crystallize and fortify resolve to push ahead. If you read for others, they should be counseled that the reading is but one way of gaining insight, and should be weighed along with other factors.

What to ask the cards

The Tarot functions best as a mirror and as an adviser. It reflects forces in motion, reveals directions, and shows possible and probable outcomes. It helps us to see when we are on a path that is straight and true, or when we have wandered off in an unprofitable direction. If asked, the Tarot will advise on a course of direction. Remember—and stress this to those who come to you for readings—that the ultimate outcome rests with the individual, who exercises the power of free will.

The Tarot peers into the future. In ancient times, the future was believed to be immutable. Today, thanks to quantum mechanics, we know that the future is fluid. In quantum mechanics terms, the Tarot does not reveal a definite outcome, but rather a probable outcome based on the forces that are in motion in someone's life. All the cards in a spread say something about the forces that are in motion. If all looks well, the client can be validated in certain courses of action to bring about the desired and envisioned future. If the probable outcome is problematic, the client can be counseled on how to change the course of events.

Astrology functions in a similar way. Astrologer Dane Rudhyar once called astrology "the algebra of life"—it does not show predestination, but is a guide to help realize potential. The same is true for the Tarot. A reader should never dictate to the client what "should" be done. Rather, the reading should help the client see things from different perspectives and gain clarity for making their own decisions.

Any question about future outcomes can be asked of the cards. I usually choose the Celtic Cross and the Seven Card spreads for the most information.

Gauging time

I feel an average reading has viability for six to twelve months. The cards look at the present, the recent past, and a probable future based on forces in motion. Once a year or more has passed, too many decisions and actions have been made, altering the forces in motion.

Calculating time is tricky, because it is a construct of our reality, and readings operate in an ever-present now that has no linear time. Everyone who works in the psychic arts develops their own sense of gauging time for forecasts. The more you do readings, the more you will develop your own linear time yardsticks for advising clients.

When more information is needed

Occasionally the spread will seem incomplete and you will wish it had one or two more positions to shed more light on the matter. On the side, turn over extra cards for a little boost. Do so after the reading has been analyzed and discussed, and if there is something unresolved that might be helped with more cards, or if the client seems to need extra assurance.

In these situations, I turn over one card and place it to the lower right of the spread. If necessary, I turn over two or three, working in a horizontal line left to right.

If the primary spread does not adequately address a question (usually it is one that the client brings up as "can you also look at such and such"), I will often employ a seven card spread, or, in a short reading, a three card spread. Sometimes it is necessary to do a second Celtic Cross.

When a spread is top heavy

If half or more cards in a large spread (such as the Celtic Cross) are Major Arcana, some readers pick up the cards and do a new spread using just Major Arcana. I do not follow this practice myself. However, I take note of "top heavy" spreads and adjust the reading accordingly. The presence of many Major Arcana often points to situations laden with significant, important, or serious factors.

Handling negative indications

Few situations in life are clear-cut, but are a mix of positive and negative factors. Sometimes the prognosis of a situation is decidedly negative. It is paramount that the client always goes away feeling helped and empowered. Do not sugar coat or avoid the negative, but frame it in a way that opens the door to solutions. The cards will always reveal a client's strengths and assets.

Stress that the reading is a snapshot of possibilities given the present direction. You can ask questions to get the client to examine his or her true feelings or motives.

For example, say a woman comes to a reading with the question, "Will I marry X?" It is obvious from her demeanor and remarks that she desires this outcome very much. The cards, however, say no or not likely, and your own psychic impressions reinforce this.

It is fair to assume that as much as the seeker professes to want the marriage, she has doubts about it coming to pass, or she would not be asking the question. All of us from time to time harbor unrealistic expectations and then look for ways to convince ourselves that what we want will come to pass no matter what. By asking a few gentle questions, you may be able to bring inner doubts and fears to light where they can be acknowledged and dealt with.

In this case, perhaps the seeker has projected a desire to get married onto the relationship. Or, perhaps she has fears that a marriage would not work out. Perhaps the relationship might well end in marriage, but has not progressed far enough. You can couch an answer like, "Right now, it does not look likely within the time frame of the reading" (six to twelve months, or whatever time frame you feel is reflected in the reading). Then go on to point out the reasons why that are given in the cards.

The important thing is that the client discovers what lies deep within the heart—that she sees things in a fresh way and feels empowered to make positive changes. That is one of the greatest benefits of the Tarot.

Topics to avoid

It is not advisable to handle questions relating to medical care and predictions of life expectancy. You will risk treading into legal territory concerning the practice of medicine without a license. It is not for Tarot readers to advise clients whether or not medical procedures or certain medications and therapies are appropriate.

Predictions of life expectancy—the client's life or anyone else they want to ask about—also are not advisable. A date for the end of life, no matter how many years in the future, can have an explosive emotional impact on a person. At the very least, they may be traumatized by the information, and in worst case scenarios may even contribute to self-fulfilling prophecy.

"While not all assessments of how long someone has to live result in life-or-death clinical decisions, addressing prognosis remains a challenge for most doctors," said Dr. Pauline W. Chen in an online article published in 2012, "Why Doctors Can't Predict How Long Patient Will Live." If doctors have difficulty dealing with this question, so will you. Every now and then I meet a psychic who insists they are always right in predicting the end of life. No one is accurate 100 percent of the time. Right or wrong, you are still playing with fire and the risk of psychological damage.

I once had the cards read by a woman who seemed to possess good psychic ability. The question I brought to the reading concerned career matters, and many of the things she said seemed to be right on target. Then she stunned me by casually announcing that one of my two dogs was going to die soon. I had not mentioned I owned dogs, but she went on to deliver an accurate physical description of the dog in question, and said that she would be hit by a car and suffer a spinal injury, and that I was going to have to put her to sleep. She estimated that this would come to pass within six months, although she allowed that her sense of time could be a "little off." The shock of this unsolicited information was bad enough, but her manner of delivery, so cavalier and without a shred of regard for the emotional impact upon me, was downright cruel. I do not believe she did this deliberately; she was just thoughtless, and had no idea of the force of what she was saying.

I cannot even begin to describe the devastation I felt. I could not fathom how such an accident could happen, because the dogs were not allowed to run loose. But, since the psychic had been so accurate about other things in the reading, I feared for the worst. I lived in absolute dread for six months. Nothing happened.

Later, I mentioned this incident to another psychic, who told me some of the woman's clients came to her for second opinions because they had been told that their spouses or children were going to die. They, too, were probably given this information in an offhand fashion. Do not be so irresponsible!

My dog, by the way, lived a healthy and happy life for years after that. One could argue that the warning was legitimate, and prompted me to be extra careful and thus avoid a probable event. However, in light of what I was told about this woman's other dire predictions of death, I believe she was off base, and was irresponsible in telling me such negative information.

I also decline financial investment questions for the same legal and ethical reasons. It is one thing to comment on the likelihood of success of a business venture, and another to advise on buying or selling specific stocks and properties.

How to make the most of a reading

By the time you start giving readings, you should be familiar enough with the cards so that you do not have to rely solely upon descriptions of their meanings. You should know the cards well enough so that the information comes to you naturally and intuitively. In readings, you are considering much more than individual card meanings. You are also examining how the cards relate to each other in a spread, and their synergism, that is, the sum total of the spread that is greater than the individual parts. In addition, the cards prompt a flow of intuitive and psychic information that comes in other ways, such as mental impressions, symbols, and so on.

If you are uncertain about the "official" meaning of a card or array of cards, allow impressions to arise within you. Draw deeper, more personal meanings from the cards. Look at them individually and collectively, and try to get a feel for the synergism of the reading. Tarot cards are like chemicals: each has its own properties, and when you put them together they react and combine to create something different. If a reading seems ambiguous or indefinite, do not be put off. There are many possibilities as to why, which are discussed further on in this chapter.

Remember, this book is only a guide to the Tarot. By working with the cards over and over again, they will speak to you in their own way, especially as you grow more comfortable with them and learn how to listen to the inner voice the cards trigger.

After you have placed all the cards in their positions, analyze the spread carefully. Look for patterns in the spread as well as similarities or wide differences in the suits or arcana that you've laid out. Talk about what you see and feel. Is the reading a surprise? Does it suggest new directions? Can you or the client make changes that will lead to another ending?

Make notes in your Tarot journal of the readings that you do for yourself. Record the date, the question that was asked, and a sketch of the spread. You can simplify the process by copying by hand diagrams of spreads onto pieces of tying paper. Number the card positions. Make photocopies. To record a layout, fill in the names of the cards that turn up in each position. It is insightful to compare readings over a long period of time, particularly if you have posed the same question at various intervals.

When reading for others, offer to record the session if they do not come with their own recorder. I use a digital recorder and then upload the file to a large file transfer service or drop box for the client to download later. It is hard to remember all the details of a reading, so clients appreciate recordings. If you store copies yourself, make sure they are secure for privacy reasons. Sometimes I find it useful to refer back to a reading when clients book sessions at later times.

Reading with a partner

Solitary work with the Tarot is rewarding, but there is no need to limit yourself to that. Working with a partner adds a new dimension to study and readings. Two persons who are in tune with one another—close friends, lovers, or spouses—can spark off each other in interpreting cards. The result is often thought-provoking, lively discussion.

My husband, Joe, and I will sometimes both do one-card draws for the day, or for quick insight into a question of mutual importance, and then discuss the two perspectives.

Handling problems

Every now and then a reading just will not gel. The cards do not add up or the message is confusing. Or, the cards seem to be talking about something else other than what the client professes to want. When that happens, it is best to be honest and acknowledge that the cards are not clear. You will not do yourself or the client any favors by struggling through a reading. Instead, suggest that there is a good reason for this and then explore these possible explanations:

The client is not clear about their questions
The client may be confused or conflicted. You may need to ascertain what is really afoot, and rephrase the purpose of the reading.

The real issue is something else
The cards indicate that something else in the client's life is more pressing and needs attention. Perhaps it is something the client has been trying to avoid. Probe with a few gentle questions or statements, such as "I'm wondering about blah blah, it seems there are some concerns or issues there."

Resolution requires more than one session
Some people wait until problems become quite entangled and complex before they tackle them. What they are hoping to resolve requires other issues to be addressed first. You may want to advise followup sessions.

You are unable to tune in to the client
It is a rare psychic who can read equally well for everyone all the time. You will find that you tune right in to some clients, and others require more effort. (Being well rested and with a clear mind are essential when you read, in order to minimize such difficulties.) Sometimes the client is defensive or angry—even if they have sought out the reading—and the negative energy throws up a wall.

And, there are just some people you will not be able to read well. On rare occasions, I get a client like this. I usually realize it before the reading starts, but I will lay out the cards, anyway. If no impressions come, or the cards seem confused, I will say to the client that for whatever reason, I am not the right reader for them. End of sitting, and no charge, of course.

Beginners have a learning curve, and may feel that a lot of readings are difficult. With practice, that eases up. You must be confident in your ability.

You are projecting onto the cards

Let the cards speak their Truth. Do not project anything you think the client wants to hear, or should hear. Do not be attached to the news. As noted above, be diplomatic, and find positive ways to convey harsh information. Remember that the reading is for the client, not you, and there may be things they need to hear.

Environmental distractions interfere

No matter how well you have learned to focus and concentrate, there are going to be times when you are unable to overcome external distractions. If the distractions are not going to abate, you are in a no-win situation and should reschedule the reading. For example, for years I had an annual reading given to me by a talented psychic with whom I shared a good working rapport. One year, I showed up for my morning appointment to find that the neighbors in the upstairs apartment were doing substantial remodeling. It was impossible to ignore the thumping of hammers, the whine of saws, and the sounds of heavy objects being dragged across the floor. My friend was upset, because she had requested that they not work during the hour of our reading. The neighbors had agreed but did not honor the agreement. My friend stopped the reading to make a phone call, but the work continued. It was upsetting for both of us, and we should have rescheduled. Instead, we plowed on, but the concentration just was not there on either part.

Do not be reluctant to reschedule a reading—but only do that when necessary and not on whim. Be judicious about when and how often you do so, of course, but recognize that a client would much rather reschedule a reading than go away feeling dissatisfied.

The client wants too frequent readings

Some clients want to come back too soon and too often for their own good. Some persons are oracle addicts, and bounce from reading to reading looking for someone—or something—to tell them how to live their lives. They defer all decisions to readings.

Many Tarot readers have policies concerning how often a client may have a reading. It is difficult to have a hard and fast rule, however, because every situation is unique. In some cases, a client will want a follow-up in a few weeks, which may be reasonable.

The red flag clients are those who start calling every week, and then multiple times a week. You will find that their lives usually are in turmoil, because they are not making their own decisions and taking the necessary actions. More and more, they will want you to tell them what to do. This is crippling for the client, so you may need to be assertive about how often you recommend follow-ups.

I do know readers who have clients on retainer. The client pays a substantial sum for unlimited access, often on a round-the-clock basis. You may decide this is something you would like to cultivate.

Most of those who become your regulars will only want readings every now and then—maybe even only once or twice a year. Periodic readings are beneficial, even if there are no pressing problems or issues, because they help the clients see their lives from new perspectives.

10

Spreads

Ever since Etteilla popularized the Tarot for fortune-telling in the eighteenth century, spreads have been developed to make the most meaningful readings of the cards. Many modern Tarot readers have developed their own spreads. The spreads in this book include some of the most familiar spreads, such as the Celtic Cross and Life Horoscope, as well as some new spreads and new variations of spreads. As you become comfortable with the Tarot, you can experiment with modifications and new spread designs.

Most clients come to readings looking for answers to specific questions. Even if they say they "just want to see what comes up," they still have specific questions behind that. Spreads position the cards to give the answers. Each card position has its own meaning, which is combined with the card meaning. In addition, spreads are examined synergistically, as a whole.

You will gravitate to favorite spreads that you feel are the most effective. Sometimes the length of the reading is a factor in determining the spread.

This chapter presents twelve effective spreads, from traditional to innovative. I have also included tips for designing your own spreads.

Celtic Cross Spread

The Celtic Cross is one of the most popular spreads, and is usually the first one learned by beginners. It is particularly suited to divination readings. The Celtic Cross has remained my favorite over the years. Its ten stations address a variety of angles. The Celtic Cross reading is a ritual that has acquired a substantial amount of psychic power from collective input over a long time. As noted earlier, the more a ritual is performed, the more powerful and effective it becomes.

In the Celtic Cross, ten cards are laid out in the form of an equilateral cross with a separate, vertical line of cards off to the right side. The cards are placed on the table upright or reversed as they are drawn from the top of the shuffled deck. The exception is the first card, which is always turned upright even if it comes off the stack reversed.

Some readers have the client select a court card that represents him or her concerning the question at hand. This is done prior to shuffling and cutting. The court card is either placed to the left side, or, in some cases, is laid down in Position 1. I seldom do this, and I have never felt it to adversely affect a reading. There are legitimate reasons for omitting this step. The client may not wish to categorize herself within the bounds of the court cards. If the client is unfamiliar with the cards, making the choice can be confusing, off-putting, or onerous, and this can generate a tension that will interfere with the reading. Your ability to read for others is influenced not only by your rapport with the cards and your inner voice, but also by your rapport with the client. Use your own judgement as to whether to include this step, and do not hesitate to omit it if it feels appropriate.

You will find minor variations in the Celtic Cross spread from book to book, and the version presented here includes my own modifications.

Here is what each of the card positions represents:

1. The Cover: The forces covering, influencing, or surrounding the person asking the question.

2. The Crossing: The immediate obstacles, influences, or opposing forces that lie ahead. The card is always read

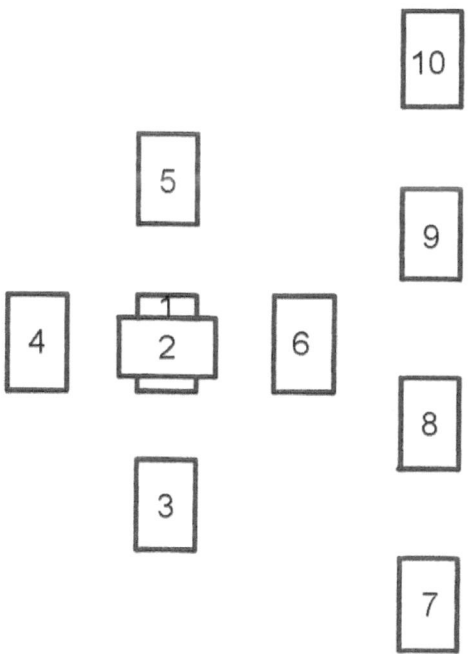

CELTIC CROSS SPREAD

right side up. Influences nonetheless may be positive or negative; and the rest of the spread will indicate which applies. Interpret the card within the context of the whole spread, and also in relation to the number 10 card, which represents the final outcome.

3. What lies beneath the surface: The basis for the client's question. Things that existed in the past that have now become part of the present and are the reason for the question being asked. Also, repressed emotions, and forces operating in the background.

4. Passing influences: Influences on the client that are in the process of passing away or are already in the past—or which need to be released.

5. Forces in motion: Factors that are shaping up on the horizon, such as a potential event or influences of others that have a bearing on the situation. This card deserves special attention, because it points to forces taking shape, which may or may not manifest, depending upon actions taken by the client. Help the client see how to make the most of potential opportunity or take steps to overcome obstacles. Again, look to card 10 for additional insight.

6. Future probabilities: Things, events, and outcomes that lie ahead. These are forces likely to manifest in the life of the client. If the changes are desirable, look to cards 3, 5, and 10 for inspiration.

7. Personal emotions: The emotions, including hopes, fears, anxieties, and apprehensions held by the client.

8. Influences of others: The opinions and actions of others, especially family, that are affecting the client.

9. Desired goals: What the client hopes will come to pass: aspirations, goals, and dreams.

10. Resolution or final outcome: Where the forces in motion are leading, depending on what the other cards in the spread have to say.

The diagram shows the order in which the cards are laid down in the spread. In some references, you will find positions 4 and 6 reversed. However, I strongly believe that 4, the position of passing influences, should be on the left, where the card is moving away from the entire spread. Position 6 suits the unmanifest future, where it can relate to other cards figuring in that mix.

For a deeper Celtic Cross reading, use only the Major Arcana.

Seven Card Spread

I often use the Seven Card Spread in short readings and also as a secondary spread in a reading. After shuffling and cutting the cards, lay out seven cards in an arc from left to right. There are three cards leading up the arc, a fourth card at the apex, and three cards leading down the arc.

The cards can be viewed as a time line: forces that are leading up to the present, and forces shaping a probable future that follow.

Three Card Spread

The Three Card Spread is ideal for quick takes and short readings. Lay them out left to right. Left is the Past, middle is the Present, and right is the Future. You can apply other unified triad meanings to the positions, such as Body, Mind, Spirit.

One Card Draw

The One Card Draw is technically not a spread, but it is a valid reading, and also a great way to learn the cards. Ask a question and draw a single card from anywhere in the pack. What does the card say about your question? Start talking and allow impressions to arise spontaneously.

I often offer the One Card Draw at workshops during breaks. I do not ask to know the other person's question, only that they focus on it in their mind. Upon seeing the card, I start talking about what it means to them. I keep it short.

The One Card Draw is uncanny in hitting something of importance or concern to the client.

I occasionally use the One Card Draw at the start of a day, for the day's message, or when I am wrestling with a decision. It cuts right through the clutter.

Yes No Spread

There are times when you want simple yes or no answers to questions. Here is a way to do that:

As you shuffle your cards, think of your question. Then count out the cards, stopping when you get to the thirteenth card. Turn that one face up. Repeat this until you reach the end of the deck and you have turned up six cards. Count the number of cards that are in upright positions. If four to six cards are upright, the answer is yes. If two to four cards are upright, the question is leaning in your favor but it is not a definite yes. If you have fewer than two cards upright, the answer is no.

Past Present Future Spread

If you want to go beyond the Yes No spread, you can take those six cards, reshuffle them, and lay out the first six positions of the Celtic Cross spread. Then interpret the cards using the corresponding meanings from that spread:

1. The Cover
2. The Crossing
3. What lies beneath the surface
4. Passing influences
5. Forces in motion
6. Future probabilities

Trinity Spread

I call this the Trinity Spread because it makes use of the powerful mysticism of the number three. As noted earlier, the triad is a common motif in myth, legend, and fairytale, and we see trinities expressed in many things, especially in the triune nature of man: mind, body, and spirit. Three is a number of forward movement and the creative force, and the ascent of consciousness into spiritual planes—all beneficial forces to harness in a Tarot reading.

The threefold elements that anchor this spread are Emotions, Thoughts, and Actions on one axis and Past, Present, and Future on a second axis. This spread is ideal for self-exploration and contemplation, because it gives you a good snapshot of your life's situation, and your progress through life.

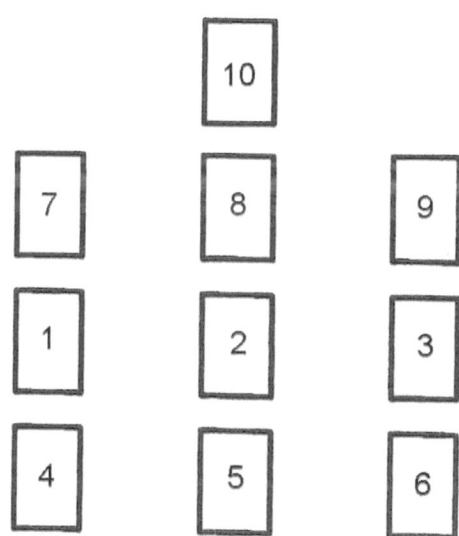

TRINITY SPREAD

Use only the Major Arcana and the court cards. The cards are laid out in three pillars with three cards each, and a tenth crowning the middle pillar. Shuffle and lay the cards out from left to right in the order shown in the figure. Let them fall right side up or reversed. Vertically, the lines represent, from top to bottom, Future, Present, and Past. Horizontally, the cards are, from left to right, Emotions, Thoughts, and Actions. These are the primary forces that shape our lives. At the top, by itself, is the tenth card, which represents the Integration of the nine cards below it.

Emotions

This category includes not only feelings, but impulses, inspirations, and intuition, the things that bubble up from our subconscious or manifest in our dreams. Hopes and fears also belong here, as do creative urges and right-brain thinking. The cards that fall here give insight into the influences driving our emotions. If court cards turn up, consider whether they represent aspects of yourself or individuals with whom you are involved.

Thoughts

This category includes our rational, logical, and analytical mental processes—the way we judge and assess, quantify, qualify, and justify. Our left-brain thinking fits here, which for most of us is the dominant means by which we make decisions.

Actions

This category reveals how we translate our emotions and thoughts into something tangible. It is particularly valuable for spotlighting passivity and indecision.

Past, Present and Future

These lines represent major forces in play at the moment (present), on the wane (past), and emerging (future). Cards may reveal attachments to the past, degree of focus in the present, and what needs to be done to manifest the desired future.

Integration

How do all these factors come together? The Integration card has something to say about it. The crown card represents forces that could come into play and affect the picture that is revealed by the lower nine cards. It can show positive or negative energies. Remember that when negatives show in a Tarot reading, they provide an opportunity to correct and rectify.

In reading the cards, examine the lines horizontally, beginning with Present, then moving to Past and then to Future. Study each card in the line individually. Now integrate them into a single picture. When you have done that for each of the time lines, you are likely to get a new perspective on areas in your life that need attention.

Suppose you are feeling stalled. The cards might tell you, for example, that you are being too heavily influenced by a particular person or persons; that you are allowing rational thought processes to interfere with intuition, or, conversely, that you are too impulsive; that unrealistic fears are holding you back; or even that you have been too lazy to act on your intentions. You will get ideas for making changes.

Eliphas Levi Wheel Spread

Eliphas Levi did not invent this spread, but it is based on his Tarot wheel, shown in the chapter on "The Kabbalah Connection." As you recall, Levi laid out the letters T, A, R, and O (standing for Taro and rota) at the ends of the arms of an equilateral cross. Draw a circle around it and you have a wheel, which represents the ever-changing cosmos revolving around an unchanging center, the Source.

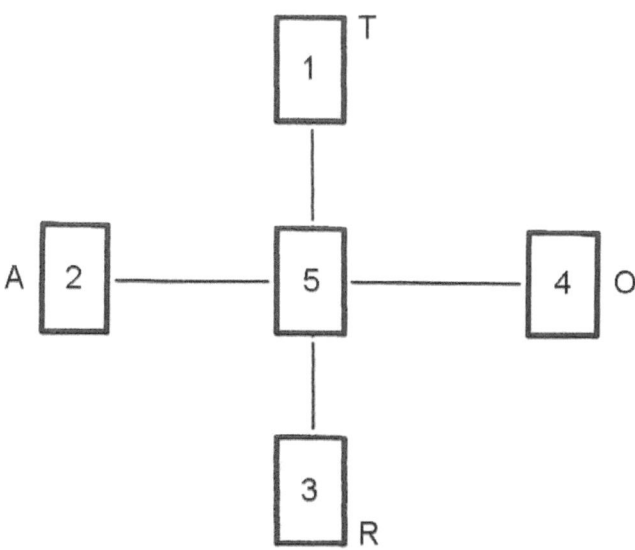

ELIPHAS LEVI WHEEL SPREAD

First, compose a question. Take the Major Arcana only and shuffle. Draw five cards at random and lay them down as though on the axes of an equilateral cross. Start at the top with one and move clockwise with the next three cards. Place the fifth card in the center.

The cards represent the following:

1. The present situation: Forces and influences immediately affecting the question. Consider people, thoughts and feelings, events, and circumstances.

2. Waning influences: Obstacles that have been overcome, aid that has come to an end, changes in emotion, energy, outlook, goals, and such.

3. Hidden or unconscious influences: What we repress or fail to recognize does not disappear, but finds other ways of expression. Here we find the stuff that usually surfaces in dreams: yearnings, fears, desires, and deepest and darkest secrets. These are fragments floating in the sea of the unconscious, waiting to be recognized and reintegrated into the whole.

4. Emerging influences: New factors looming on the horizon. Again, consider people, thoughts and feelings, events and circumstances.

5. Synthesis: What is needed to reconcile and unify the other four factors.

Mandala and Alchemical Spreads

The mandala is an ideal form for organizing and expressing the inner world. In Eastern meditation, the mandala expresses complex realms of higher consciousness, whereas in Western psychotherapy it helps people deal with forces welling up from the unconscious. In this spread, the mandala is used to examine the inner impulses that arise out of the self. This is a spread for contemplation.

The spread features nine cards. Nine is the number of man (nine months in gestation), and mental and spiritual achievement. The perimeter of the circle is formed with eight cards. Eight represents regeneration, renewal, and eternity, the Alpha and Omega, the beginning and the end, a meaning that is further reinforced by the circle itself as the symbol of unity and continuity. The ninth card is placed in the center as the Self.

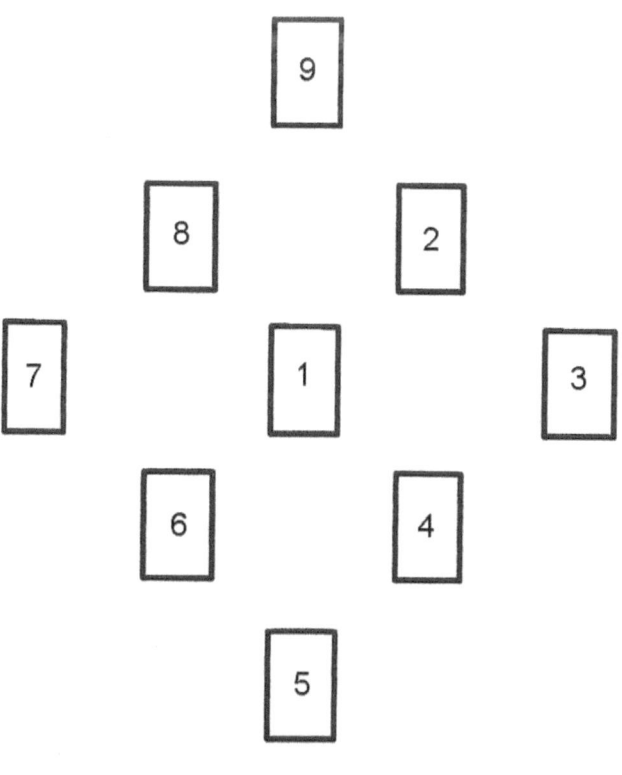

MANDALA SPREAD

In laying the cards out, begin with the Center as card number 1. Then move to the upper right and continue around, until you have card number 9 at the top of the circle. There should be four cards marking the quarters of the circle, with a card in between each quarter point.

As you go around the circle, you will see how the cards build on each other progressively. Here are associations for the card meanings:

1. Self: The unifying principle within the human psyche, the totality that embraces both conscious and unconscious. Through the Self, we make contact with our anima and animus, and confront our shadow, that part of us which is split off and repressed and needs to be reintegrated.

2. Desires: Our instinctive urges and basic needs.

3. Dreams: What we ideally want to be, accomplish, have, or give to be a human being in the fullest sense: love, happiness, compassion, health, and so on.

4. Pursuits: Despite our dreams, the things we decide to pursue: careers, hobbies, volunteerism, and so on. How do the pursuits match the dreams?

5. Attachments: Things we pursue that hold us back from achieving our true dreams. Attachments typically are to false values, such as money, prestige, fame, and possessions. How many pursuits are attachments?

6. Qualities: Our good points.

7. Sorrows: Our faults, attributes, and behavior that need improvement.

8. Self-image: Our overall view of ourselves. This card relates to the previous seven, and to the Self card. How does the self-image conform to what the cards in the other positions have to say? What areas need to be improved?

9. Soul's urge: Our true sense of purpose and destiny that transcends all else.

By adding another four cards, you can create the Alchemical Spread. The four cards are placed on the outside of the circle at the quarter points, thus forming a square around the circle. These cards stand for the four elements. In alchemy, this configuration represents the squaring of the circle, the great alchemical work, or the Philosopher's Stone. The cards that comprise the square should be interpreted for clues to forces that can be tapped for positive change.

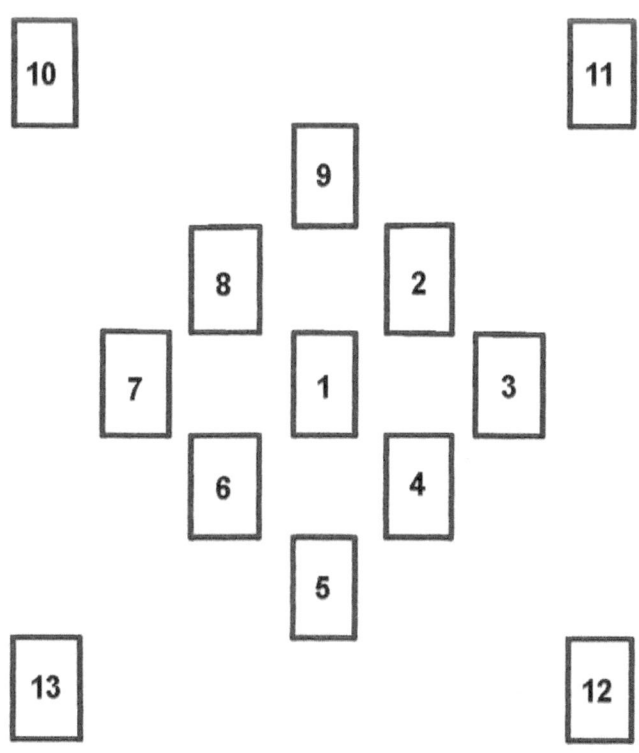

ALCHEMICAL SPREAD

1. **Earth:** Darkness, mystery, the unknown, secrecy, the unenlightened state
2. **Air:** Spiritual illumination, intuition, enlightenment, mysticism, the eternal
3. **Fire:** Intellect, rational thought, will
4. **Water:** Creativity, emotions, fertility, courage.

Chakra Spread

The Chakra Spread makes use of Tarot symbols as applied to the seven primary chakras. In yoga, chakras are centers of energy that permeate the physical body and funnel *prana*, the universal vital force, throughout the body. Invisible to the ordinary eye, chakras are aligned along the spine and are shaped like wheels; *chakra* is Sanskrit for "circle." The chakras rotate and draw in *prana*, which influences physical, mental, and emotional health, and spiritual development. If the chakras rotate sluggishly, illness results. Chakra activity is refined and developed through the practice of yoga, and can be treated in energy medicine healing.

Each chakra governs a spiritual function, and so the chakra system provides a good structure for Tarot application.

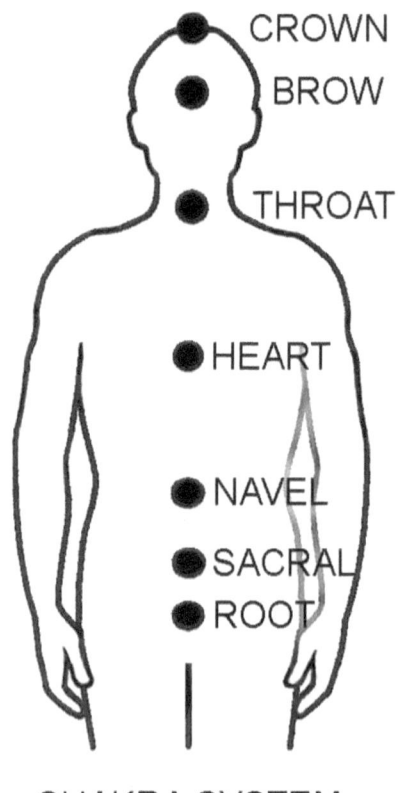

CHAKRA SYSTEM

To do the spread, lay out seven cards in a straight, vertical line to symbolize the spine, moving from bottom to top. Each card represents a chakra, and the cards are interpreted in light of those functions.

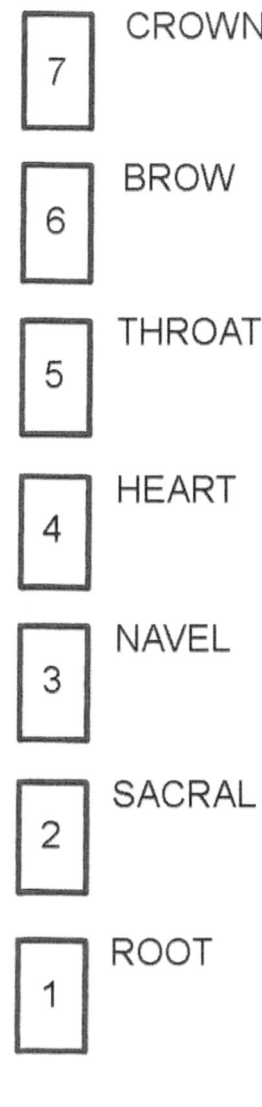

CHAKRA SPREAD

You can do this spread with the entire pack or just the Major Arcana. This is an excellent self-knowledge spread that lends itself well to contemplation. Here are the chakra associations:

> **1. Root chakra:** Located at the base of the spine, it is the seat of the kundalini, an intense and powerful force that is awakened in enlightenment. The root chakra governs self-preservation, one's animal nature, taste, and smell.
>
> **2. Sacral chakra:** This center is located in the vicinity of the spleen, and govern sexuality and sexual expression, assertiveness, drive, ambition, and personal power.
>
> **3. Naval chakra:** Located near the navel, this chakra is associated with the emotions. It governs the adrenal glands, pancreas, liver, and stomach.
>
> **4. Heart chakra:** The heart chakra governs the thymus gland and influences immunity to disease, and is linked to love and unconditioned love. It is the first "upper" chakra related to higher consciousness.
>
> **5. Throat chakra:** This chakra is associated with creativity, self-expression, and the search for Truth. It influences the thyroid and parathyroid glands, and the metabolism, and is associated with states of expanded consciousness.
>
> **6. Brow chakra:** The brow chakra between the eyebrows is the third eye and influences psychic abilities and spiritual enlightenment. It governs the pituitary gland, the pineal gland, intelligence, and intuition.
>
> **7. Crown chakra:** The highest chakra is located just above the top of the head. It is not associated with any glands or body functions, but reveals the individual's level of consciousness. It is activated when all the other chakras are in balance and harmony, and brings supreme enlightenment.

In reading the cards, examine what each says about the chakra and how well it is functioning.

Life Horoscope Spread

The Life Horoscope Spread is ideal for self-readings as well as for others. It can help you gain valuable insight into how the various influences on your life and the different aspects of your personality are shaping your future. In this reading, you interpret the meaning of the cards in relationship to where they fall in the horoscope. You are not seeking specific yes or no answers, but rather answers to larger questions about life. A knowledge of astrology is essential to get the most out of this spread.

HOROSCOPE SPREAD

First shuffle the pack, then lay out twelve cards, counterclockwise in a circle in the order shown in the figure. Each of the positions corresponds to one of the twelve houses of the Zodiac. You may include an optional court card to represent yourself or the client, to be placed in the center of the circle.

Here are the aspects of life governed by the houses, and the natural signs of the Zodiac that rule them:

First House (Aries): Personality, outward appearances, interests, attitudes
Second House (Taurus): Money matters, financial situation, material possessions
Third House (Gemini): Communication, relationships with brothers and sisters, travel
Fourth House (Cancer): Birth and death, home life, mother and father
Fifth House (Leo): Love, children, creativity
Sixth House (Virgo): Health, service
Seventh House (Libra): Relationships, partnerships, contracts, and agreements
Eighth House (Scorpio): Outside influences, death, inheritance
Ninth House (Sagittarius): Search for truth, long journeys, dreams, spiritual growth
Tenth House (Capricorn): Career, profession, ambitions
Eleventh House (Aquarius): Friends, associations, hopes, fears
Twelfth House (Pisces): Unconscious mind, karma, limitations

Allow the Tarot cards to provide insights and commentaries from the perspective of each house.

Designing your own spreads

Spread design is based on patterns and flow. The building blocks are shapes, numbers, and the association that relate to card meanings. Spreads do not have to be elaborate and complicated—in fact, some of the most effective are the simplest. Laying out cards in a spread is a ritual, and the more you do it, the more ingrained it becomes in your consciousness and the more psychic power it acquires. You should not have to stop and think what comes next, or what a position means.

Here are the five components of a spread, and the order in which they should be put together:

1. The purpose of the spread
What do you want the cards to reveal? Most traditional spreads are yes/no or are broad enough to cover a wide variety of situations. However, you may want to develop very specific spreads to use in certain circumstances. For example, you can design spreads solely to examine career matters, relationships, money issues, and such.

2. The time frame
What time period will the spread embrace? Will it cover past, present, and future, present and future, or present only? Spreads can be narrowed down further to seasons, months, and weeks.

3. The pattern
All Tarot spreads are organized according to lines and shapes. The cards are always laid out in a certain sequence, and each position in the pattern carries a certain meaning. Decide how you want to express the purpose and time frame.

Start by drawing up a list of position designations, that is, what an individual card position will represent in either purpose or time. You can use number and shape symbolisms to determine how many cards you will have in a spread. For example, a spread that deals with relationships might be expressed with six cards that are laid out according to the points of a hexagram, a shape that symbolizes the union of opposites.

Sixteen Basic Spread Patterns

Five to twelve or thirteen cards will give you plenty of options to explore. Beyond thirteen, spreads can become cumbersome. You can certainly tackle larger spreads, but in the beginning it is best to stick to simpler and smaller ones.

Experiment by arranging the cards in patterns. The simplest is a linear spread, a single line upon which the reading moves horizontally or vertically. A little more complex is a multi-linear spread with two or more lines stacked one on top of another, like the Trinity Spread. Geometric shapes work well, such as circles, triangles, squares, pentagrams, and hexagrams. Other good candidates are equilateral crosses, zigzags, arcs, and compass points. You can combine shapes, such as placing squares or triangles within circles, or a circle within a circle, or a circle within a square.

4. The sequence of the layout

Decide the numerical order in which the cards will be laid down. The flow should be smooth. The order will be governed by the shape and the position designations. If you have chosen a circle, what determines the starting point? The twelve o'clock position, the top, is a logical point. Or, you may have divided the circle into quadrants according to cardinal points or seasons. Perhaps you would rather start at three o'clock, which is the east, the direction of the rising of the sun and, symbolically, of illumination, spring, renewal, and beginnings.

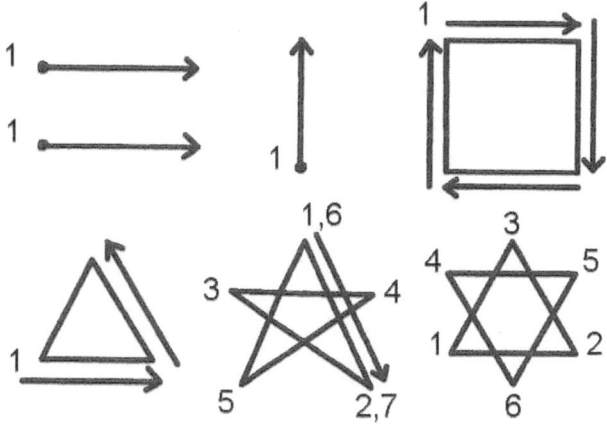

SEQUENCES

Whatever you choose as the starting point, it is logical and natural to move to the right or clockwise. If you are using horizontal lines, start at the left and go right. For a triangle, form the base from left to right, then move up to the crowning point. For a square, start at the top left corner and then move to top right—then bottom right—then bottom left. You get the picture. Whatever sequence you use, make sure it has a natural flow, as though you draw the shape every time you lay the cards out.

5. The position designators

Decide what each position in the spread sequence means. These should be arranged in a progression of revelation that has meaning to the overall pattern.

As an example of how the design process works, consider again the Trinity Spread. Its purpose is to provide a mirror for contemplation, a picture of the Self based on three key aspects of Emotions, Thoughts, and Actions against a backdrop of past, present, and future.

Practice, practice, practice

You may think of other patterns that lend themselves to good spreads. The only way to find out whether or not a spread is effective is to do it over and over again, posing a variety of questions. Do the pattern, sequence, and position designations enable you to arrive at a meaningful interpretation? Is the sequence natural? Are there enough cards? Too many? Does the spread feel forced? Be ruthless in your evaluation and make changes accordingly. Throw out what does not work and add in new elements. Try the spread out on your family and friends. Are they satisfied with their readings?

Some spreads may look great on the drawing board but do not work well in practice. Chalk it up to an interesting experiment and design another spread. Keep records of all your designs, even the ones that do not work. Reexamine those at a later date—you may get ideas for changes that will turn the spreads into winners.

11

Developing Your Psychic Ability

Psychic ability is vital to reading the Tarot. Everyone is born with psychic ability, some with more than others. All of us can develop and strengthen our natural psychic ability, and working the Tarot will accomplish that.

Intuition is another term for psychic ability, one that many people prefer. They will talk about their clear hunches, gut instincts, and other signals, but they all boil down to the same psychic faculty.

Your psychic sense is a clear and direct knowing that often comes suddenly and without explanation. It is unerringly on target and accurate. It transcends time and space, which sometimes makes it seem paradoxical or puzzling, because it cannot be rationalized and may contradict what one thinks. At some point, circumstances bear it out.

We all know certain individuals who seem to be endowed with an abundance of good luck. These people are always having hunches that prove to be correct and, what's more, they have the courage to act on their hunches and use them to their advantage. It is easy to assume that these folks were just blessed at birth, but the truth is, as just stated, *everyone* has psychic ability. Most people have learned to repress it by overriding it with ego and analytical thinking. We receive psychic information all the time, but most of it is lost in the shuffle of our busy minds. How many times have you said to yourself, "I *knew* I should have done (or not done) that..." or "I had a feeling he was bad news, but..." or "I had a hunch that was going to happen but I didn't believe it..." Your psychic faculty gave you guidance and you ignored it because it contradicted the "should," "wants," and "oughts" in your head.

Research has demonstrated that the right hemisphere of our brain processes emotions, creativity, and insights, whereas our left hemisphere processes logic. Thus, the psychic faculty is a right-brain function. Psychic awareness is often strongest in childhood, when imagination and emotions are given free reign without attachments. As we grow older and conform to the expectations of society and the demands of the workaday world, this attunement fades. We base our decisions and actions on what we are told to do, have to do, and need to do in order to adapt and survive. We become attached to our decisions, emotions, attitudes, and desires, and we pay less and less attention to the hunches and gut feelings that tell us otherwise.

A fortunate few of us manage to stay in touch with this marvelous hot line to the inner voice, and are more successful as a result. In 1962, a study of extrasensory perception among business executives undertaken by the Newark College of Engineering revealed that highly successful executives have a strong sense of intuition, believe in it, and rely upon it more than those who are less successful (though they avoided the term "psychic"). Others who retain their ability and develop it are those who work in the arts, which requires use of altered states and imagination.

You will find psychic ability to be an essential ally in your work with the Tarot. It connects us to the Higher Self, a source of wisdom and illumination that knows precisely what is best for us. The Higher Self functions as an interface between the worlds of Spirit and Matter; and is ever ready to serve as a beacon and guiding light. It is in touch with the collective unconscious, where archetypes reside as a form of inborn intuition. Accessing this source of wisdom will help you read the cards and go beyond what is apparent on their surfaces to probe their deep mysteries. Your psychic sense will help you with insights in determining the message of a spread. In self-help, it will help you use the Tarot to plumb your own depths. In readings for others, it will deliver impressions that will enable you to read the client on many levels.

If you think you are not psychic, dispel that notion right now. No matter how distant you have become from your inner voice, it is possible to reclaim connection to it by cultivating it. Psychic ability is like a muscle: the more you exercise it and use it, the stronger it becomes. When you get in touch with it, its impact upon you is unmistakable. The psychic sense functions holistically on physical, emotional, mental, spiritual, and environmental levels, and involves a wide variety of internal and external cues.

Everyone experiences psychic cues in a unique way. For some, the cues may be mild, whereas for others, they are attention-grabbers. You may have physical sensations, such as a tingling of the skin or the feeling of leaden weights in the stomach. You may hear clairaudient or inner voices. You may feel seemingly inexplicable attractions or aversions to persons you have just met without knowing any facts about them. You may get inspirational solutions to problems, or get sudden creative ideas. You may suddenly feel close to the Divine. You may think of someone, without reason, just before they call or appear. You may have dreams that come true. You may have visions, either external or projected onto the screen of your mind.

Regular readings and study with Tarot cards will strengthen your psychic ability. In addition, there are many simple exercises and other things you can do to strengthen it, and the following material will help you get started. It is useful to keep a record of your psychic experiences in your Tarot journal, noting whether or not they proved to be accurate. Over time, you will be better able to recognize that special quality that accompanies psychic information.

Here are ways to develop your ability. For a comprehensive self-study guide that covers ways to develop all five senses for psychic input, see my book *Guide to Psychic Power*.

Tips for psychic development

Be in the moment
Most of us go through daily life somewhere else besides the present. We rehash the past and anticipate the future. Our thoughts are often not focused on where we are at the moment. Yet, all we ever have is *now*. The past is over and done with, and the future has yet to arrive and may not

arrive as we anticipate. By not living in the now, by not giving ourselves fully to the moment, we are letting life pass us by.

This is not to say that you should not daydream, plan for the future, or analyze the past in order to help yourself. There are times when those mental diversions are appropriate. But psychic function is a product of the now. It may provide a peek into the future, of a potential yet to be fulfilled, but unless you are present in the now you are likely to miss the message.

Make a commitment to live more in the moment. As you go about your daily affairs, invest yourself in them fully. Give them your total attention. You probably will be surprised at how much time you spend doing things you do not want to do, but feel obligated to do, or how much time you waste out of laziness. When you realize how precious the moment is, you will be more careful about how you spend your time, and will feel better about yourself. Being centered and in the moment creates conditions in which the psychic faculty can flourish.

Let go of attachments

Attachments to emotions, especially negative ones such as anger, fear, and guilt, prevent us from having access to psychic information and intuitive guidance. Being attached to certain outcomes will cloud your guidance. Allow impressions to arise and pay attention to them.

Many emotional attachments belong to events or circumstances long past. By living more in the moment, you will be less likely to carry a lot of emotional attachment baggage around with you.

Meditate

Regular meditation is one of the best ways to cultivate the psychic faculty. Meditation is a discipline of the mind and body in which the body is stilled and the mind quieted. In mystical meditation, one seeks to transcend thought to higher realms of consciousness. On a more mundane level, meditation can be applied to any number of purposes, such as improving psychic skill, gaining self-knowledge and spiritual insights, and improving health.

Scientific studies from the 1960s to the present have demonstrated that meditation has a beneficial effect upon the body by lowering the metabolism, blood pressure, and heart rate, and slowing brain waves to levels experienced in deep states of relaxation. Individuals who regularly practice meditation, even for a few minutes a day, attest to an overall improvement in their lives, such as greater resistance to stress, improved personal relationships, greater self-confidence, and an overall enhanced sense of well-being.

Here are steps to take:

1. Sit in a comfortable chair or couch, ideally one that allows you to keep your back straight. Place both feet flat on the floor and let your hands rest in your lap, either loosely folded or with your palms turned up. Close your eyes. It is appropriate here to petition and thank the Divine.

2. Allow your weight to sink fully into the cushions. Become conscious of every part of your body. Let the chair absorb all your tension, worries, and distractions.

3. Become conscious of your breathing. Breathe deeply and slowly, allowing the belly to expand with each intake of breath. Hold the breath for a moment, then release it slowly through the nostrils. Repeat this several times, then allow your breath to come naturally, still expanding the belly on intake.

4. Relax the parts of the body progressively. Begin with the feet. Feel all the tension drain away. Let it flow out through your feet into the earth. Move up to your ankles, then your calves, knees, thighs, and buttocks. One by one, release tension in each area and let it drain into the earth. Continue up your torso, relaxing the abdomen, stomach, chest, and shoulders. Relax your arms, wrists, and fingers, letting the tension flow out through the fingertips. Relax the neck, jaw, face, forehead, and top of your head, and send the tension down into the earth.

5. Now that you are physically relaxed, visualize a stream of white and gold energy pouring down from the heavens, entering you through the top of your head. It flows to every part of your body, filling it with white-gold, energizing, healing light. It flows out your extremities, into space and out through your feet and into the earth, nourishing everything it comes into contact with. Surround yourself with the light. Allow yourself to feel good. You are light and buoyant, hardly aware of your body at all. You are protected from negative influences.

6. Quiet the chatter in the mind. Let go of thoughts and worries. Many people find this difficult, especially in the beginning, so do not be discouraged if you have trouble. One centering technique is to count your breaths. When you get to ten, start over again with one. If thoughts arise, do not be dismayed; just let them dissolve or disintegrate incomplete and continue counting your breaths. If emotions arise, allow them to happen, examine them without attachment, and let them go. Another centering technique is to think of an object, such as a pearl or diamond, and hold it in your mind. When thoughts arise, let them go and return to the image.

You are now in a meditative state, a state of altered consciousness. Stay with it. In the beginning, this may only be for a minute or two. The more you practice, the longer the meditative periods will last. The meditation will calm and center you, and clear obstacles to the reception of psychic information.

Visualize Geometric Shapes

The visualization of geometric shapes is a right-brain, intuition-enhancing exercise that you can do during meditation, or during a quiet moment. Imagine a white screen before you and project onto it a shape, such as an equilateral triangle. Hold it steady for as long as you can (this is not as easy as it may seem). Try a variety of shapes— circles, squares, pentagons, hexagrams, and so on. Make them increasingly complex: put a circle inside a square, a triangle inside a circle.

Manipulate Your Consciousness

If you had to locate your "consciousness," where would it be? Most people point to their head. That is an oversimplified answer, but it is a good starting point for this exercise, which will help you develop an awareness that extends beyond the physical senses. This works best in meditation.

Visualize your consciousness as a small sphere of light deep in the center of your head. What is it like? Is it sharply defined or soft and fuzzy? What color is it? Is it warm or cool? Gradually enlarge the sphere until it fills your entire cranium. Feel the light pressing gently against your skull. Now contract it to the size of a marble. Enlarge it again, but this time go beyond the bounds of your head and body. Fill the space around you. Now let your consciousness expand farther out until it fills the entire room with light.

You can also try moving the sphere around inside your body. Let the sphere drop to your heart center. Feel it expand in your chest. Move it down to the solar plexus. Now move it back up to your throat. Then let it return to the center of your head.

Free Associate

This exercise will help you loosen your thought processes so that you think more spontaneously. Do this exercise with a partner. The partner throws out words. Say the first thoughts that come to your mind, no matter how bizarre they sound. If you hesitate, you are allowing your left brain to interfere, weighing and analyzing what you should say. Instead, do not judge. Be detached.

Absorb Your Environment

Most of us live in environments that are filled with noise and distractions. As a consequence, we learn to shut out our environment. In the process, we also shut out environmental signals that may be part of our psychic process.

Devote a quiet period to doing nothing but absorbing your environment, indoors or outdoors. Relax and open your senses to the stimuli around you. Notice colors, shapes, textures, temperatures, breezes, smells, and sounds. Take note of people, animals, flora, machinery, objects, and vehicles. Look at the ceiling, the floor, the sky, the earth. Experience everything around as though you were just born and were sensing for the first time. Be fully in the moment. Be detached. Allow impressions to arise and fade without attachment or judgment.

The strengthening of your psychic ability will benefit you in all aspects of your life, not just in Tarot work. Ideas and inspirations on all manner of things will come to you more easily. They will always occur at the most convenient times, so it is a good idea to keep a small notebook handy wherever you go so that you can jot them down. Psychic hits are often are like dreams—unless you write them down, they fade quickly. If you record them, even a few key words, you can recover the ideas later when you have more time to devote to them.

12

Meditation, Visualization, and Affirmations

Tarot readings are informative and enlightening, but only one aspect of what the tarot is capable of delivering. Some of the most powerful work you can do with the Tarot involves inner work in meditation, and with visualizations and affirmations.

Meditation

The Tarot is a wonderful tool for meditation on matters of self-knowledge and personal growth. I recommend two meditation approaches. The first is contemplation, which is thinking about the meaning of something: a word, a concept, an image, and so on. The second is concentration, which is the focusing of the mind on one thing, such as a mantra, a yantra (a geometric image used in yoga meditation), a symbol, or a candle flame. In formal meditation practice, concentration seeks not to discover the meaning of the object of concentration, but to use the object as a means of transcending thought to an absence-of-thought state.

Most Tarot meditation work is contemplative, in which you are seeking the deep meaning of the cards in relation to yourself and your life path. The Major Arcana, with its archetypal images and mystical symbols, provides riche territory. When I meditate on the Tarot, I prefer to work primarily with these cards. They are endless in their potential and will take you deep within yourself. Certainly, you can include the entire deck in your meditation work. Meditation on the pip cards is most fruitful if they bear pictorial images rather than just numbers of patterns or single symbols.

To meditate on the cards, examine the card as a whole, and then look at individual details. Relate the card to yourself and to aspects of your life and goals. Spend fifteen to thirty minutes on the card. Close your eyes and feel the energy of the card. Think of the card's symbols and meaning. What are its mysteries? What are its positive aspects? What are its negative aspects? How does the card relate to you? Do you see yourself in the card? How do these forces operate in your life—or are they missing and in need of manifestation? For example, how are you The Hierophant—or do you need to embody The Hierophant?

Allow thoughts to arise freely. Do not dismiss anything, no matter how offbeat—it may prove to be a valuable piece in a jigsaw puzzle picture that emerges over time. Let the images in the card speak to you. Let the birds, animals, plants, and landscapes talk to you. What are they trying to tell you about themselves? About you? If you were to go on a journey with them, where would they take you? Let mental pictures come to you. When you are ready to end the exercise, give thanks for all you have learned.

If you have trouble getting the juices flowing or staying focused, re-center yourself on the card by examining its individual symbols and thinking about their meanings.

Treat Tarot meditation like a ritual: establish a routine and practice it frequently, even on a daily basis. Refer back to the chapter "Tarot Rituals" for ideas. Music, chant, and sacred sound can intensify your experience. As I mentioned earlier, I prefer a continual OM chant.

To keep the energy flowing, place the card where you can see it frequently at home. Meditate on it again prior to sleep, with the instruction to your dreaming mind that you will experience more insights and benefits from the card's symbolism while you sleep.

Here are three approaches to selecting cards:

1. Choose a card at random, knowing that the one you draw answers a need, perhaps not recognized consciously, within you. Consider what the card has to say about you, both in positive and negative ways.

2. Make a deliberate card choice based on an analysis of what you need to address. For example, if you are going through a difficult time, you might choose The Tower as a way of connecting with the strength to not break.

3. Take the Fool's Journey and start at the beginning of the deck and work your way sequentially through the Major Arcana, following the suggestions above.

All three methods have their rewards, but number three, the Fool's Journey, is the most exciting. You never know exactly how the journey will go and what you will find along the way, and it is never the same twice. The Fool's Journey is best undertaken when you are fairly confident of being able to meditate on a daily basis for continuity until the Journey is completed.

You can spend months, even years, meditating upon the Tarot, with new territory continually unfolding before you. You may never want to venture beyond one deck, but if you do grow tired of one or feel you have learned as much as possible from it, then switch to another. The core archetypal meanings of the cards remain the same, but different artists interpret those archetypes in different ways via the images they create.

Include your meditation insights in your Tarot journal. By referring back to your records from time to time, you will be able to see your changes and growth. What have you learned? What new questions have arisen for study?

For concentration meditation, select or randomly choose a card. This is your gateway to the spiritual planes. By concentrating on the image, you can step through the card, like a doorway, to a different state of awareness.

After choosing a card, enter a state of meditation and then gaze steadily at the card, asking for it reveal something significant and of benefit to you. Allow impressions to arise, and follow their flow. The gateway may take you into territory not related directly to the card image; rather, the card has acted as a catalyst for a deep spiritual experience.

Visualization

Formulate action plans based on what you have learned from your meditations. Creative visualization is the use of positive thoughts and mental imagery to achieve desired goals. Thoughts and pictures of a desired result are held firmly and vividly in the mind, as if the result were already realized. Visualizations release energies in both the conscious and subconscious that will help you realize your goals by putting you in attunement with forces in motion that will attract the desired circumstances.

Creative visualization has been found to be a powerful force with many applications. In addition to enhancing manifestation of goals, it can help a person change course, get through obstacles, and weather great difficulties by visualizing the desired end result as though it has already happened. It is used in alternative healing modalities to help people see themselves as already healed, thus speeding the healing process in many cases. And, psychical researchers have found that mental imagery is a channel of psychic information, especially during meditation, when the mind is an alpha state, and during certain stages of sleep.

Incorporate creative visualization in a daily plan of meditation and action-planning.

Affirmations

Affirmations are positive phrases and sentences that function in much the same way as creative visualization. They are couched in language that asserts the affirmations are already realized: "I can..." "I am..." "I do..." Affirmations permeate the consciousness when they are written down and repeated often. However, mental pictures and positive words in and of themselves will not produce results. You must totally *believe* in them and in their eventual manifestation, *and* do whatever you can to bring them into being. You must invest in them your will to accomplish them. The more firmly you believe, the more likely you will reap what you believe. Doing the exercises once is not enough—they must be done repeatedly and frequently, and also combined with action, until the goal is attained.

How do you specifically apply affirmations to the Tarot? Let's say that you wish to incorporate into your life the qualities expressed in a Tarot card—perhaps the power of The Magician to create and influence your own destiny. Visualize yourself as The Magician, shaping your own destiny. See yourself as part of the card. See yourself as The Magician in the external world, going about your daily affairs. Now visualize yourself achieving the desired goal. The importance of this cannot be underestimated. *You must see yourself as having achieved the goal.* It is tangible and real, not something projected into a hazy future. Make the image as vivid and as detailed as possible. An affirmation might be, "I have the power to create my own destiny. I use this power wisely and use it now to achieve_____. I give thanks now for my achievement." Say the affirmation out loud and repeat it while holding the image firmly in your mind.

Creative visualization and affirmations are most effective when incorporated into meditation and journal writing. Because they require an investment of time and energy, choose them wisely and work on one or a few at a time.

All of these exercises and procedures described in this chapter can be adapted to suit your own style and taste. It may take you awhile to settle on those that feel the most comfortable and productive.

Major Arcana meditations

The following are descriptions of some of my own meditations on the Major Arcana. They are intended to give you a starting point, and ideas for your own meditations.

0 The Fool

As the innocent, The Fool represents an open mind. This combination of innocence and an open-mind guides our search for deeper knowledge free of the judgments and biases we carry with us from our previous experiences. The ideal meditation with The Fool card is to become The Fool and seek the answers to our questions from the experience of life itself as someone who has yet to experience life. To become The Fool in a meditation brings a sense of excitement about the discoveries that await us and the adventures yet to begin. That is because we approach these meditations without attachments to any ideas or things and are willing to let our minds explore the unknown.

With The Fool as your guide, your meditation can take you to unexpected places and open doors you did not know existed. You have no fear of the unknown, only a thirst to learn.

In my meditations with The Fool, I begin with an image of myself surrounded by a golden aura as bright as the sun. I know that this golden light will protect me, even light my way, which is why I fear nothing even though I have no idea where my journey will lead. As I settle more deeply into my meditation, I feel myself fully transformed into The Fool, filled with a sense of happiness because I know there is much to learn on my journey.

Even though each journey as The Fool is different, they all begin with the same question: Where will my meditation lead me today and what will I learn about myself, about life, about the challenges ahead?

In these travels, I sometimes find myself in places that I know, or in situations that are still unfolding as well as some from my past. In any event, I always feel like I am visiting these places or seeing these things for the first time. I become a neutral observer. This fresh look allows me to see things I have overlooked before when my eyes were clouded with preconceptions, false judgments, and an unwillingness to learn. At the same time, I frequently journey to places unknown and places that may not even exist, at least here on Earth. To my mind, this is a reminder that there is more to learn or experience about life than I can ever imagine.

I always emerge from these meditations with an understanding that whatever path unfolds, it is mine to walk down. I also feel a renewed desire to plunge deeply into life and to experience all its different wonders. I yearn to discover. I do not fear the problems and obstacles that will block my path. Instead, I recognize that there is always a way to get where I am going—and not necessarily as The Fool. That is why it is essential to approach all meditations with this card with an open mind and a willingness to learn.

I The Magician

When I select or draw The Magician card in a meditation, I always remember a basic truth: it is within my power to create my own destiny, even if fate has its role to play. The Magician reminds me that I can influence outcomes.

The Magician symbolizes the ability to harness the creative forces that exist in the universe—both within and outside ourselves—so

I approach a meditation on this card with a great sense of awe and feeling charged with energy. This will not be a quiet or serene meditation, but one filled with purpose and determination. I will want to bring all the powers The Magician possesses to bear on whatever problems or challenges I face.

In meditation, I lay out my problems or questions before me with a belief that I can solve them. While I try to be objective in understanding the problem or question confronting me, I let my mind suggest solutions based on past experiences that are similar or that seem like the best possible approach from the tools at my disposal.

Because the focus is on the solutions and not the problems, I imagine the different outcomes that are likely to result from various approaches I could take. The Magician never leaves anything to chance—there always is a formula that can be applied—so the question becomes, "What works best?" The answers may not come automatically and the solutions may not present themselves immediately. But once you begin the process—with an eye toward resolution—the answers will come eventually.

In many respects, meditations as The Magician reflect the basic nature of the card itself—the ability to draw on forces that we cannot see, but which surround us, and channel that power through ourselves. Meditation, after all, helps us draw on the hidden forces within and then provides a way to bring them to the surface so we can apply them to our lives.

When meditating with The Magician, it is also wise to keep in mind that reversed the card suggests you are blocking your creative energies and are fearful to experiment. These meditations can help you remove those blocks between you and your creative self. In a meditation you can allow your mind to suggest new possibilities that otherwise remain hidden in your subconscious. Over time, the walls will fall and you will be able to harness the creativity that exists within.

II The High Priestess

It is only through meditation that you can truly appreciate the deeper meaning of The High Priestess. The symbol of the unseen, life-giving forces in nature, The High Priestess communicates without uttering a word or sound. She is pure thought and action. Through meditation we learn to speak her language—the language of silence and tranquility—and see the world as it really is. She will reveal to us the deeper mysteries of the universe.

When I pick up this card to meditate, my mind fills immediately with a sense of the power that flows through all things. It is not the same kind of power that The Magician represents, but rather the power The Magician taps into in order to create. I feel I am standing at a gateway to true knowledge, with The High Priestess beckoning me to walk through.

The High Priestess represents the invisible in nature, so I begin my meditation with a tangible image of some aspect of nature—perhaps a flowing river, or a flower unfolding in the morning sun. I become whatever image I visualize, allowing myself to experience the world as it does. If it is the river, I allow myself to merge into the water and flow along with it. As a flower, I let myself root deeply in the soil.

These experiences teach me that I am not separate from nature but a part of it, and that all things are connected. These experiences also teach me that I will grow in life by becoming part of life, not standing to the side and watching, or thinking of myself as separate and distinct from everything that surrounds me.

Meditations with this card remind me to have trust in myself and be patient as I go through life. Also, the more I meditate on the symbolism of The High Priestess, the more I learn of the power of silence. By being quiet, I can hear so much more around me. Instead of seeing the void as empty, I see it filled with the mysteries of life.

III The Empress

The Empress is the principle of creation. She is the merging of the invisible life forces into the visible. She gives life its myriad forms. In our meditations with The Empress we strive for the same. We want our ideas to be transformed from thought into reality. We want them to nurture and grow under her protection.

The Empress also represents the process of life itself, the ebb and flow of all things. So, we must be willing to allow our ideas to come and go, to be born, grow, and then die. We cannot cling to that which we have outgrown.

The Empress can be a very comforting card for a meditation. Her mothering role appeals to our emotions, making us feel warm, secure, and whole.

In a meditation with this card, I always begin with a prayer of thanks for all things in the world that spring from her. Then I ask for her guidance as I meditate on questions about the directions my life is taking. Am I moving forward or standing still? Is this the right direction for me? Is it time to move on or stay a little longer?

In asking these and other questions, I am seeking emotional, not intellectual responses. I want to do what feels right in my heart. I want to know that the soil is fertile and it is a good place to plant the seeds of a new idea, thought, or plan.

Sometimes I meditate with The Empress card free of any questions. I seek instead to appreciate more fully the process of life, to better understand how things pass from one stage to the next and that nothing stays the same. I just want the comfort that comes from knowing that all is well and that things are unfolding as they are meant to. I also want to know that The Empress will look out for me. Like all mothers, The Empress will care for her children.

IV The Emperor

Unlike The Empress who speaks through our hearts, The Emperor speaks to us through our intellect. He is the manifestation of the constructs of the mind—rational thought, logic, and the order that man imposes on the natural world.

Meditations with The Emperor follow a more structured path than they do for any other cards of the Tarot. The questions are more basic and deal more with the form of our lives, rather than the substance—the how instead of the why. Questions are also less probing and deal only with surface issues of life. We do not try to understand what we are doing, but rather we want to be aware of the consequences of our actions, especially if they are wrong.

My meditations with The Emperor card have a stern quality to them. I use these experiences to review my life or a particular situation that I am in. I seek to explain or justify my actions, particularly if they are contrary to the normal way of doing things. I also seek approval—I ask The Emperor to tell me if what I am doing is right. If I am wrong, I want to know that as well.

A meditation with The Emperor can be a healthy exercise at the same time because it lets you outline things in an unemotional, almost detached way. In other words, "Here is the problem or opportunity. This is the way logic says to handle it." Then if you act, you do so with the sense that you are proceeding properly. On the other hand, if you choose to go a different route, you have had the chance to consider the alternatives.

Similarly, a meditation with The Emperor can provide the impetus for making a break with the past, for changing directions. Because things are so clearly laid out in The Emperor's world and we know where they will lead, a meditation can focus on the benefits of moving down an entirely new path. There are risks, of course, but at least we have been forewarned.

V The Hierophant

The Hierophant is as complex a card in a meditation as it is in a reading. There is enormous room for latitude in interpreting its meaning and what you wish to draw from it for your meditation. For some, it is a card of prayer and spiritual growth, with The Hierophant as the guide. For others, the card serves as a reminder that there is a higher authority and that The Hierophant is the link between you and that power.

For my meditation, I straddle both meanings and use the card to help me grow spiritually. I approach this card without any preconceived notions or particular beliefs in a divine power. Instead I start with the premise that there is some divine power at work in the universe, and The Hierophant serves as a visible symbol that it exists. Although I cannot define this power, I know that whatever is there, I will learn how to integrate its presence into my life through meditation with The Hierophant. I recognize him as the link to this hidden mystery. I respect his ability to open doors to the unknown by giving myself to him.

My meditations with this card focus entirely on a desire to grow spiritually. I accept The Hierophant as someone who knows how I can achieve this growth. In each meditation, I ask him to reveal the path I am seeking. Each time, of course, I receive the same answer: "I know the answers, but I cannot tell you. You must keep seeking them for yourself." In this way, The Hierophant becomes a constant reminder that the answers are not there just for the asking, but that someday they will come.

VI The Lovers

The Lovers card symbolizes the combined forces of the male and female sides to our personalities—the male represents the intellect and the female the unconscious self—and the tension that exists between the two.

When I meditate with The Lovers card, I focus on the dynamics that these male and female forces create in my life and how they influence my decisions as well as my growth. Ultimately what I am striving for is the same sense of harmony between the two that is represented on the card.

I usually meditate on a matter I am trying to resolve. First I try to see the possibilities from the two different perspectives: what my intellect says is right because of the way it adds up, contrasted by what I feel emotionally is right. Because there is rarely agreement between the two, I continue my meditation and allow an answer to form that falls somewhere between the two halves—something that intellectually I can live with and that also feels right.

Not all my meditations with this card, however, are limited to solving problems or answering questions. I also use meditations with this card drawing on one of its other meanings: the importance of love in my life as a nurturing force. In these meditations, I ask myself some basic questions, such as "Am I a loving person?" or "Am I loved?" What I am ultimately striving for is an assurance that I am both giving and receiving love in my life, to myself and from myself, as well as to and from those within my life. Often from these meditations I realize that I cannot make all decisions alone no matter how personal they may be, but instead I need the help of my partner, the person I love.

VII The Chariot

Meditation with The Chariot can be an exhilarating experience. That is because The Chariot represents the drive for success that exists within each of us. Although we hope that many of our other meditations with the Tarot will lead to a positive outcome, clear direction, or a better understanding about where we are going, The Chariot is only about winning. A meditation with The Chariot begins with a feeling of power and ends with a sense of accomplishment. It is a fulfilling experience.

Not surprisingly, I select this card for meditation whenever I am going to tackle a new challenge or begin a new task. I use this card to feel good about what I am about to undertake, to fill myself with a sense of power and accomplishment.

In a meditation I actually see myself as the charioteer. I see no obstacles in my path, just success. I adopt the single-mindedness that the charioteer wears on his face on the card. I begin my contemplation by visualizing the task or project that I will be doing. The whole time, I envision its successful outcome.

You can also use this card to meditate when you feel blocked by a challenge. To begin, look deeply into the image on the card and, for the moment, try to forget the problem you face. Close your eyes and think only of the charioteer. As you feel yourself transformed, then begin thinking about the problem or obstacle. Ask yourself, "How would the charioteer handle this situation?" "What tactics would bring him success?" "How can I be like him?" This change in your attitude can help you see things in a whole new light, with the focus on success, instead of defeat or despair.

It is important when meditating with The Chariot to keep in mind that the successes it can help us achieve have to be put in perspective. Although the card is about power and accomplishment, this accomplishment is limited to material gain. Do not forget that our spiritual side needs nurturing, too, and there are many other cards in the Tarot that will help us achieve that.

VIII Strength

Most of us accept the fact that life is often a struggle, that few things come easily to us, and that it is essential to be strong in all that we do. That is the message of the Strength card—and what we are looking for in our meditations with it.

Meditating with this card gives us the strength we need by showing us how to draw on the forces that exist within each of us, and that we do not have to look beyond ourselves for help.

This is an entirely different force and sense of power than that which we draw from meditations with The Chariot card. That card is about outward strength. The power of the Strength card is the strength of self-confidence—the inner strength that comes from accepting ourselves for what and who we are. Also, while the charioteer is singly-focused and thinks only about winning, this card is about strength in all situations, even defeat.

When I meditate with this card, I use these experiences as opportunities to assess myself. I am especially interested in addressing my fears that are counterproductive to my growth and that I know have no place in my life.

Sometimes I start by focusing on something that troubles me or something that I do not feel I can accomplish. Then I question myself, asking why I really feel that way. I allow my mind to suggest other instances when I have faced odds that seemed just as difficult, yet I was able to overcome them. Over and over again, I watch as the negative is replaced with the positive until I feel I am firmly in control of myself and am ready to tackle what faces me.

There is more to be gained in these meditations than just a sense of strength. You can also develop a better appreciation for the process of life and its many challenges. But do not lose sight of the fact that whatever you do, you must have faith in yourself. That way, win or lose, you still progress.

IX The Hermit

The Hermit card provides one of the deepest meditative experiences of the entire Tarot deck. That is because The Hermit is a representation of the very essence of the meditative process itself—the withdrawal from our day-to-day existence to ponder the deeper truths of the universe.

While The Hermit himself represents the extreme and total withdrawal from daily affairs—something that few of us are prepared to do, or even want to—we can still borrow from his experience and enrich our lives, even for the briefest moments.

The Hermit has dedicated his life to breaking through to a higher plane of thought and consciousness. Just like the great mystics, he strives to reach the highest possible peak of knowledge.

When I meditate with this card, I become like The Hermit and push my mind as far as it will take me. I reach for the unknown, seeking just as The Hermit does, to come face to face with the ultimate force that empowers the universe.

I begin by imagining a void, completely empty and without form. As I continue to meditate, I visualize myself drifting into this formless space. Eventually I feel cut loose from my earthly bonds, free to float deeper and deeper into this darkness. I never feel afraid, but rather I am drawn deeper and deeper into it, attracted by the unknown. Also, in this state, I no longer feel as though I am a physical being. In fact, I have no conception of myself—my individuality seems to disappear and I become a part of the void, without form of my own.

These meditations can be the most serene and peaceful of all. Because, like The Hermit, I leave all behind to experience the ultimate, to scale the highest peak of knowledge.

Meditations with The Hermit card are invigorating, too, because they open my mind to an awareness that there is far more to our universe than can ever be described in words. There are some things that you can only experience. And once experienced, you must lead the way for others to follow.

X The Wheel of Fortune

Throughout our lives we are constantly asking, "Where am I going?" and "What am I supposed to do in life?" We spend a great deal of time in our meditations asking these same questions. The answers, although different for each of us, especially depending on when we ask the questions, all have a thread in common. That is, we are all spinning on The Wheel of Fortune, the wheel of life. Things come and things go. Our lives begin and end over and over again.

We can meditate on this card in several ways. We can use the experience simply to get a focus on the many changes occurring in our lives—to assess where we have come from and to prepare ourselves for what is next. On a deeper level, we can use these meditations to measure our growth and to see if we have progressed in our development as the wheel has spun over and over again. We can also seek reassurance that, despite the turmoil that may be occurring in our lives, it too will pass. Finally, we can meditate on how our own actions have influenced the unfolding of events in our lives.

I approach a meditation with this card with a sense of neutrality. I come to learn, not to question, accepting the fact that the wheel spins with or without me. I just want to know if my life is in sync with the turning of the wheel. I find these meditations particularly helpful when I feel uneasy or if I am stressed. By closing my eyes and allowing images to flood my mind of the many random events that have occurred over the days, months, and years of my life, I am comforted by the fact that I can discern growth and positive change. I am reminded that all things in life provide a lesson, and these lessons can be integrated into the next stage of the turning of the wheel.

XI Justice

The world operates on the principle of justice—that is, when all is balanced, all is well. When things fall out of balance, when the scales of justice are tipped to one side, they must be righted once again. This is the message of the Justice card and the key for our meditations with it.

I use these opportunities to meditate on the quality of my life, to find if I am living it in harmony or if things are out of balance and need correcting. I recognize that maintaining this balance is my responsibility and I am liable for the consequences when I allow disharmony to enter the picture.

I find that a meditation with this card—particularly when things are out of balance—allows me to put my life in perspective. When things need correcting, I can either make those corrections or risk the consequences. Either way, the decision rests in my hands.

In general, though, I appreciate the opportunities to head off trouble by meditating on the direction in which I am moving and looking for signs that danger might be coming my way. I start by focusing on the current state of affairs in my life, whether it be my work or my relationships. I allow scenes to play out in my mind and imagine where they will end up if they continue in their present direction. In a meditation, my mind presents different scenarios, allowing me to choose what I think will be the best course to follow in the long run.

Sometimes I just use meditations with this card to reflect on the meaning of justice, to make sure that I am practicing it sufficiently in my life. The more we show an understanding of justice in our dealings with others, the more we move closer as a society to living in equilibrium with one another.

XII The Hanged Man

Life is a transitory process. Things come and go. Sometimes we are instruments of this change. Other times we are simply swept along. Major change usually entails a break with the past, often involving moving in new directions or doing things differently. Almost always, change concerns personal growth and development. The Hanged Man card represents ourselves in the early stages of this change, in a state of suspension, caught between the world we are leaving and the one we are about to enter.

This is an excellent card for meditation when we sense change coming and are looking for reassurance from ourselves that this change is right for us. By becoming The Hanged Man, we thrust ourselves into the unfamiliar and begin the process of integrating new things and experiences into our lives.

In a meditation, I literally feel myself in a state of suspension. Instead of hanging from a tree, I imagine myself walking through a door into a dark room. I tell myself that once I walk through that door I cannot return from where I came. I know I must walk through a new door and welcome the experiences that await me.

These meditations are especially helpful when I feel apprehensive about what I will face. I find that if I can use this meditation simply to convince myself that the decision has been made and there is no turning back, the feelings of discomforts ease considerably and I am well on my way toward the new direction.

Also, meditations involving The Hanged Man card fill me with a great sense of purpose in my life. As long as I know there is movement, I know there will always be growth.

XIII Death

The Wheel of Life could not spin, The Hanged Man would have no reason to be suspended between the known and unknown, and we would have no growth in our lives without the power represented by the Death card. Death, in Tarot symbolism, is not something to be feared. Rather, it is an empowering force that clears away the old to make way for the new.

Meditations with this card can be both useful and enriching. They are useful because they help us move on. Similarly, they are enriching because they open our eyes to the underlying dynamics of change at work in the universe, reminding us that nothing stays the same forever.

I welcome meditations with the Death card, seeing them as opportunities to tap into the life force that guides my destiny. I begin by looking back over my life at the big and little changes I have made. I review the different events that seem relevant to me at the time of my meditation. I let the images come and go at their own will. I am more an observer and less an actor, watching these comings and goings. All I want from a meditation with the Death card is a sense of the unfolding of the new from the passage of the old. I do not seek any answers to questions about the current direction in my life. Those can be answered with other cards from the deck.

I always find that a meditation with the Death card is a liberating experience. Too much time is spent clinging to old ideas, thoughts, and values long after their usefulness has gone from our lives. Yet we are always afraid to let go, thinking it is fine to hold on to them for just a little longer. "Who knows," we tell ourselves, "we might need them again." The Death card stands in opposition to that belief, reminding us that the old can only stand in the way of progress, of growth, of true learning.

XIV Temperance

The Temperance card is more a state of mind and thought than anything else. It is a symbolic representation of a merging of all the forces in our lives that influence our daily activities—our likes and dislikes, successes and failures, what we want and what we have.

By meditating with the Temperance card, we have the chance to see our life from its total perspective. We see all the forces that come into play and how they affect us, how they define our personalities, how they color our thoughts, and how they make us what we are or prevent us from becoming what we want to be.

A meditation with the Temperance card is a passive experience. We do not use these opportunities to judge ourselves or make conclusions. Rather, we are only interested in taking the temperature of our inner self. We want to know if all the ingredients are there to ensure that we are in harmony, that equilibrium reigns in our life.

I usually meditate on an image of myself as I think I appear to others. I accept this image with all of its negatives as well as positives. I visualize myself functioning in different situations—at home, at work, when I am happy, and when I am sad. I want to learn about my strengths and identify my weaknesses. I am seeking knowledge about myself that I can apply to making myself a better person.

Ultimately, if I can apply what I learn from these meditations, I can make changes that will help me grow and become the person I want to be. I will have a better understanding of life and how to live it in harmony. I will be able to make wiser choices, because I'll know myself better and have a stronger fix on what's right for me.

Also, meditations with this card can remind us of the basic virtue of temperance: Living in equilibrium brings peace and a greater sense of self-worth to our lives. Living in disharmony causes pain, discomfort, and self-doubt.

XV The Devil

Despite its ominous look and evil foreboding, The Devil card can help us deal with our fears, weaknesses, and other restraints that we place on ourselves. We should welcome a meditation with this card because it can help us purge ourselves of all the obstacles we have placed in our path, the things that block our growth and cloud our vision and leave us feeling without hope or sense of purpose.

Each of us carries our personal devils around with us. Fear of change. Fear of commitment. The fear that we cannot progress or that we cannot better ourselves. All of these are illusions—just like The Devil. He does not exist. We only invent him as an excuse to explain our failures and fears.

A meditation with The Devil card can help us get beyond all that and see reality for what it is and to appreciate all that life has to offer.

When I meditate with this card, I ask myself questions such as, "Am I making progress with my life or is there something holding me back?" "What is it that I am afraid of?" "Is it really as bad as I imagine?" I should know the answers to these questions—the fact is, I do, because they are with me every day of my life. But until I meditate on them—and see them as the devils they are—I keep them alive and with me. I do nothing to get rid of them.

By confronting these fears and doubts in a meditation, I put them in their proper perspective and recognize that they have no place in my life. I see how they prevent me from growing spiritually, from enjoying life. I learn through meditation that I have the power to rend them powerless, to exorcise them from my thoughts, to be rid of them.

Once I recognize 1 have this power, I can go much further in my mediation and shift my focus from the negatives in my life to the infinite possibilities that await me.

XVI The Tower

Try as we might to protect ourselves from change, there comes a time when it is unavoidable. Ready or not, we find it descends upon us with the fury of the heavens and with a flash of lightning from above. The Tower of our lives that we thought was impregnable comes crashing to the ground.

Is this something to fear? No. Because from the ruins of The Tower emerges liberation. Without walls to hold you, you are free to grow.

In meditations with The Tower card, there are three ways to apply its symbolism. First is the idea that we must break free of the walls we have built around ourselves. By seeking inner guidance, we can find a way to shatter the artificial barriers holding us in.

On another level, The Tower is a metaphor for the sudden enlightenment that meditation can bring. The image of a lightning bolt destroying our image of reality is more than appropriate.

Finally, the image of the lightning bolt exploding across the sky can symbolize the way sudden inspiration and creativity come to us after a meditation.

You can choose any or all of these different approaches to meditating with The Tower card to suit your personal situation and needs.

When I meditate with this card, I do not distinguish among the different meanings. I allow the experience of the meditation itself to determine that.

Sometimes I start with a series of questions about my life. These questions often relate to a specific situation that I am in, and I will ask, "Am I trapped or am I free to make changes?" At other times, the questions can be more broadly focused and I might ask myself, "Is my outlook toward life open or is it narrow and hemmed in?" From there, the meditation takes its own course and the answers flow from within, providing the direction I am seeking.

Sometimes these answers explode across my mind like the lightning bolt in the card, and other times they come long after the meditation. Either way, the experience brings me a greater self-awareness and sense of purpose.

XVII The Star

The Star is our link to higher knowledge and enlightenment. Its light pierces deep into our unconsciousness, illuminating the hidden truths that we seek in our journey through life. Thus, when we meditate on the symbolism expressed by the card, we are merging our minds with the universe as a whole, opening ourselves to an infinite number of possible experiences and new directions. The Star also symbolizes the world of our imagination, the world of the unseen that we can only experience by looking deep inside ourselves.

Meditating on The Star has the same effect as looking upward to the night sky and being dazzled by the light of the heavens. We know there is so much more there than we can see. What we cannot see, we imagine.

In my meditations with the card, I use the light from The Star to guide me in new directions. I allow it to bring me in touch with the unknown thoughts that reside deep inside. I close my eyes and let the light from The Star flood through me and illuminate the darkest regions of my mind. I say to myself, "I am ready to learn, to explore the unknown. Please take me where I have never been. I am open, I am ready."

Often I feel myself transported out of my body, floating in the heavens far above the earth. When I look down, I see the earth as I have never seen it. New paths appear before me. I see new opportunities for growth. I also feel I am a closer to understanding the cosmic order and the reason for all things. It is an experience that leaves me deeply inspired.

XVIII The Moon

The Moon is a card of dark secrets and illusions, dreams and shadows, images not fully formed, and phantoms of the night that make us feel uneasy. The card provides the chance to meditate on some of the things in our life that unsettle us, that chip away at our strength. A meditation with The Moon card can be a test of faith and a demonstration of strength.

We must be willing to plunge ourselves into the darkness, using the eerie reflection from the moon to light our way. We must prepare ourselves to be confronted by illusions that seem as large as life. And we must use these experiences to prove to ourselves that we are strong, that we have faith, that we can continue the journey.

A meditation with this card can be like a dream in which all things seem real, but yet you know they are not—or so you want to think.

I find meditations with this card are an ideal time to confront those hidden fears, those self-doubts that I carry with me but don't want to deal with openly. I let these images come into my mind, as they would in a dream. But unlike a dream, this time I am in control and can direct the outcome. I show myself that there is really nothing to fear—the things that frighten me don't exist in the real world, they only live in my mind. I remind myself that if I am strong and have faith, I can overcome all my fears and doubts.

I find that I had little to fear in the first place, but I am glad I had the opportunity to be reminded of this truth once again.

XIX The Sun

The Sun is one of the most joyous cards of the Tarot deck, a quality that carries into meditations with it. It is a card of warmth, happiness, hope, and enrichment. Its image is one of boundless energy and a fulfilling life. The Sun is also the symbol of the life-giving powers of the universe. Under the light of The Sun, things are constantly being reborn. By gazing deeply into this card, we can feel the revitalizing powers of The Sun, how its energy lights up our soul and gives life to our deepest wishes and dreams.

The card also exudes a sense of innocence and freedom. This is not the same as The Fool, whose innocence comes from a state of not knowing anything. Rather, this is the innocence of a new day and new beginnings. We have traveled quite a distance on the road of life and reached another level of development and consciousness.

Our meditations with this card should give us the chance to examine our life and the progress we have made. We should use these meditations to say a prayer of thanks for the richness of the experiences we have had. We should also meditate on the new experiences that await us.

Knowing that I am going to meditate with The Sun card, I instantly feel good. I know it will be a rich experience and that I will feel as free as the young children pictured on the card at play.

I call these my "thanksgiving" meditations. It is my opportunity to feel grateful for the wonderful bounty of my life, the richness of my discoveries, the growth I have experienced, and my freedom to grow more. I am also thankful for all that awaits me as my journey continues. We should all be blessed with the sun to light our path, to warm our soul, and to fill us with the same energy that courses through the universe.

XX Judgement

The Judgement card reflects the coming together of our life experiences. We use this card to meditate on the myriad events that have passed before our eyes and receded into our memories, and take account of what we have accomplished and apply it to understanding the purpose of our existence on this planet.

Despite the title "Judgement," the card is not judgmental. Similarly, our meditations are not judgmental, either. Instead, we should use the experience to understand that all that we have done has been leading somewhere, that we have been fulfilling our individual destiny, even if its true meaning has been kept hidden from us.

When we meditate with this card, we can feel the stirring in our soul from the trumpet's blast. We are being called—and we must answer that call. Our life has reached the point at which we are ready for answers to our deepest questions. It is important, however, to keep in mind that this does not imply an end to life. Instead, the Judgement card usually implies that we have reached the end of a cycle or the passage from one stage to the next, and it is time to begin The Fool's journey again. Meditation with the

Judgement card helps us prepare for this new stage. It provides a chance to see how things have led to where we are and where we are going next.

To meditate with this card, I look for a common thread that binds my life's experiences. I look for some acknowledgment that I have been moving in a direction leading to a sense of purpose. I take from these meditations a feeling of fulfillment and self-satisfaction. I also prepare myself for changes that may be on the horizon. I say, "This is what I have done. I am ready and waiting for what comes next."

XXI The World

The World card symbolizes the essence of life—how all things come together to form the whole and how we are one part of that larger picture. If we lived a thousand lifetimes, the one thing we would see in common as we passed from one life to the other is that the life process is eternal. We do not make life, we live life. We flow with it. All the forces we encounter on our journey through time, all our experiences, all the knowledge we gain, we draw from life. Our lives spin forever just as The World spins round and round.

When we meditate with this card, we tap into the cosmic flow. We see our lives as part of the world, not as unique or distinct. We allow our minds to separate from our bodies and become a part of the eternal process, to experience the coming and going of all things, to see how the ebb and flow comprise the whole.

To meditate with this card, I picture a river flowing endlessly. I become part of this river and flow with it. It leads me nowhere, and I seek nowhere to go. I just want to experience the flow. From it comes an appreciation of the eternal flow of life itself.

I find these meditations help me put things in perspective. They teach me to be humble and not to think of myself as supremely important, but one of the many living things on this planet. I seek no answers to any questions. Rather I use the experience to affirm the life process, to get a sense of the purpose in my life and to feel connected to the greater whole. These meditations leave me feeling grateful for the time that has been afforded to experience life and learn all the lessons it has to offer.

13

Dreams and the Tarot

Dreams and the Tarot are made for each other: both speak in symbols; reach into personal and archetypal levels of meaning; comment on the timescape in terms of past, present, and probable future; and contain valuable information for guidance, enlightenment, and healing. Could a better partnership exist?

The Tarot adds great dimension to dreamwork, enabling a deeper probing of meaning and richer insights. Even if you think you thoroughly understand the message of a dream, the Tarot will always reveal more. In addition, a regular practice of dreamwork involving the Tarot can improve dream recall and stimulate more productive dreaming.

Frequency of recalled dreams and the amount of recalled detail vary from person to person, and even wax and wane according to the inner energy we have available to devote to dreams. Sometimes periods of stress and change can temporarily depress dream recall. We still dream even if we do not recall them. Working with dreams, such as in conjunction with the Tarot, will for many people increase dream recall.

Dreams address how to restore or maintain balance and harmony in life. They are symbolic in content, using "day residues" from our daily activity, themes, and activities that have personal meaning, and many symbols from the archetypal realm. Once you understand their symbolic language, dreams make complete sense—and they are full of wisdom and power. Tarot augments dreamwork in powerful ways by serving as a messenger from the archetypal realm that bridges the worlds of spirit and matter.

Dreams rarely present complete stories with a beginning, middle, and end. We do not need to have whole story dreams for them to be helpful, however. Fragments can reveal a great deal. Frightening dreams also contain helpful and healing information.

For a complete course in working with dreams, consult my book *Dreamwork for Visionary Living*. I have included here an introduction to dreamwork that will get you started with the Tarot.

Guidelines for interpreting dreams

First, practice interpreting some of your own dreams with basic dreamwork techniques. Everything in a dream—even inanimate objects—is a symbol that potentially says something about the dreamer. Start keeping a journal of your remembered dreams, even those that are short and fragmentary, regardless of how much sense they make to you. You will find that all dreams make sense when viewed from the perspective of symbols.

Follow these steps to unravel a dream:

1. Give the dream a title that expresses the action.
2. Describe the high concept of the dream.
3. Analyze all the elements: people, objects, actions, emotions, colors, and so on.
4. Describe all elements as though you are explaining them to someone who knows nothing.
5. Ask yourself how all elements might represent yourself.
6. Describe your emotions, both within the dream and upon awakening.
7. Describe the archetypal content of the dream.
8. Look for elements that suggest a personal myth.

9. Describe the overall message of the dream.
10. Conceive a conclusion or plan of action based on the dream.

Dreams often contain puns and plays on words, so use your powers of free association to consider all possibilities. Nothing is out of the question!

Tarot dream interpretations

Once you have analyzed your dream, use Tarot cards to add new insights. You can do card draws and analyze the meanings of the cards in relation to the dream. I prefer either a one-card or three-card draw, but you can experiment. You can even do a spread for the dream, such as the Chakra Spread or Celtic Cross.

Allow the cards to talk about the dream—let impressions arise spontaneously. Here are tips:

> **Court cards** are personal guides, mentors and models, the trusted people who dispense advice and try to steer us in the right direction.
>
> **Major Arcana cards** point to the big picture. Sometimes we cannot see the forest for the trees. The Major Arcana help us to pull back to a broader perspective. They are impartial to outcomes. They call us to examine ourselves and situations more thoroughly.
>
> **Minor Arcana pip cards** fill in the lines with details, especially pertaining to personal matters. Use the symbolisms of the suit signs and numbers to examine dreams from specific angles.

If you apply the Tarot regularly to dreamwork in this fashion, you are likely to see certain cards turn up again and again. Dreaming also follows patterns, with certain themes and symbols that repeat. The repetition may point to unresolved situations, or to patterns in your emotional reactions to certain situations. Both dreams and the Tarot are oriented to revelation, guidance, and solutions. Together they are a powerful combination to help you steer your path through life.

Remember that both Tarot and dreams invite an action response: what are you going to do with your insights and revelations?

Tarot and incubated dreams

We do not have to wait for lightning to strike in spontaneous dreams—we can solicit specific guidance from our dreams through the ancient practice of incubation. Dream incubation involves asking dreams in advance to answer questions. Dream incubation was widely practiced in the ancient world, such as by the Egyptians, Greeks, and Romans. Many dreamwork enthusiasts today use the same techniques when they want clear guidance for creativity, decision-making, and problem-solving.

Here are the steps to incubating a dream:

Choose an important matter and be willing to explore it

Dream incubation is an activity of the sacred. The ancients undertook dream incubation when something important was a stake, such as healing or a major decision. Approaching dreams for answers to questions is akin to pilgrims approaching the oracle at Delphi. One does not come to the temple with trivial questions. So, we go to our inner temples with questions that have weight.

It is also important that, in choosing a question, we are completely clear on our willingness to have it examined by the truth that is expressed in dreams. There is always the possibility that we will receive answers that we might rather not hear.

If you are not clear in your intent, your dream oracle will not be clear, either.

Phrase a question you would like your dreams to answer

Keep the question short, simple, and direct. The more complicated the question, the higher the risk of receiving ambiguous answers. Ask for specifics. If you are trying to decide between two courses of action, it is best to inquire about one course. Ask, "Should I do Plan A?" and not "Should I do Plan A or Plan B?"

Here are some examples of effective phrasing of questions:

- Should I (proposed action)
- How can I heal myself
- How can I solve (problem)
- What is the status of my relationship with (name)
- How can I improve my relationship with (name)
- How can I make (project or venture) a success
- How can I manifest abundance and prosperity

Once you are practiced at incubation, try more open-ended questions. Some examples are:

- What shall I do now
- Show me my path
- Why... (do I... am I...)
- What is the divine purpose for me

Write the question in your dream journal
Writing down the incubation question helps to "set" it in consciousness and start the alchemical process of incubation. The question cooks away on the back burners of your mind. Writing down the question also helps to crystallize focus and intent. Do not be surprised if you get ideas for improving the question, or even decide to ask something else.

Prepare the body, mind, and soul
Dream incubation should be undertaken when you have the time to devote proper attention to it. Choose a day and night when you will not be stressed, hurried, or involved with activities close to bedtime. During the day, follow the ancient wisdom of eating lightly or fasting. Abstain from alcohol and stimulants all day or at least close to bedtime.

Meditate on the question, which continues the alchemical cooking. Be sure to give thanks for the answer that will come, which helps prepare the way for receiving the answer. Think about the question throughout the day.

At bedtime, do an incubation ritual
Small rituals will help set forces in motion. Light a candle, spend a few minutes in meditation to still your mind. If you wish to read, choose something that is inspirational or spiritual—this is not the time to read an adrenalin-raising novel or news magazine.

Before you go to sleep, repeat your incubation question either silently or aloud. Both thought and sound set forces in motion. You may also want to write out your question again, which is another way of focusing intention and marshalling forces in motion.

As you fall asleep, visualize a ball of blue light at the base of your throat, and breathe into it to energize it. This is the seat of the throat chakra, which governs self-expression and the search for Truth.

Record and interpret your dream
Upon awakening, record your dream immediately so that details will not be lost. Dreams evaporate quickly, so do not count on your ability to bring it from memory later in the day. Record everything you recall, including fragments and emotions.

Interpret your dream using the guidelines given in this chapter.

Consult the Tarot
Dream incubation is a "big" process, so draw a card from the Major Arcana. What does this dream messenger have to say about your dream? You can also do multiple-card draws and spreads with the entire deck as well.

Watch for extra information that comes later
Dream incubation sometimes seems a peculiar process, operating by its own rules and timetables. The answer to your question may not be in the dream you have on the incubation night. Or, perhaps you do the incubation process, but do not recall a dream the next morning.

Sometimes the answer pops up in your mind later. It may come in a dream the next night, or even weeks later. It may come via intuition in a sudden flash that hits you while you are not thinking about the situation. It may come via synchronicity, or "meaningful coincidences." Synchronicity can come through things other people say to you, in which a message seems to be hidden; or something you read; or some other "chance" event (such as an opportunity).

And, the answer may come from a subsequent Tarot card meditation or reading.

Do not give up if success is not immediate
If you do not receive an immediate answer, repeat the entire incubation process again the next day. If you still have no results, repeat it a third time. If three tries produce no results, there may be one or more reasons why:

- You are not clear on the question or your willingness to examine it
- You have received the answer but have not recognized it
- You will receive the answer at another time
- You need to ask another question first

If you have remembered dreams but do not feel they answer your question, reexamine them for clues you may have missed. Remember that dreams are often subtle in their messages.

Many times, answers must come at the appropriate moment. Trust in the process and allow yourself to ride with the flow. Be observant for signals.

In conclusion

You now have a comprehensive program for developing a multi-faceted, powerful strategy using the Tarot. The cards will serve you well. You will go through cycles of intensity and even less use, based on your needs, but you will always come back to the cards, for they hold the keys to Truth, wisdom, and enlightenment.

Appendix
Glossary of Symbols

The following is a glossary of symbols commonly used in the design of Tarot decks that follow the Western occult tradition. Some of the symbols presented are complex with multiple meanings. In such cases, meanings most appropriate to the Tarot have been selected. Use the glossary to enrich and deepen your understanding of individual cards.

For more symbols, consult my *Dream Guide and Dictionary*, which features more than 1000 symbols.

Anchor Salvation, stability, security, hope, good luck.

Androgyne *See* Rebis.

Animals Mankind's animal nature, instincts, and subconscious self. Qualities they symbolize are true to their own natures, such as gentleness, loyalty, ferocity, and so on.

Ankh Egyptian looped cross meaning "life" or "hand mirror," symbolizing life, the universe, regeneration, resurrection, immortality, and the union of the male principle (the staff) and the female principle (the closed loop).

Apple Forbidden knowledge, earthly desires, evil, untransformed power, magic, eternal life.

Arrow Energy, solar rays, divine power, a phallic symbol of creative energy.

Bag (also Sack). Vessel or container of wisdom, inspiration, transformation.

Banner Freedom from material bondage, victory, self-assertion, a heightened spiritual significance.

Barley Fruitfulness, fertility.

Bee Industry, diligence, creative activity, productivity, orderliness, discipline, sweetness.

Beehive Industriousness, creativity, unified community.

Birds The soul, messengers to the gods, thoughts and aspirations in flight.

Black Death, destruction, humiliation, negation, inertia, beginnings.

Blue Heaven, contemplation, godliness, spiritual qualities, numinosity, inspiration, the unconscious, darkness made visible.

Boat *See* Ship.

Brown The earth, foundation, renunciation of the world.

Bull Fecundity, regeneration, brute strength.

Butterfly The soul, resurrection and rebirth, attraction to light (spiritual).

Caduceus Spiritual enlightenment and illumination, transformation of consciousness, immortality, healing, the four elements, balance between positive and negative, equilibrium.

Cave The womb, containment, the unconscious, the center, embryonic development, inner transformation, security.

Chariot Divine power in motion, triumph, glory, drive, ambition.

Cherub Youth, life, the innocence of childhood.

Chimney Access to heaven.

Circle Oneness, completion, perfection, the cosmos, eternity, the ever-renewing cycle of life, the sun, the Self, the totality of the psyche, the process of individuation, spiritual protection.

Clouds The unseen God, Divine Omnipotence.

Cone *See* Pine cone.

Cord Incarnate life; the force that binds the soul to the body, circle.

Crab Dreams, a bridge between the unconscious and consciousness.

Crocodile Fecundity, power of the unconscious, destruction and fury, knowledge.

Cross World axis at the mystic Center, conjunction of opposites, the binding together of heaven and earth, spirit, and matter; ascent to God, suffering and sacrifice, protection against evil.

Crossroads The union of opposites.

Crow Prophetic vision, creative power, spiritual strength, beginnings, solitude.

Crown Preeminence, divinity, spiritual illumination, light, closeness to God, victory over sin, death, the self and the material.

Cube The earth, the manifest universe.

Dog Fidelity, guardianship, obedience, companionship, guide to the underworld.

Dolphin Resurrection of the soul, salvation.

Dove The soul, purity, peace, wisdom.

Dragon Evil, the Devil, dark forces, temptation, the element of earth.

Eagle Renewal, regeneration, the illumined spirit, imagination.

Egg The cosmos, the earth, the seat of the soul, life, archetypal feminine symbol of world creation.

Eight Regeneration, spiritual illumination, never-ending cycles of cosmos.

Eleven Sin, transgression, excess, instability, imperfection, master number of intuition and spiritual insight.

Eye The all-seeing divine, protection against dark forces, disease, misfortune, evil.

Fire Spiritual energy, illumination, purification, destruction.

Fish The unconscious, spirit, life-force, fecundity.

Five The microcosm, the Quintessence or fifth element of Spirit.

Flag *See* Banner.

Forest The unconscious, darkness, the mysterious, unknown territory, realm of unfamiliar and possibly dangerous beings, wild growth.

Forty Spiritual trial and initiation.

Four Foundation, stability, solidity, the earth, rational and logical achievement, hard work, the human body.

Fox Cunning, shrewdness, guile, stealth.

Fruit Fertility, abundance of nature, Goddess.

Garden The conscious, controlled, orderly growth in the sun's light.

Goat Sinners, the damned, stubbornness.

Goose Descent into hell, the soul of the dead in flight to the underworld, messenger to the gods, magic, providence, vigilance.

Grapes Fertility, pleasure.

Gray Mourning, neutrality, penitence, humility.

Green Fecundity, fruitfulness, harmony, youthfulness, prosperity, energy, healing, magic and the supernatural, the halfway point in the spiritual journey.

Hands Action in the world; right hand: masculine, positive, and active forces (including intellect, reason, and creativity); left hand: feminine, negative, and passive forces (including intuition, emotion, psychic nature, and fecundity).

Hare Fecundity, procreation, frequent companion of Goddess; fleetness, diligent service, lust and physical passions.

Harp (also Lyre) Divine music, bridge between heaven and earth.

Heart The center of the body, mystic Center of love and illumination, center of eternity, source of emotions, courage, understanding, sorrow, happiness, the sun center of man, light, intellect, seat of intelligence.

Hermaphrodite *See* Rebis.

Heron Generation of life, patience, silence, speed, secrecy, solitude.

Hexagon/Hexagram Union of opposites.

Horse Instinct, intense desires, lust, uncontrollable instinctual drives arising from the unconscious, health and vitality of the physical body, powers of clairvoyance, power and motion of solar energies, omen of death, carrier of souls of the dead to the underworld. Winged horse: vehicle of consciousness.

Indigo Advanced spiritual qualities or wisdom, psychic faculties, intuition.

Iris Purity.

Ivy Fidelity, immortality, attachment, undying affection, a force in need of protection.

Key Passport to knowledge, the unconscious, spiritual realms, immortality, the act of discovery.

Labyrinth Death and rebirth, the mystical Center, secrecy.

Ladder Access between planes of being or levels of consciousness, ascent of consciousness to spiritual realms, descent to subconscious and underworld.

Leaf Fertility, regeneration, prosperity, abundance, well-being.

Lemniscate Eternity, infinity, regeneration, the Holy Spirit, infinite wisdom, higher consciousness, the alpha and omega, no beginning and no end, the endless spiraling and balancing of opposing forces in the universe.

Light Spirit, spiritual strength, morality.

Lightning Divine power, revelation, fertility, the generative force.

Lily Purity, sweetness, virginity.

Lion Majestic strength and courage, solar light, latent passions, the kundalini force.

Mandorla The equilibrium between equal forces, interpenetration of heaven and earth/spirit and matter, the divine, the sacred, virginity, the vulva, gateway to the mysteries of sex, life, and birth.

Mask Outward appearance or persona, concealment, transformation.

Maze *See* Labyrinth.

Moon Intuition, emotions, fecundity, the psychic, magical powers, Goddess, illusion. Crescent and waxing moon: beginnings, endeavor, energy, promise, growth. Full moon: fruition, fulfillment, boon, maximum potential. Waning moon: deterioration, decrease, diminution.

Mountains Dwelling places of the gods, the ascent of the spirit.

Narcissus Self-love, self-contemplation, introversion, indifference, coldness.

Nine Attainment, fulfillment, truth, incorruptibility.

Octagon Rebirth, regeneration, transition from matter to spirit.

One God, Spirit, creation, unity, light, beginnings.

Orange Pride, ambition, egoism, flames, luxury, ferocity, health, vitality, energy.

Ouroboros Eternity, the self-sufficient and endless cycle of Nature, the continuity of life and time, union of opposites.

Owl Death, the forces of darkness, night, passivity, wisdom.

Ox The earth, self-sacrifice, patience, submissiveness, cosmic forces.

Palm Triumph, victory, fecundity, the anima.

Path *See* Road.

Pentacle/Pentagram The dominion of intelligence and mind over the forces of man's lower nature, the five senses of man; the four elements plus spirit; the five physical points of man (head plus limbs). With point down: the lower nature.

Pentagon Wholeness, the microcosm.

Pig Companion and guide to hero, king, and magician; link between earth (body) and air (mind).

Pillars Connection, support, the ceremonial chamber. Single pillar: the world axis or World Tree that connects heaven, earth, and underworld. Twin pillars of white and black: opposites of life and light and passivity and darkness.

Pine cone The creative and generative force, fecundity, good fortune, phallic symbol.

Pink Love, the mystic heart Center.

Pomegranate Rejuvenation, resurrection, fertility, multiplicity contained within Oneness.

Purple Royalty, imperial power, pomp, pride, truth, justice.

Rain Fertilizing forces, purification, descent of spiritual forces to earth.

Rainbow Bridge between heaven and earth.

Ram Strength, victory over obstacles, and dark or negative forces.

Rebis The union of opposites to attain unity or wholeness; the Philosopher's Stone, the attainment of enlightenment.

Red Blood, life-force, lust, eroticism, anger, passion, sensuality, materialism, animal life, human animalistic nature, courage, willpower, strength.

River Passage of time, life journey, spiritual journey.

Road The life/spiritual journey.

Rocks Solidity, firmness.

Rose Victory, pride, triumphant love, erotic love, the mystic center of the heart.

Salamander Power of transmutation.

Scales Equilibrium, balance, immanent justice.

Scorpion Evil, treachery.

Serpent Wisdom, resurrection, guardian of the spirit and great mysteries transformational energy for spiritual illumination, the kundalini force, enlightenment, temptation.

Seven Mystical man, the perfect order, the macrocosm, the highest stage of illumination, the psychic, luck.

Shell The feminine principle, the unconscious, fertility, the moon.

Shield Spiritual defense and protection.

Ship Vehicle of the soul through the waters of the unconscious, carrier of souls of the dead to the afterlife.

Sickle Mortality and death.

Silver Psychic qualities, lunar power and magic, the feminine principle of the cosmos, protection against dark forces.

Six Equilibrium, harmony, balance, health, union of opposites.

Snow Purity, spiritual qualities, frozen emotions.

Sphinx Power, the mysterious and enigmatic, wisdom, vigilance, strength, royal dignity, the four elements, the combined physical, intellectual, natural, and spiritual powers, the union of physical and intellectual powers, subduing animal instincts.

Spider Skill, creativity, aggression, cycle of life and death/building and destroying.

Spiral The waxing/waning, cyclical powers of the cosmos, growth, evolution, flexibility, the need for change.

Square Firmness, solidity, organization, becoming whole, secured, stabilized, the four elements, four seasons, four quarters.

Staff Support, a branch of the Tree of Life.

Stag Regeneration, renewal, the Tree of Life, messenger of the gods, heavenly and spiritual light.

Stairs Connections between different worlds or different levels of consciousness. Descending: access to the underworld or unconscious. Ascending: access to heaven or higher, spiritual consciousness.

Standard *See* Banner.

Star The spirit, especially the spirit in its struggle against dark forces, a light in the darkness, the light within, the celestial realms.

Stork Herald of good news, birth, spring.

Storm The creative power, especially sacred. Fertilization.

Sun Spiritual illumination, heroic and courageous forces, the creative principle.

Appendix | Glossary of Symbols

Swan The mystic journey, mystic Center, self-sacrifice, the complete satisfaction of desire, the union of opposites.

Ten Perfection, the cosmos, the law, container of all things, return to unity.

Thirteen Betrayal, unlucky (traditional meaning); lucky (in some traditions).

Three The generative force, creative power, forward movement, the totality of beginning, middle, and end, multiplicity, ascent to spiritual realms.

Tiger Cruelty, wrath, darkness of the soul, defender against the forces of chaos.

Tower Ascent, intellectual fortress, security, isolation.

Tree The inexhaustible life of the cosmos, center of the world and universe, World Axis, connections to others, grounding, realm of nature.

Triangle Ascent to spirit. Tip up: fire, the masculine principle, the Trinity, the upward aspiration of all things to the Source, vision, seeking, planning. Tip down: water, the feminine principle, emotions, intuition, the unconscious. Inverted with tip cut off; earth, foundation, solidity.

Trident The unconscious.

Twelve The cosmic order.

Two Duality, opposites, balance, the dawning of something new in the consciousness, the conjunction of opposites.

Unicorn Purity (especially in the face of great temptation), female chastity, the word of God.

Vesica Piscis The vulva, creation, equilibrium between equal forces, the interpenetration between heaven and earth and spirit and matter, the opening to the Void.

Vessels Regeneration, regeneration, transmutation.

Violet Religious devotion, sanctity, temperance, knowledge, sorrow, grief, old age, mourning.

Wand Power, doing, creating, manifesting.

Water The unconscious, intuition, emotion, the psychic, access to the unconscious, life-giving and generative force.

Wheat Bounty of the earth, fruit of the womb of the Goddess.

Wheel Divine power, the eternal turning, the sun, spiritual illumination, equilibrium of contrasting forces.

White Purity, innocence, joy, light, life, light and illumination.

Wolf Valor, guardianship. wild energy, instincts.

Wreath Nature, the Goddess, victory, celebration.

Yellow Glory, fruitfulness, goodness, wisdom, illumination, light, intellect, generosity.

Zero Nothingness, the unmanifest, the Cosmic Egg.

Zodiac Continuity, wholeness, oneness, perfection, the attributes of circles and wheels, renewal and rebirth, wheel of life.

About the Author

Rosemary Ellen Guiley is a leading expert in the metaphysical and paranormal fields. She works as an author, researcher, and investigator, and has published more than 60 books on a wide range of topics. She has been studying the Tarot, dreams, and symbols for much of her life, and became a student of alchemy in the 1980s. She has been a professional Tarot reader since the early 1990s.

Rosemary also conducts research in ufology, entity contact experiences, afterlife studies, spirit communications, and past lives and reincarnation, among many other subjects. She is a certified hypnotist and does past-life regressions, and also does dreamwork consultations. She lectures internationally and makes numerous media appearances, and is a frequent guest on *Coast to Coast AM* with George Noory. In addition, she runs her own publishing house, Visionary Living, Inc.

Rosemary's website is www.visionaryliving.com. She lives in Connecticut with her husband, Joe Redmiles.

Bibliography

Barrett, Francis. *The Magus*. Secaucus, NJ: The Citadel Press, 1967.

Bonewits, Isaac. *Real Magic*, rev.ed. York Beach, ME: Samuel Weiser, 1989.

Budge, E. A. Wallis. *Amulets and Superstitions*. New York: Dover Publications, 1978. Reprint. (First published in 1930.)

Butler, Bill. *The Definitive Tarot*. London; Rider & Co., 1975.

Campbell, Joseph. *Myths to Live By*. New York: Viking, 1972.

Campbell, Joseph and Richard Roberts. *Tarot Revelations*, 2d ed. San Anselmo, CA: Vernal Equinox Press, 1982.

Case, Paul Foster. *The Tarot: A Key to the Wisdom of the Ages*. Richmond, VA: Macoy Publishing Co., 1947.

Cirlot, J. E. *A Dictionary of Symbols*. New York: Philosophical Library, 1971.

Connolly, Eileen. *Tarot: A New Handbook for the Apprentice*. Van Nuys, CA: Newcastle Publishing, 1979.

Cooper, J. C. *An Illustrated Encyclopedia of Traditional Symbols*. London; Thames & Hudson Ltd., 1978.

Eliade, Mircea. *From Primitives to Zen: A Thematic Source Book of the History of Religions*. San Francisco: Harper & Row, 1977.

_____. *Rites and Symbols of Initiation*. New York; Harper & Row, 1958.

_____. *Symbolism, the Sacred, & the Arts*. Diane Apostolos-Cappadona, ed. New York: Crossroad, 1988.

_____. *Patterns in Comparative Religion*. New York: New American Library, 1958.

Ferguson, George. *Signs & Symbols in Christian Art*. London: Oxford University Press, 1961.

Gawain, Shakti. *Creative Visualization*. New York: Bantam Books, 1982.

Gray, Eden. *A Complete Guide to the Tarot*. New York: Crown, 1970.

_____. *Mastering the Tarot: Basic Lessons in an Ancient, Mystic Art*. New York: New American Library, 1971.

_____. *The Tarot Revealed*, rev. ed. New York: New American Library, 1988.

Greer, Mary K. and Rachel Pollack, eds. *New Thoughts On the Tarot*. N. Hollywood, CA: Newcastle Publishing, 1989.

Greer, Mary K. *Tarot for Yourself: A Workbook for Personal Tranformation*. N. Hollywood, CA: Newcastle Publishing, 1984.

_____. *Tarot Constellations: Patterns of Personal Destiny*. N. Hollywood, CA: Newscastle Publishing, 1987.

_____. *Tarot Mirrors: Reflections of Personal Meaning*. N. Hollywood, CA: Newcastle Publishing, 1988.

Guiley, Rosemary Ellen. *Guide to Psychic Power*. New Milford, CT: Visionary Living, Inc., 2015.

———. *Dreamwork for Visionary Living.* New Milford, CT: Visionary Living, Inc., 2014.

———. *The Encyclopedia of Magic and Alchemy.* New York: Facts On File, 2006.

Hall, Manly P. *Meditation Symbols in Eastern & Western Mysticism: Mysteries of the Mandala.* Los Angeles: Philosophical Research Society, 1988.

———. *The Secret Teachings of All Ages.* Los Angeles: The Philosophical Research Society, Inc., 1977. Reprint. (First published in 1925.)

Hamilton, Edith. *Mythology.* New York: New American Library, 1940.

Hope, Murry. *The Psychology of Ritual.* Longmead, Dorset, England: Element Books Ltd., 1988.

Jayanti, Amber. *Living the Tarot.* N. Hollywood, Cal.: Newcastle Publishing, 1988.

Jung, C. G. *Psychology and Alchemy,* 2d ed. Vol. 12 of The Collected Works of C. G. Jung. Princeton: Princeton University Press, 1968.

———. *The Archetypes and the Collective Unconscious,* 2d ed. Vol. 9, Part 1 of The Collected Works of C. G. Jung. Princeton: Princeton University Press, 1968.

———. *Man and His Symbols.* New York: Anchor Press/Doubleday, 1988. (First published in the United States 1964.)

———. *Memories, Dreams, Reflections.* Recorded and edited by Aniela Jaffe. New York: Random House, 1961.

Junjulas, Craig. *Psychic Tarot*. Dobbs Ferry, NY: Morgan & Morgan, 1985.

Kaplan, Stuart R. *The Encyclopedia of Tarot*. New York: U.S. Games Systems, Inc., 1978.

Knight, Gareth. *A Practical Guide to Qabalistic Symbolism*, vols. I and II. New York: Samuel Weiser, 1978.

Lammey, William C. *Karmic Tarot: A New System for Finding and Following Your Life's Path*. N. Hollywood, CA: Newcastle Publishing, 1988.

Masino, Marcia. *Easy Tarot Guide*. San Diego: ACS Publications, 1987.

Neumann, Erich. *The Great Mother: An Analysis of the Archetype*, 2d ed. Princeton: Princeton University Press, 1963.

Nichols, Sallie. *Jung and Tarot: An Archetypal Journey*. York Beach, ME: Samuel Weiser, 1980.

Ouspensky, P. D. *The Symbolism of the Tarot*. New York: Dover Publications, 1976. Reprint. (First published in 1913.)

Peach, Emily. *Tarot for Tomorrow: An Advanced Handbook of Tarot Prediction*. Wellingborough, Northamptonshire, England: The Aquarian Press, 1988.

Place, Robert Michael and Rosemary Ellen Guiley. *The Alchemical Tarot*. London: Thorsons/HarperCollins, 1995.

Place, Robert Michael. *Alchemy and the Tarot: An Examination of the Historical Connection with a Guide to The Alchemical Tarot*. Saugerties, NY: Robert Michael Place, 2012.

_____. *The Tarot: History, Symbolism, and Divination*. New York: Tarcher/Penguin, 2005.

Pollack, Rachel. *Seventy-eight Degrees of Wisdom: A Book of Tarot.* Parts I and II. Wellingborough, Northamptonshire, England: The Aquarian Press, 1980, 1983.

Sargent, Carl. *Personality, Divination, and the Tarot.* Rochester, VT: Destiny Books, 1988.

Schueler, Gerald and Betty. *The Enochian Tarot.* St. Paul, MN: Llewellyn Publications, 1989.

Sharman-Burke, Juliet and Liz Greene. *The Mythic Tarot.* New York: Fireside Books, 1986.

Silberer, Herbert. *Hidden Symbolism of Alchemy and the Occult Arts.* New York: Dover Publications, 1971. (First published in 1917 as Problems of Mysticism and Its Symbolism.)

Smith, Caroline and John Astrop. *The Elemental Tarot.* New York: Dolphin/Doubleday, 1988.

Symonds, John and Kenneth Grant, eds. *The Confessions of Aleister Crowley, an Autobiography.* London: Routledge & Kegan Paul, 1979.

Trigg, Elwood B. *Gypsy Demons & Divinities: The Magic and Religion of the Gypsies.* Secaucus, NJ: Citadel Press, 1973.

Von Franz, Marie-Louise. *Alchemy: An Introduction to the Symbolism and the Psychology.* Toronto: Inner City Books, 1980.

Waite, Arthur Edward. *The Pictorial Key to the Tarot,* 2d ed. London: Rider & Co., 1971.

——————. *A New Encyclopedia of Freemasonry.* New York: Weathervane Books, 1970.

Wang, Robert. *The Qabalistic Tarot.* York Beach, ME: Samuel Weiser, 1987.

Wang, Robert. *Tarot Psychology: Handbook for the Jungian Tarot.* West Germany: Urania Verlags Ag, 1988.

Wanless, James. *Voyager Tarot.* Carmel, CA: Merrill-West Publishing, 1984.

Whitmont, Edward C. *The Symbolic Quest: Basic Concepts of Analytical Psychology.* Princeton: Princeton University Press, 1969.

Williams, Thomas A. *Eliphas Levi: Master of Occultism.* Birmingham: University of Alabama Press, 1975.

Woudhuysen, Jan. *Tarot Therapy: A New Approach to Self-Exploration.* Los Angeles: Jeremy P. Tarcher, 1979.

www.ingramcontent.com/pod-product-compliance
Lightning Source LLC
Chambersburg PA
CBHW021143080526
44588CB00008B/188